FOOD & BEER

DANIEL BURNS
AND
JEPPE JARNIT-BJERGSØ

FOOD
&
BEER

WITH
JOSHUA DAVID STEIN

FOREWORD BY RENÉ REDZEPI

PHOTOGRAPHS BY
GABRIELE STABILE AND SIGNE BIRCK

FOREWORD
BY RENÉ REDZEPI

Let's turn back time. It's a bitterly cold November day in 2003; there's a strong wind howling through the narrow streets of Copenhagen, and a persistent rain keeps slashing at my face as I try to bike through this typically Danish weather.

I'm on my way to a beer tasting.

We're about to open Noma and we've decided that when we do, we want to offer the best beers from all across the Nordic landscape.

While I was battling the weather in Copenhagen our sommelier was traveling through Scandinavia, and had spent the better part of a month researching, trying all the small breweries, and shortlisting the best. It was an exciting time for us: we were trying to build a new restaurant, to forage a new flavor, and of course we needed drinks that complimented this new mindset.

On opening night, we debuted a menu with two drink tastings: one was a full wine pairing—the traditionally accepted route—while the other option featured predominantly beer. I think we sold two beer tastings during that whole first month and it took us just six months before we stopped serving that option altogether. Not because we didn't believe in it, but because people just didn't want it. The snobbery around what to drink was simply too strong, and the traditional "wine cartel" in Copenhagen laughed so hard that I think they scared away everyone who might have been curious.

It's hard to understand today, reading through the pages of this book, how different the perception of beer was not much more than a decade ago.

Beer was really just something you got in a six-pack for the game, or binge drank with your buddies. It was perceived as a simple brew of humble grains, one that lacked any sort of refinement, and few thought it could match the sophistication of a nice meal. Maybe a hearty stew, some fish and chips, or a messy hot dog with ketchup on a Saturday night—but that was it.

We did our best, but we still didn't have a full understanding of the drink, or a great breadth of options to choose from. Still, we kept trying here and there when we had a bit of time on our hands. It wasn't a focal point, but we never forgot about it.

The first time I felt we actually nailed a food and beer pairing came with the help of Daniel Burns. He'd just come to us from The Fat Duck, a long and lanky redheaded Canadian with piercing eyes and a stout attitude. A bit like grown-up Simba from The Lion King. With Daniel also came a small revolution—at first it swept through our pastry kitchen: all recipes were tightened up, the wording corrected, measurements adjusted, and the sugar downsized. Daniel helped reorganize the section: more hands on deck, the clock-in time changed to one hour earlier. It was time to step it up.

Maybe this was the divine factor we'd been looking for; because with him we did this jellified buttermilk soup, an adaptation of a classic Danish summer serving. On top of the jelly we had raisins that had been soaked in aquavit, a scoop of ice cream made from dark sugar-beet molasses and paper-thin flakes of malt chips on top. The beer we served with it was from the Faroe Islands, a little brewery in picturesque Klaksvík. The beer was called Black Sheep, a dark lager with quite a malty flavor and a nice tarty, fruity finish. The malty tones, especially, really helped to accentuate the dark molasses. To this day it's one of the best matches that I've had between beer and food.

Some years passed by and Daniel was getting ready to finish his tenure with us. He wanted more, something of his own. Meanwhile, Denmark and most of Scandinavia had gone through a speedy renaissance of microbreweries. Suddenly it seemed that in every corner of every city somebody was setting up shop: microbrews had become a thing of quality. People started asking questions about strands of yeast, about who was the brewer, or sharing the latest news about the guy who started growing his own hops.

For the next five to six years, this new beer appreciation continued to grow and transform much faster than most of us could keep up with. But it was still mostly restaurants that served hearty fare, places with fat steaks and good burgers, that were the ones that focused on beer.

Meanwhile, Daniel was in New York, heading up the Momofuku test kitchen for David Chang. Daniel and I were in steady contact, and every few months we'd speak about the highs and lows. One time we were on the phone, and he was super depressed; he'd been dreaming up a plan for a restaurant, but it had come crashing down. "Don't worry buddy," I said, "things will always turn out right for people blessed with a talent like yours." Unfortunately he was beyond consoling, and when he hung up the phone I felt he still wasn't convinced.

Right around the same time—for all I know it could've been the same day—our good friend and frequent beer supplier to Noma, Jeppe Janit-Bjergsø, (one of the local brewers) emailed Lau, our restaurant manager. He explained to Lau his own bold move to America and that he was starting over in New York. Lau replied something like, "Great news, go for it! But you should really hook up with Daniel—he's our former sous-chef and he's also in New York right now."

The next time Daniel and I spoke, the mood had shifted and he was totally upbeat about this new secret project. He couldn't say much; "I don't wanna jinx it," he said, but he felt it was good now that the old project had crumbled. "I'm so excited!"

And that I guess is the real prologue to what this book is about. The chance meeting of two remarkable individuals. One of the best brewers in a generation of greats, with a good sense of business, and fresh attitude, and the other a creative, driven chef with crazy good work ethics. But it also signified the start of a new style of restaurant, a place in which light, creative cooking, Michelin-star-worthy stuff, was at home with beer. I'm pretty sure that individually both would've succeeded in own right—Jeppe creating great brews, and Daniel with a Michelin star or two doing something else—but together I believe they've created something truly special. Something new.

INTRODUCTION
BY JOSHUA DAVID STEIN

Ours is a time in which so-called unconventional pairings are gaining the wider recognition they deserve. From the idea that two people who love each other have the right to get married to which nation-states can be allies, past practice is increasingly losing its luster. For many, the path to acceptance was that two-word inquiry so often asked with rhetorical flip, "Why not?" Unable to come up with a compelling reason—"Because I guess I never really thought about" holds no water—attitudes shifted with remarkable speed. Thank God.

I'm not suggesting any sort of equivalency between that and the subject of this book—the pairing of beer and fine dining—except that both benefit from the posing of the question, "Why not?" For many people, beer, even if it is really good beer, isn't considered an adequate pairing for fine dining. Despite the rise of gastropubs, some of which serve refined riffs on burgers, and despite a burgeoning craft beer scene, beer has been relegated to inferior status. The sorry state of the American brewing industry since Prohibition—that is its consolidation into large brewers churning out bland lagers—might be partially responsible. But since the domestic craft beer scene has been flourishing for at least forty years, and since European, especially Belgian, beers are now widely available, the problem lies not in the quality of beer but in our perception of it.

It's one thing to have a moment of revelation. It's another thing completely to open a bar and restaurant to test the hypothesis. And that's what Daniel

Burns and Jeppe Jarnit-Bjergsø have done at Tørst, a bar that serves Daniel's more casual food with a curated list of beers, and Luksus, the fine-dining restaurant in the back in which the tasting menu is paired with beers selected by Jeppe and his team. When I first entered the world of Luksus, shortly after it opened in 2013, I was on the job, as the restaurant reviewer for the *New York Observer*. It's hard to be shaken as a critic and harder still to be stirred. And even before I had my first snack—it was the Lobster Relish (page 136) and it walloped my tongue—the very idea of Luksus had made me question my own assumptions and biases against beer in the fine-dining context.

Traditionally, fine dining has been a luxury, accessible only to those with the disposable income to afford it. Fine dining's traditional companion, wine—and I speak for Jeppe, Daniel, and myself when I say we respect wine a great deal—contains a history of privilege. To make wine one must have grapes and vineyards and years to tend them and years to age it. There are AOCs and DOCs and DOCGs and often pictures of castles on the bottle labels. As a companion, wine is ideally suited to fine dining, one assumes, because of its indisputable complexity and the constellation of exclusivity that surrounds it. Not so with beer. Beer can be made quickly, cheaply, and even at home. The ingredients—hops, malt, and yeast—are readily available and affordable. The process of brewing is unbelievably simple and intuitive. There's a reason many of

the best new breweries in the world started in someone's house or garage. The barriers are, therefore,
low. Beer is the great democratic drink.

Leaving aside that this notion is often disproven
by many of the beers in this book—beers brewed in
150-year-old casks, beers released in limited quantities for which men and women furiously scrum,
then feverishly trade—this has been the reputation
of beer. What Daniel and Jeppe do at Luksus is to
force one to ask why we associate affordability and
accessibility with inferior quality. Both men zealously fight for the guest at Tørst, and at Luksus, to
see the uncommonly beautiful in the common ingredients, be they food or beer.

In the first half of this book, Tørst, we've picked
ten flavors that beer and food most closely share.
Jeppe explains which styles, and which beers, em-
body these flavors and why. Daniel illustrates how
those flavors are used in his kitchen. Then, continu-
ing the discussion, Jeppe picks a beer, and Daniel a
recipe from Tørst, sometimes complementary—
sometimes contrasting—for each other's selection.
It's a dialogue between the two, beer and food,
Jeppe and Daniel.

The second half of the book, Luksus, is focused
on Daniel's even more refined recipes taken from
some of the three hundred recipes that Daniel and
his team have developed in the two years since
Luksus opened. These are accompanied with specific beer pairings chosen by Jeppe. There are only
sixteen seats at Luksus and we wanted to mimic as
closely as possible what it is like to sit in one of
those seats for an evening.

But this isn't just a book about food and beer.
It's also a story of the men, Jeppe Jarnit-Bjergsø and
Daniel Burns, and the wondrous exciting project
they created, the first restaurant ever to earn a
Michelin star that serves only beer—no wine or
cocktails. Daniel and Jeppe themselves are an unconventional pairing. Each has his own history that
colors who each man is today—and what each
makes. Daniel frequently returns to childhood
memories to create dishes. Jeppe instead plows
forward, headlong into the future. Daniel divides
the world into neat compartments, governed by
predictable and unalterable rules. Jeppe delights in
flouting process. Tørst and Luksus is where they
meet; and Jeppe and Daniel are two guys who
opened their minds and asked themselves,
"Why not?"

WHO IS JEPPE?

It's pronounced yep-pay and this my story. I was born in Copenhagen and grew up in a town called Nivå, in the so-called whiskey belt of Denmark, a stretch of palatial estates and thick forests twenty miles north of Copenhagen. The area is well-off but my family was not. My mother was a secretary for the Danish Prison and Probation System. My father was a warden at Vestre prison in Copenhagen. I have a twin brother, Mikkel, and four other siblings as well. Mikkel was born two minutes before I was. He cut in line. My father left when we were eight. He found a new family a few hours north.

When I was twelve, my brother and I started middle-distance running seriously. We were small guys with long skinny legs and an unconventional form. But we were fast. And more than fast, we never gave up. We ran almost every morning at six a.m. It didn't matter if it was sunny, raining, snowing. Hot or cold, the Bjergsø brothers ran. That's what was needed to be the best, so that's what we did. In a couple of years, we were recruited by Sparta Atletik og Motion, one of Europe's best running clubs. We took a train down to Copenhagen to practice at the Østerbro stadium a couple times a week.

When you run as seriously as we did, you learn to shut off all the signals in your body telling you to stop. It's not natural to run as far or as fast or as often as we did. Lungs burn, muscles turn to fire then finally feel like lead. Still you run. I read somewhere that the most successful runners are those

most inured to pain. Within our bracket, Mikkel and I were the best runners in our age cohort in Denmark. Naturally we competed against each other. He pushed me. I pushed him. Eventually, we joined the Danish National Team and ended up competing in the World Junior Cross Country Championship in 1994 in Budapest. Our lives were devoted entirely to training. Everything we ate or drank, when we went to sleep, and when we awoke was dictated by what could make us run faster, better. All things outside of the track passed by in a blur. And in some ways, I'm glad they did. Our family struggled, financially and emotionally. It was not, I would say, an idyllic childhood. But at least on the track, where the objective was clear and the terrain free from impediment, I felt at ease.

After high school, Mikkel and I applied for, and received, scholarships to run track in the United States. I had never been outside Europe but I wanted to get as far away from it as I could. I chose Arkansas State University in Jonesboro, Arkansas, because I wanted to meet real Americans, not tourists. Mikkel chose Kansas State University. At ASU, I clashed heads with the track-and-field coach. He was a very hardheaded man—and so was I. But I was the fastest on the team and he knew it. He preached technique. But I didn't give a shit about that. Whatever works, works.

After a year, Mikkel and I moved back to Denmark. It was 1995 and I wanted to become a teacher. I've always been good with kids because I understand that children need structure and discipline, but also that they like to be spoken to on their level. Mikkel went to teacher's college too, in the north of Denmark. We rejoined the running club Sparta because we didn't want to give up running. But shortly after my return, I injured my knee. I had surgery, healed, ran, but then reinjured it. That was it. If I can't be the best, I have no interest in doing it. What's the point? Soon Mikkel quit too. He had no one to compete against.

I was twenty-one and I had been an athlete for most of my life. I had never really had a youth. Finally, I discovered drinking and dating and what it meant to be free. It didn't hurt that I also happened to be at Blaagaard Statsseminarium in Søborg. It's the most fun teacher's college in Denmark. Those guys partied hard. A few of the other teaching students and I even formed a band. We called ourselves Poison Ivy 2. We'd sing punk versions of kid songs and then go to bars. And, sometimes, we would just go to bars.

This was 1996. Beer was shit in Denmark. Already in the United States craft breweries were popping up, but where we lived it was a Carlsberg monopoly. I am not fond of Carlsberg. There were, however, a few bars that had some interesting stouts on occasion and that's where we'd go. Perhaps because I came to beer so late in life—especially when so many of my compatriots had spent their adolescence drinking it—I became obsessed. I took to beer with the passion of a convert. I searched for good beer bars in Copenhagen and when I quickly exhausted those options, I took to the road. Thankfully, Denmark geographically is somewhat close to the heart of beer: Belgium. It was only a ten-hour trip through northern Germany and the Netherlands to Flanders, where I could load up on beers like Rodenbach, or to Pajottenland, with its famous lambic breweries. I say "only", because for me, ten hours was nothing compared to the pleasures of a good beer.

Around 1998, I had the idea to start a beer club. It was nothing too serious, but a group of us—my brother and a bunch of other teaching students— would meet every other month with one interesting beer we could find. We even made a magazine, *The Beer Nut*.

Eventually I got tired of driving for hours to find interesting beers, so a friend of mine from teaching college, Michael Peyk, and I decided to brew our own. The first one we ever brewed was a wheat beer we called Doppel Wit, an easy enough style to make. Michael and I did it just for fun, but Mikkel, too, decided to start brewing and formed a company called Mikkeller with his friend, a journalist named Kristian Keller. What appealed to me about brewing is that, just like running, making beer is something you just do. It's not like vinifying grapes or distilling spirits. One doesn't need a great deal of equipment or time or land. There is no sense of inherited wealth or onerous prerequisites. Anyone can make a tremendous beer wherever he is, whoever he is. Ingredients are, of course, important, but no one has a stacked deck. Brewing is like running: At the end of the day, you, and you alone, are responsible for your locomotion.

Though beer-making is frequently a solo effort, happily my life was becoming less one. In early September 2002, I met Maria Jarnit. Frankly, I can't say why she liked me—craft beer fanatics don't always make the best boyfriends. But I can say that when I saw her sitting at an outdoor table at Luftkastellet, a bar by the Copenhagen waterfront, she seemed to me an island of peace amidst a raucous sea, and I was in love. She was a twenty-three-year-old student studying literature; I was a twenty-seven-year-old unemployed teacher. But we had the world in front of us, and we had each other. Unlike me, she is not outspoken and plays her cards close to her chest, but when she finally speaks, what she does say is often either wickedly funny or tremendously insightful—and usually both. Soon, I had proselytized her to beer and she had planted the seed that perhaps it could be more than just a side project for me. More important, having Maria in my life made me realize that though results are important, so too is the process. Up until that point, my impulse had been to train my eyes on the finish line and run hell-for-leather. But being in love means it's not enough just to win the race; it matters who you finish with. I knew I wanted her by my side.

Gradually, I entered into the beer-trading subculture, which functions as an informal shadow distribution system. Around the world, Byzantine laws regulate how beer is sold but hundreds of bottles pass freely from enthusiast to enthusiast, bypassing arcane regulations. Through forums on websites like Rate Beer and Beer Advocate I hooked up with American beer nerds. I would send them beers like Westvleteren, and, in return, receive bottles of big American stouts and IPAs. These new beers that arrived by post furthered my conviction that there was a world of beer to explore.

In 2005, Michael and I decided to open Ølbutikken, Danish for beer shop, a closet-sized beer store in Copenhagen with about 250 beers on the shelves. We imported beers from the same Belgian breweries I visited like Cantillon, Drie Fonteinen, Struise, and, occasionally, Westvleteren. Though traditional in their native Belgium, these sour beers with complex flavors and rich though unknown histories were exotic to Danes. Still laboring under Carlsberg's near-monopoly, Denmark had never seen beers like these or a store like ours, and the incipient beer culture drank up thirstily. Immediately, Ølbutikken had long lines that formed outside whenever we opened. Of course, it didn't hurt our mystique that we were open only a few hours a week. Little did anyone know that was because Michael and I were still teaching school full-time.

A few years later, in 2008, I decided to commit myself to building a beer empire. At Ølbutikken, we were bringing traditional Belgian beers to Denmark. Now it was time to start formally importing the drastically different radical beers I had been receiving from upstart American breweries. A whole country hadn't heard of Jolly Pumpkin, Hopping Frog, and Alesmith! I approached Henrik Boes Brølling, a guy I had become friends with after running into him at Antwerp's Kulminator, one of the most famous beer bars in the world. "Another Dane, here?" I thought, "He must be a kindred spirit." It turned out he was. Though Boes Brølling was an architect by training, he, too, saw the soft spot in the market. In 2008 we went into business together, calling our import concern, Drikkeriget, a play on the Danish phrase "drinking kingdom" that could also mean, "binge drinker". We were a bit of both.

As for my own personal kingdom, that was growing too. Maria and I were married in 2006 and our son, Elliot, a bright-eyed blonde sprite, was born in January 2007. Ølbutikken and Drikkeriget were successful, but I wasn't ready to throw my fate to the beer gods. So I was still teaching at the time, spending eighteen hours a day at the school, or loading and unloading pallets for the import company, or at Ølbutikken selling beer to the growing beer enthusiast population. Things were tight and I was tired and overworked. But I knew we were on the forefront of a new beer movement and I would not yield. Ølbutikken was literally one of the best beer shops in the world and I wanted it to be even better. Drikkeriget was one of the biggest and definitely the best importers of American microbrews to Europe. Yet I wanted more.

By this time, Maria and I had traveled across the United States in a circuitous route that took us to many of the craft breweries from Florida through Texas and up to Arizona and to California. That so many of them cared so little about the established rules of brewing really appealed to me. At breweries like Pizza Port in Carlsbad, California, and Stone Brewing Co. in Escondido, California, anything went as long as it worked. Compared to the process-obsessed Old World, America's craft breweries were results oriented.

I decided it was time to start brewing professionally myself. I had been exposed to thousands and thousand of beers from around the world. I had the knowledge, and the connections, strong opinions, and passion. But I didn't have a partner. By this time, Mikkel, whose Mikkeller had grown to be one of the most hyped breweries in Europe, and I were at odds. Anyway, I wanted to run my company alone, at least professionally. On April 1, 2010, the same day our second son, Melvin, was born, I became the owner and sole proprietor of Evil Twin Brewing.

I am what is known in the industry as a gypsy brewer, though I prefer the term "contract brewer." That means I'm not saddled with the costs of owning and maintaining my own facilities. Contract brewing has existed since the early 1980s, when the New Amsterdam Brewery, one of the early New York City craft breweries, farmed out their brewing operations to another brewery, F.X. Matt, in Utica, New York. Over the years, contract brewing has been repeatedly villainized and rehabilitated. At the end of the day, contract brewing simply makes making beer more accessible. Some contract brews will be worse than conventionally brewed beers, some better, some the same. But in general, I think, democratization is a force for good. The secret to my beers isn't in the execution but in the recipes. So my job as a contract brewer is to develop the recipes and find partners who can execute them. I say partners, instead of contractors, because that's what they are. I think of guys like Ryan Witter-Merithew at Fanø Bryghus, or Menno Olivier at De Molen, as a director might think of his cinematographer. The product isn't just my vision, but ours.

The work I do with Evil Twin Brewing, the beers that I make, are an extension of who I am. Actually, since it is Maria who puts her copywriting skills to use (and her staunch non-beer nerdism) in naming the beers, they are an extension of who we are. They are irreverent. Some have silly names like "Christmas Eve in a New York City Hotel Room" and "Wet Dream." Other beers are silly like "Mosaic Single Hop Imperial India Pale American Wheat Lager." Now, that's a mouthful but it makes sense. We don't take anything seriously except results. The flavors must be excellent. Whatever it takes to get there, whatever "rules" get broken or conventions scorned, are immaterial to me. There's nothing arrogant or conceited in recognizing when something is good, whether you made it or not. There's nothing callous or malicious about doing whatever it takes to be excellent.

Inevitably, I found American breweries to be more like-minded than their European counterparts. Guys like Ed Westbrook in South Carolina and Phil Markowski at Two Roads in Connecticut are as daring and unorthodox as I want my beers to be, and one reason they now account for over ninety percent of the beer I make through Evil Twin Brewing. Ideas that would be dismissed quickly at the conservative brewers in the Old World were taken up with gusto. Cram a porter with doughnuts? Why not? Add beef jerky? Okay! Eventually, I was so focused on the United States, it didn't make sense any longer to stay in Denmark. Anyway, there was nothing left for me in Copenhagen. I now had a family of my own.

By this time, I had met Brian Ewing, an American as passionate about beer as I was. Brian worked at a marketing firm during the day and sold craft beer out of his Toyota Prius on nights and weekends. Like me, he was drawn to the far-out beers of Belgium and was obsessed with bringing them to the States. He was also an early supporter of Evil Twin, buying cases of my beer and proselytizing the gospel of my weird vision to anyone who would listen. In four years, Brian helped make Evil Twin a nationally renowned brand and, in the process, we became best friends. It was his encouragement and hard work—and his sponsorship of our visas—that made our move to New York possible. "Jeppe," he would say, "think of what we could do together!" Somewhere deep inside, I had always known I'd end up in America and had always hoped that New York, with its burgeoning beer scene, was the ideal place for me to pursue my passion. At the time of our arrival, New York was still in the throes of mixology. But there were a few shops like Bierkraft and Beer Street, and bars like Blind Tiger Ale House and Spuyten Duyvil, with their well-thought-out beer lists, that gave me hope.

Only a few weeks after we moved, and settled into an apartment in Williamsburg, Brooklyn, I hosted a tasting of a small selection of Evil Twin beers at a little Brooklyn bottle shop called Beer Street. The shop, on the corner of a quiet street and run by a former professional point guard, Lorcan Precious, was like finding safe harbor in a new land. So I served beers close to my heart, an IPA named by my son Melvin (its unpronounceable title, the result of his infant mashing on keys, is "DEVFFC, MQAL9,.8" though it's often called Melvin's Brew) and another, inspired by changing Elliot's diapers, called Soft Dookie, a vanilla-laced Imperial Stout. That the crowd responded with enthusiasm was important to me. But even more important, Beer Street was where I met a quiet Canadian chef I had heard so much about from my friend, René Redzepi. His name was Daniel Burns.

THE LIFE
OF DANIEL

A series of additions and subtractions, divisions and multiplications, had brought me to Williamsburg the night I met Jeppe. The algebra of a life, the isolation of that variable, x, is who you are. Isolate x and solve. The phenomenological world has always made the most sense to me when written as a formula. Though formulas are close cousins to recipes, it's not because I'm a chef and it is my duty to create and communicate complicated procedures in the clearest possible way. I was a mathematician long before I brunoised my first carrot or braised a pork shoulder.

For the first half of my life, I thought I would spend my days in the company of numbers. That would have suited me fine. Numbers are clean and uncompromising. They follow rules, are predictable, dependable, lifeless only to those who fail to recognize their hidden character. A life spent in their abstract company would be a life well lived. Some boys dream of being astronauts or firemen. I dreamt of being a math professor. Obviously it didn't turn out that way. Instead of in a classroom or a cloistered study, I've spent most of my adult life in the best kitchens in the world: The Fat Duck in Bray, England; St. John in London; Noma in Copenhagen; and Momofuku in New York.

But in the spring of 2012, I was looking for my equal sign. What had my life amounted to? After a long period of accumulation, I had gone through a series of subtractions and divisions. Three years prior, I had arrived in New York from Copenhagen with the chance to run the research kitchen of David Chang's Momofuku. It was a chef's dream: access to any ingredient I wanted and liberated from the constraints of nightly service. I was free to chase my thoughts from ether to paper to pan. And I did, five days a week for three years. But that April I resigned, disillusioned, and disheartened. It wasn't Dave, who was a gracious, supportive boss, and it was not the work itself—my explorations

grew ever deeper into the arcane corners of the culinary world I very much enjoyed. My research wasn't being put to use as much as I'd like. Toward the end of my time there I had felt ill at ease and off balance. It turns out the missing quantity had been the plate. I was developing exciting new skills and techniques, but few of my ideas made their way in front of diners. And what is a chef if no one eats his food? The question of who I was, and what I was doing, was unresolved, and so I set out on my own to find that answer.

I grew up in a household where the abstract and the applied were held in equal regard. My father, John Terrence Burns, was a high school chemistry teacher. My mother, Arlene Elizabeth Ellen DeGrace, was a high school home economics teacher. We lived in Dartmouth, a small city adjacent to Halifax, Nova Scotia, in a tidy house with a two-car garage on Beckfoot Drive, at the end of a cul de sac. From a young age, I listenened to my father discussing chemistry at dinner with my older brothers, Sean and Bryan, in one ear; in the other, I'd absorb my mother carefully explaining to me how she calibrated our family meals to align with Canada's nutritional guidelines. Hers were the hands helping mine precisely mark off perfect eight-millimeter dice. My father's were the hands holding mine as we gently squeezed pipettes for the home chemistry experiments that were our constant activities.

When I wasn't in the house, I was on the pitch. Football (which Americans call soccer) was a big part of my life. In fact, all sports were. Hockey is a given; basketball, too, since my dad, JT, was a college ball player, and also football. My days were marked by morning practice and evening practice, drills and exercises. Not only did I play varsity at university, but all throughout my youth the teams I played on did very well. I got used to winning and it made me want to strive for excellence in everything I did. My football team made the National Championships in every one of my formative years, from age thirteen to nineteen—which meant winning the provincial championships and being crowned the best team in Nova Scotia. We traveled across the country to compete, far beyond the small-town confines of Dartmouth. The only thing that made all of that possible was that we were driven, we were precise, we would not give up, and we would win.

At home or on the field, at the table or in the kitchen, my childhood, though warm and loving, had no accommodation—or allowance—for the introduction of error or imprecision.

So well before I had encountered my first proof or my first pudding, the world had resolved itself into objective truths and the consequences that followed. The word *must* was engraved in my psyche from an early age, for I remember everything I did—from the hours of ball hockey I played nightly, to the football (soccer) pitch—or the basketball court where I spent most of my time, and even how I ordered my sweaters in their drawer had to be done with technical precision. I was fiercely competitive, and as my brothers will attest, hard on myself and others. But that is because it was always the ideal to which I compared myself. There could be no margin of error, no justification for suboptimal performance. That is, I think, what attracted me to mathematics, and ultimately, along with a side of luck, to the kitchen.

Hoops brought me to Beer Street. I was at Beer Street that night because the guy who runs it, Lorcan Precious, is an extraordinary basketball player. The former point guard for European Professional Leagues, Lorcan is tall, friendly, has a killer three-point shot. Shortly after moving to New York, and settling into a small one-bedroom apartment on the river's edge in Greenpoint, Brooklyn, I had joined a league sponsored by the local bookstore, Word. There were eight teams with clever literary names like The Spaulding Greys, The Oranges of Rathe, and The Purple Pros. Lorcan and I were guards on the Brown team called Like Water for Chocolate. I didn't know it at the time but Lorcan's father, Bob, founded Ginger Man, one of the first real craft beer bars in Texas back in the '90s. After his pro career wound down, Lorcan also took up his family trade, opening a tiny beer store on a residential street in Williamsburg.

Lorcan asked if I'd be interested in making some food for a Danish brewer he had coming in. I said sure. My affinity with Denmark was strong. After all, for three years I had called Copenhagen home and the kitchen at Noma, my office. That I had found my way into some of the best kitchens of the world from a small town in Canada still seems hard to figure out.

Even as mathematicians struggle to generate random numbers, my trajectory thus far has been stochastic. At twenty-four, soon after graduating university with a double degree in Philosophy and Mathematics, I realized math no longer added up. I was never going to win the Fields Medal and there's no minor league for mathematicians. Ten years of banging my head against the wall for a PhD was unfathomable. Plus, fuck, man, I wanted to make something. With my hands. But what? The question of what I should make was dauntingly broad. After talking it over with my mother, I thought perhaps I could cook. Years of her meals had left me competent in the kitchen, with an ingrained appreciation for preparation as well as an attunement to the subtle balance of flavors. But where? Thankfully, in 1999, I convinced a Buddhist barista in Halifax to let me make soup for his café. I wanted to find out if I might like working in a kitchen at all. It turns out I loved it. The kitchen is a well-ordered universe with documented methods and preparations, where clarity and neatness are prized almost as much as creativity. It felt, in other words, like home.

After a few months of making carrot-ginger soup, I moved across the country to Vancouver with my girlfriend, a ginger-haired tree-planting philosopher named Andrea Purton. I ended up in the kitchen of Century Grill, one of Vancouver's better restaurants. I had zero experience in a professional kitchen, but I knew how to hold a knife and, importantly, I paid attention to detail. Though I was only a commis, a position on the lower rungs of the kitchen brigade, I closely observed all the stations, from the fiery intensity of the grill to the relative calm of the pastry station. I found the rhythms and the monastic monotony of the professional kitchen comforting.

Life outside the kitchen wasn't so neat. Subtractions. Two years prior, when I was twenty-three years old, my father unexpectedly died, after choking on a piece of meat, and I was still mourning his loss. Andrea left in 2001. Sometimes people just leave you. In the kitchen at least rules were inviolable; routines were established. And the fruit of this discipline wasn't simply the pleasure of a job well done but actual genuine comfort: food, an expression of love. That alchemy was addictive.

After Vancouver, I followed a British girl named Cassie—whom I had met whilst she was studying English literature in Victoria—back to England. She lived in Bristol; Bray is only an hour and a half away. So I arranged a week-long stage, an unpaid internship, at The Fat Duck, Heston Blumenthal's lauded restaurant. I had no home, no money, no plans. But I wanted to learn from the best, and Heston was one of the best. I kept my knife roll in a tent I pitched by the Thames River at Amerden Caravan Park, a campsite within walking distance of the restaurant. Every morning I felt a little bit like Huckleberry Finn as I grabbed my backpack and walked along the river away from the site, up the long stairwell to the M4, across the Thames; then back down on the other side toward the kitchen. Every night, I'd decline a ride and walk back to the encampment, stumbling through the darkness.

Heston is a mad genius with a mathematical mind, and I quickly took to his method of cooking. He taught me that even the most scientific processes can summon powerful childhood memories. In dishes like his famous "Egg & Bacon Ice Cream" and "Sounds of the Sea," he used innovative means to thrust diners back to their youths. While I was there, a Scot named James "Jocky" Petrie took a shine to me. Jocky was the pastry chef, and I think he enjoyed our banter. As a chef, you spend nearly all your waking hours in close quarters with another person. You've got to like each other or it's hell. I was new to cooking but older than my contemporaries and I could carry on a conversation about Hegel (which we never did), ratios (sometimes), and football (often). He offered me a job in the pastry department and like that, I worked in one of the best restaurants in the world.

By the time I moved to Copenhagen to work in the kitchen of René Redzepi's Noma, I was no longer just a savory chef but I wasn't quite a pastry chef either. I had added sweetness to my arsenal, but, above all, I was after balance. Equilibrium is something Noma does exceptionally well, whether by closing on Mondays so the staff could spend time with family, or carefully calibrating flavors and ingredients into structurally improbable but sturdy formation. Right away, I fit into a kitchen culture, which was quiet, modest, and intensely focused. This was a time of additions and multiplications, obsessively developing new dishes, and happily sharing them with the world. It was my job to set up the pastry program, working with René to apply his philosophy of flavors to desserts just on the sweet side. In so doing, I began to develop my own philosophy.

Any chef who deserves to be in a kitchen can showcase an ingredient. But what I was looking to solve were multivariable formulas in which the respective flavors of many ingredients created a well-balanced plate. It was not enough to showcase, for instance, dulse, a seaweed common in Scandinavia, or a cut of meat by simply roasting it. I wanted to offset, complement, tease, prod, poke, multiply,

divide, square, cube, and find the square root of that flavor and scores of others.

At Beer Street, I had free rein – though limited resources – to bring my philosophy to the table. I made a Hunter's Salad, chicken and pickled mushrooms served on rugbrød, using a friend's kitchen for prep. I had never met Jeppe. He's a tall guy with a somewhat severe mien, quickly softened by his sense of humor. Jeppe knew René from Copenhagen and oversaw the beer program at Noma. When he left to move to New York, Lau Richter, the restaurant manager said, "Hey, if you ever run into Daniel Burns, say hi." Laughing, Jeppe replied, "It's a city of eight million. I'll never see him." And yet, a couple weeks after he landed, here we were, in a tiny crowded beer store in Brooklyn.

I was not, at the time, what you'd call a beer man. I grew up drinking Schooner and Oland's in Nova Scotia. But when Jeppe asked me why craft beer in this country was never considered a suitable mate for fine dining, I couldn't give him an answer. Mentally, I lined up all the variables, knocking one down after the other. Beer was just as complex, just as varied, just as capable of differences in tenor and timbre as wine was. And yet . . . certainly nowhere that I had eaten or cooked was it given its due.

That night, the idea of Tørst and Luksus was born. Jeppe and I would make the case, not through words nor drunken disquisitions, but through showing it could be done. I was excited, more excited than I'd been in a long time. Finally, I would be able to return to what I do best and enjoy most: serving people food my way. This meant a return to the restaurant kitchen, to the rituals and routines, to the demands and the rewards of a fine-dining environment. This was vital for me then and it still is now. The best way I can describe what I feel like in a professional kitchen is weightlessness. It's the only environment in my life in which the fierce external pressure of my surroundings equals, and balances out, the high internal pressure I exert on myself. A life of no allowance for errors prepares one well for the kitchen. It's handiwork, and that's what I love about life in restaurants and in the kitchen on the line. It's where I am, at last, a balanced equation.

Food & Beer

A DAY AT
TØRST & LUKSUS

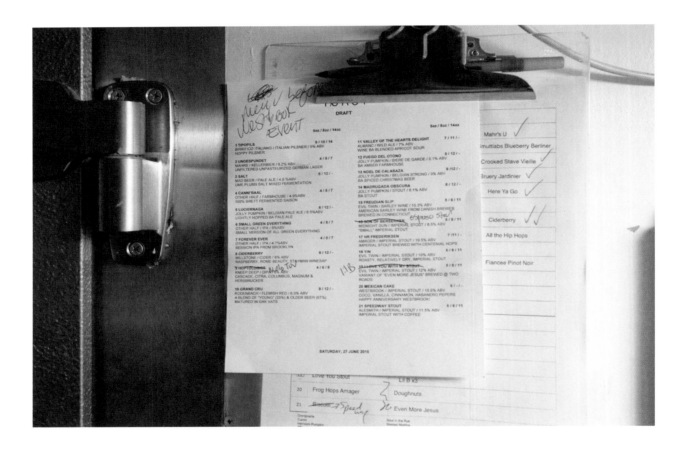

Since the late nineteenth century, Greenpoint, Brooklyn has been a predominantly Polish neighborhood where Polish immigrants settled to work the shipyards that once lined the waterfront. The last shipyard closed in the 1960s, but the neighborhood is still charmingly Slavic. A sign reading Mowimy Pol Polsku—We Speak Polish—is displayed in the windows of many stores. Tørst is located on the main artery, Manhattan Avenue, which runs westerly from the Newton Creek, a deeply polluted estuary of the East River, through the heart of Greenpoint to the imposing colossus of the Woodhull hospital in Williamsburg.

Greenpoint has a sense of grit, character, and community. It's both Polish and unpolished. Tørst is located on the last block before McCarren Park, tucked between Café Amaranth, a Thai restaurant, and Fortune Cookie, a cheap Chinese food take-out joint. A few doors down is the Brooklyn Slovak American Citizens Club. "Members Only," the sign says, and they mean it. On the other side is the New Warsaw Bakery, makers of the city's best Polish rye bread. You have to look closely to find Tørst.

There's no number on the door and the only signage is a lightly engraved marble slab over the threshold. There's no signage for Luksus either, but it's just as well. A few months after Luksus opened, we realized there's also a hair salon down the block with the same name. Turns out it's the same word in both Danish and Polish: luxury.

We're a small crew—five guys in the kitchen, seven bartenders, and three servers—stretched thinner by the fact we're running two discreet restaurants, each with its own set of needs and expectations. The symphony of the kitchen is already a complicated polyphony, as cooks balance labor-intensive mise en place (preparations) with orders being fired. As at any restaurant, the goal is to have all the elements on a plate come together in one perfect moment, but that confluence takes a lot of work and forethought.

What we serve at Tørst is informal and hearty. The menu is available, without pause, from when we open at noon to when we close at midnight. At Luksus, on the other hand, it is a tasting menu. It is served in two seatings according to precise, predetermined choreography.

In order for Tørst and Luksus to function in harmony, our staff works extremely hard. As the sun rises and Manhattan Avenue rattles with buses and delivery trucks, already our basement doors are flung open to receive heavy steel kegs and boxes of neatly packed bottles. Daniel spends most mornings at the Greenmarket in Union Square. We work with a few main farms and have about twenty suppliers. Some Daniel has known since his days at Momofuku and others are new friends. Farmers like Lani's Farm in Burlington County and the Upstate Farms cooperative have worked with us since we opened, and we've come to develop a strong rapport. Ordering is done by quick text exchanges or rapidly written emails. But still, a chef must walk the Greenmarket like a farmer his fields. Those tented stalls with tables laden with produce are the umbilical cord that connects us to the seasons. Though Union Square's is the largest farmers' market in the city, there are over one hundred such markets scattered through the five boroughs of New York City. Today, Daniel visits the small farmers' market at McGolrick Park, an elegant if overlooked park deep in Greenpoint. There, around a monument to fallen soldiers of the Battle of Argonne, gather just a handful of vendors every Sunday. Thankfully, they often include Norwich Meadows Farm, among other longtime friends of ours. Today, at the height of summer, there are fava beans—thick, vibrant green, slightly fuzzy. Daniel buys a bunch.

This morning's a particularly good one, because Annie Novak stops by. Annie's greens are great, her purslane is perfect, and her radishes are rad. She comes about once a week, rolling up on her bicycle with a plastic crate under her arm. Annie founded Eagle Rooftop Farms on the roof of an old warehouse in Greenpoint back in 2009. She was one of the earliest adopters of commercial urban farming in New York City and a fervent champion of Greenpoint. Far more than a supplier of our salad greens, Annie is more like a partner. In the peak of summer, when many vegetables and herbs are no longer fruiting, she'll drop off little flowers from coriander flowers or mustard plants and challenge Daniel to find a use for them.

We adjust the menu at Luksus according to seasonality, which means the main dishes change about ten times a year. Changing the menu so often keeps the cooks on their toes and it's also a reason for customers to keep coming back. Nearly twenty-five percent of our customers are repeat visitors. Daniel often develops recipes here, in the back room at Luksus in the quiet moments after he returns from the Greenmarket. He starts with an ingredient at the height of its season, say plums or ramps, and thinks how best to extend it. Sometimes it becomes salted and set aside to be preserved;

other times it gets pickled or serves as the base for a broth. It can manifest as a self-contained side dish or perhaps an ancillary element. Of course, each addition to an existing dish sets off a reconfiguration of flavors. Once an idea occurs to Daniel, he'll write a preliminary recipe in terse shorthand and share it with the cooks. There is a long process of tasting, testing, and refining before it is ready for service.

Because Tørst's proposition is so unique, we don't get a lot of apathetic bartenders—and we wouldn't hire them anyway. Most of our staff is made up of avid homebrewers, and if they aren't, they are steeped in beer and breweriana. They can geek out on beer if needed, but generally are pretty modulated in their geekery. The early morning for them is taken up by the usual bar prep, polishing glasses (customized for us by Martin Justesen, who does all the graphics for both Tørst and Luksus) making sure the low boy coolers are full, and that the beer lines, running from the "Flux Capacitor" downstairs, are functioning. Once a week though, there's the Changing of the Board. Behind the bar is a large mirror where we write the twenty-one beers we have on tap in white marker. Once a week, when we change over our beers, we wipe it entirely clean and scrawl, hopefully legibly, what's on tap for the upcoming week.

Today Joey Pepper and Ramon Huang are working. Between the two of them, Joey has the nicer handwriting, so he gets to be the scribe. Ramone will get his chance another day. As the kegs run out, we gradually introduce new selections. When the bar is busy, we'll go through between one to four kegs a day. Every Monday, Mike Amedei, a nice and extremely beer-knowledgeable guy who likes listening to Green Day really loud, makes the orders in consultation with Jeppe. It's been trendy lately for beer bars to have insane numbers of beers on tap. Forty, sixty, one hundred-twenty. But just like when a restaurant with a six-page menu won't be any good, the same is true for a beer bar. When you're as selective as we are at Tørst, twenty-one is more than enough. We divide up our beers into three groups—light, medium, and dark—of seven each. In the light section are easy-drinking lagers, Pilsners, wheat beers, and Berliner Weisse. The medium tranche consists of brown ales, and bigger IPAs. Stouts, barleywines, porters, as well as the occasional Quadruples, are found in the dark section.

Besides what we offer on tap, we have an extensive bottle list. All the beers we use in the Luksus pairings are bottles, for no other reason than that it allows us to guarantee availability.

One of the unique things about Tørst is our "Flux Capacitor." It's a complex system for getting the beer from the kegs to the tap, which allows us to control the pressure of each of the kegs, as well as to modulate the mixture of CO_2 and nitrogen used to carbonate the beers. Beers are carbonated on draught since they tend to flatten in transport and storage. The "Flux Capacitor" was developed by Gabe Gordon, a friend of Jeppe's, and a fan of the *Back to the Future* films. (Gabe also happens to own Beachwood Barbecue in Long Beach, California.) It is up to the bartender to modulate the pressure with which a beer is dispensed as well as the ideal balance of CO_2 and nitrogen. Gabe is the Doc Brown of the beer world.

Our bartenders' days start early for the industry, around 10 a.m. Here are Joey and Ramone, with Joey enjoying a bacon, egg, and cheese sandwich from Peter Pan Donuts, the donut shop down the street, rated among the top doughnut shops in the country. Joey calls this sandwich the "the bartender's special."

Because Jeppe has so many relationships in the beer world from Drikkeriget, Evil Twin, and now, Tørst, we frequently host brewery takeovers, in which we showcase the offerings of one of our favorite breweries, or special releases of rare beers.

Beer lovers can generally be divided into people who will wait in line for beer and those who won't. These days, we see a lot more of the former.

Today, for instance, Ed Westbrook from Westbrook Brewing Company near Charleston, South Carolina, is here with his wife, Morgan, who also runs the brewery. We're tapping Westbrook's cult favorite, Mexican Wedding Cake, an Imperial Stout infused with cocoa nibs, vanilla beans, and cinnamon sticks. New and vintage kegs are on tap, both of which are nearly impossible to get anywhere else. Also on tap are some of their more outré experiments, like Weisse Weisse Baby, a beer with lime, vanilla, and cinnamon. By 11 a.m., there's a long line of thirsty beer lovers waiting for our doors to open.

Meanwhile, down a steep flight of stairs—but a world away—five cooks crowd into a workspace no larger than 225 square feet. No matter what is going on upstairs during the day, the prep kitchen operates at a steady and focused frequency. With so little space, the men must move as octopus tentacles: independent but well coordinated. Because Daniel worked for so long in a pastry kitchen, and because the staff and space is so limited, there is no strict hierarchy or airtight division of labor. But there is a long list of things that need to get done. These tasks are kept on a blue clipboard hanging on the wall, and each man works until each task is crossed off. This means a cook might work on a compression pickle, emulsify a vinaigrette, then turn around and make blueberry ice. Throughout the day, "kits" are compiled that need to be processed into the components for each dish at Luksus. From them, marinades, pickles, brines, and broths are cooked and cooled, ready for use. Completed projects are stored in square plastic containers, labeled, dated, and stored in the reach-in refrigerator—the ready-to-go mise en place. Though it is "all hands on deck", typically one cook will act as butcher, ensuring all the meat and fish are properly marinated, cooked, and portioned. Two cooks, who have the benefit of an open window that looks out on our backyard, pay for it by doing double duty, both preparing kits for Luksus and turning out Tørst dishes. Whoever works in the corner with most of the outlets is, by default, a purée guy since that's where all the blenders and food processors are plugged in. Frequently, there's a stagiaire who does whatever he's told to do, usually clipping herbs or doing vegetable knife work.

On any given night, there are fifteen courses on the Luksus menu, each consisting of eight to twelve elements, each with its own prep. Beef Tartare (page 148), for instance, consists of fourteen different components and scores of man-hours. The meat must be scraped, weighed, and flattened. The razor clams must be shucked and portioned. A stagiaire keeps busy picking all the foraged greens, whose leaves—six leaves per portion—will top the tartare. Today, those include bitter cress, yarrow leaves, ground ivy, field mustard, wild watercress, arugula flowers, and stone crop that our forager, Evan Strusinki, delivered. Meanwhile, another cook chops the pickled green almonds, slices fresh green almonds, and cleans the wild garlic chives.

Today the squad consists of Lincoln Clevenson, a serious Southern Californian; Joshua Plunkett, a tall, angular Irishman; a new kid, Nathan Casas; and a quiet Danish stagiaire, Christian Petersen. It's up to Lincoln to assign which cook prepares what—though most already know— but it is up to each chef individually to juggle the timeline. Each chef is responsible for keeping track of his own recipes too. Joshua, for instance, writes his in beat-up little Moleskine notebooks. Lincoln manages his recipes online. Over the years, we've probably developed nearly four hundred recipes, enough to fill two large folio notebooks Daniel keeps in his apartment. Every kitchen has a shorthand cooks use to describe how dishes are made. That might mean Daniel will explain a new preparation as "chip" or a "pickle" and the team will intuitively fill in the tens of steps needed.

Today, the team is well versed in the current menu but they know things will soon change. When they arrive, Lincoln gets to work on the Lobster Relish (page 136). He quickly kills a Maine lobster, starts the marinade (which needs to sit four hours), and later dices the lobster flesh. Oysters need to be shucked and marinated. Day-of pickles must start early.

Meanwhile, upstairs, it's already a party by 1 p.m. Beer bars have a bad reputation for being sausage fests, but that's not the case for us, perhaps because Tørst has done away with the traditional trappings of a testosterone-soaked bar. An elegant Carrara marble bar and intricate wall paneling made from reclaimed wood forestall any incipient bro-ness. There's no neon; no sports; little shouting. With Ed and Morgan here and their rare beers on tap, it's particularly busy. Usually the meat and cheese plates and the flank steak salad are our biggest sellers. But the hoppy tart beers of West-brook—especially that Key Lime pie one—work well with the duck. In the kitchen, Nathan and Joshua are busy balancing their Luksus prep with slicing meats, cutting cheese, and making sand-wiches. While behind the bar, Joey and Ramon are a constant blur. There are three sizes—five, eight, and fourteen ounces—of beer available, which is important, because our customers are having many of these beers for the first time. Martin cannily designed the glasses to incorporate subtle pour marks. As they pour the beer, it is also the job of the bartenders to observe how the beer is flowing, as well as to adjust the gas mix and pressure ac-cordingly, using our "Flux Capacitor."

Daniel has disappeared into the Luksus kitchen as he quietly prepares the flødeboller by squeezing meringue into small towers atop silver dollar–size cookies. These will be covered in chocolate. All the baking is done in this space, from bread to desserts. Periodically, Daniel is visited by the downstairs chefs, who are busy with their mise en place, since the only six-burner induction unit, a piece of equip-ment integral to many of our preparations, is to be found upstairs.

It's usually empty back here in the afternoon, but today Jeppe and his friends have taken over the back room for lunch. Jeppe and his wife, Maria, have two children, Elliot, who is eight years old, and Melvin, who is five. Like his father, Elliot keeps track of everything. If something changes on the menu at Luksus, Elliot notices. Melvin, meanwhile, is never shy about asking for something sweet. Today he's in luck: Daniel has a flødebolle waiting for him.

Elliot and Melvin are well behaved in restau-rants; they've had a lot of practice, as Maria and Jeppe bring them all around the world, wherever Jeppe's brewing takes him. This year, Elliot wrote a special Father's Day message in a card for his fa-ther: "My favorite thing(s) to do with my daddy is . . ." said the prompt, "eat at a restrant." Cute little dude.

Today the crowd consists of a Swedish set de-signer, a Swedish furniture collector, Ed and Mor-gan Westbrook, and a few others. Daniel prepares a selection of dishes from Luksus and Tørst that complement the complexity of the Westbrook beers. Everybody digs in.

At 3 p.m. every day, Daniel starts the sourdough bread that forms an integral part of the Luksus experience. The bread takes twenty-five minutes to bake, and is reheated as soon as the guests sit down for snacks. At service it must be hot enough that the butter melts on contact. Though it is labor-intensive and the space is small, we normally make two loaves per person. The bread-and-butter serving is the only one we oblige requests for seconds.

During the day all cooks wash the dishes that come down from Tørst. For Daniel, it's an import-ant component of the range of a chef's responsibili-ties that keeps them grounded. But when we're

running two services, the sheer volume becomes unmanageable without help. A porter comes in at 4 p.m. Among his responsibilities are ferrying dishes from upstairs to the basement and keeping the chefs supplied with clean pots and pans and plates. A restaurant of this size can't afford the space for new plates for every course, so throughout the night it is a constant quick churn. On his days off, Daniel frequently scours the junk shops of Williamsburg looking for discarded quality porcelain. When Jeppe and Maria are in Denmark, they, too, haunt the flea markets of Copenhagen looking for plates. This results in a hodgepodge of disparate plates but stays true to the mission of Luksus: reveal the hidden value of the overlooked.

If everything is going smoothly, the red bin makes its way upstairs at 4:30 p.m. The red bin contains the entire mise en place needed for the first service at Luksus. This is a signal, signifying the countdown clock has begun. If the red bin is late, everything gets delayed and the night can quickly spiral downward. Today Lincoln carries up the red bin at precisely 4:27 p.m. It will be a good night.

The true measure of a restaurant is the quality of its staff meal. At Luksus we take this very seriously. Historically, there was even a member of the brigade called a communard, devoted to its prepa-

ration. At Luksus—and most kitchens these days— it is a rotating duty. But cooks love to do it. A staff meal is a rare chance for cooks to make whatever they're excited about at the moment, even if it's a world away from what is on the menu. It's their chance to freestyle. Tonight, Joshua Plunkett is making banh mi and agua fresca. Between preparing the night's mise en place, he's been painstakingly clipping the leaves of mint he's grown on his rooftop garden in Bushwick. He improvises a mayonnaise infused with cilantro and minces some extra pork from the walk-in. With such a small team, staff meals really are like cooking for your family.

At 5 p.m., when everybody gathers to eat, sometimes, especially when the night is nice and the backyard is open, the cooks sit around and swap stories about life back home. Often, though, the staff meal is the one moment the cooks have to themselves. Tonight the banh mi is eaten illuminated by the light of smartphones, as each man peers into his life outside the confines of the kitchen.

We know whom we'll be serving on any given night. At the 6 p.m. preservice meeting, Daniel and the front-of-the-house team go over who is dining tonight. What do they do? Have they been in before? If so, when? James, our beer host for the evening, spends the first part of his shift Googling, looking up Twitter profiles, and following Facebook links. This is also the time when Daniel goes over the preparations and elements of each serving with the front-of-the-house staff. The menu at Luksus is on the terse side and that's by design. Daniel would prefer the guests to explore first through taste. But the servers must know each step of each element, from whence it came, and what was done to it in case a guest inquires. Generally, servers try to limit their initial explanation to a few sentences rather than extended rhapsodic soliloquies. A bite should yield jouissance, not just plaisir.

Aprons go on. A quiet calm settles in Luksus. During service, Daniel is accompanied in the open kitchen by two of his cooks. Tonight, it's Lincoln and Joshua. Lincoln focuses on the snacks portion of the tasting menu; Joshua hovers over the induction oven. Daniel remains at his station in the corner, where he roasts, plates, quenelles, and controls the flow of service. It is a small room with an open kitchen and, therefore, the atmosphere is intense. There isn't space for the focused energy of the kitchen to dissipate and there isn't a barrier, save a narrow counter, to insulate the guests from it. An open kitchen means it's open not just visually and aurally, but also energetically. It's a fluid exchange between the kitchen and the diner and this is something that many patrons—and certainly many chefs—enjoy. At Luksus, diners are encouraged to ask questions. In fact, that's partially why the menu is so laconic—it forces interaction.

Obviously, one of the things that makes Luksus unique is our beer pairing. Jeppe curates the selections, drawing not just on the offerings of Evil Twin Brewing but also on the extensive bottle list stored in the basement room. Many of these beers are difficult to get anywhere else, but we try not to belabor that point. As with a wine pairing, the beer is a character with which the character of the food interacts. At Luksus, there is absolute parity between the food and the beer. Since we are the only Michelin-starred restaurant in the world to offer a full beer pairing, and only a beer pairing, the vast majority of our guests avail themselves of it.

One of the pleasures of service is watching guests try new beers—like the Del Borgo's Enkir, an Italian-made Belgian-style pale ale made from an ancient grain—for the first time. Some close their eyes, trying to grasp the flavors. Others' eyes widen in surprise, marveling at the complexity of the flavors. It's a pretty rare sight that a guest will drink a beer and not notice it.

Service at Luksus ends after the last guest leaves, which on most nights is around 11:30 p.m. The menu at Tørst, however, continues until midnight. As soon as the last guests leave Luksus, the chefs who worked service at Luksus transition from service to cleanup mode. By 12:30 a.m., all surfaces have been cleaned, all dishes washed, and all food properly stored. It's time for the post-service meeting. Daniel gathers the chefs upstairs to go over notes: Where do they stand for the following day's mise en place? How could the workflow be tweaked for better service? What are the sticking points? What worked well and what didn't? Does the plating need to be altered?

By 1 a.m., Daniel and his team leave the building they entered fourteen hours before. Manhattan Avenue is still bustling in the early morning. Though the Polish bakeries, hair salons, and most restaurants have shuttered, the bars that cater to local Greenpointers are still open. Music spills out. Revelers gather in smoking clumps outside entrances. On Friday and Saturday nights, last call at Tørst is 2 a.m. After the last guest leaves, the bartenders take stock of their glasses, wipe and clean the bar, sanitize the taps, and finally, close up. It's 3 a.m., just a few hours before the day will begin all over again.

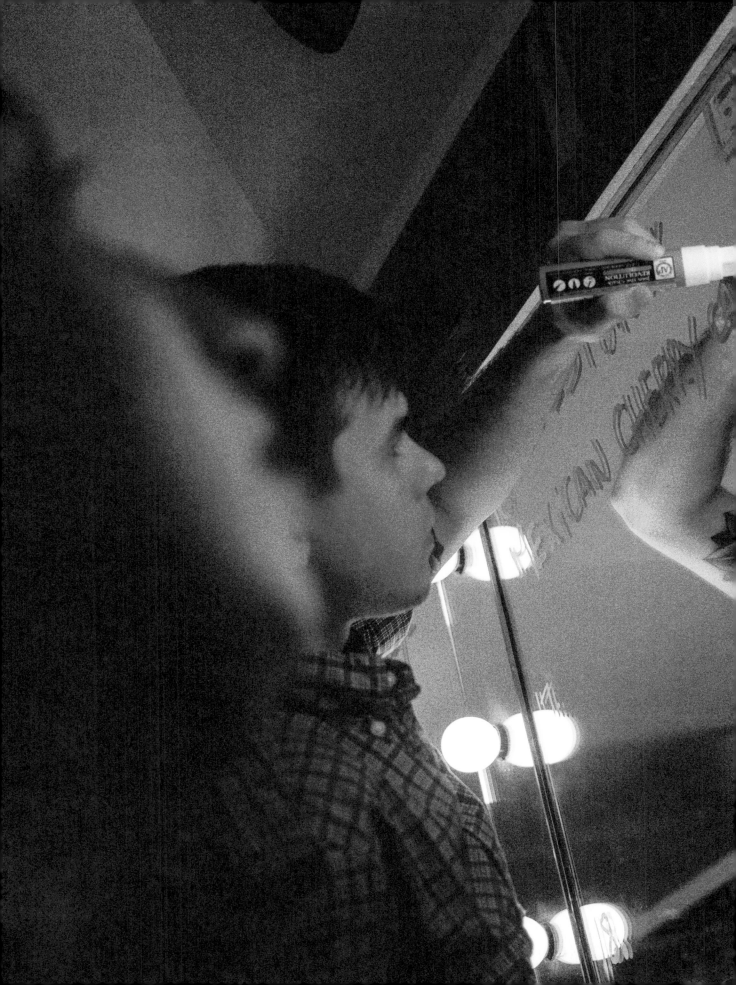

PART I

TØRST

BITTER

JEPPE   We spend most of our lives fleeing bitter: bitter experiences, bitter truths, bitter flavors. But beer embraces bitterness. There couldn't be beer without it, and without it, sweetness would have no meaning. Welcome to the Zen of Brewing.

Deep bow.

In beer, there are notes—caramel, floral, cocoa. But bitterness is the musical staff on which those notes hang. It is perhaps the most important, existential flavor in beer. Not simply because this embrace is one of the biggest differentiators in terms of flavor with our kind cousin wine, but because bitter flavors in beer are the result of a necessary structural element of its brewing: hops. You can't have beer without hops; hence, you can't have beer without some degree of bitterness.

In life, hops are flowering vines with dark green delicately serrated leaves, whose flowers are called cones. They look, perhaps unsurprisingly, like a wonky, bright green pine cone. Like holly trees and power outlets, hop vines are sexed. Since only the females produce a cone that can be used in brewing, they are much more prized and cultivated.

In beer, hops add structure and stability. The structure is based in bitterness, which comes from acids in the hop plant; the stability is born from hops' ability to ward off deleterious bacteria that causes beer to spoil. As with underseasoned food, beer without hops tastes flaccid and dissolute. And it would go bad quickly—but who cares, it wouldn't be that good to begin with. How much bitterness hops deliver into a beer is based on the makeup of the hops themselves, as well as how they are treated before, as well as when, they are added to the beer. Most hops are dried and formed into pellets before they are added to the beer. Sometimes, during harvest periods, hops are added fresh. This is called wet-hopping. Either way, the hops contain alpha acids, which yield bitterness. The longer the hops are boiled with the beer, the more bitter it becomes. When hops are boiled with the wort—the unfermented liquid mixture of malt and water—they add not only aroma and flavor, but also, since more alpha acids enter the beer, increased bitterness. When they are mixed in later in the process to already fermented beer, the process is called dry-hopping, and they contribute mostly to the aroma of the beer. Some hops are bred with an eye toward bitterness, and some for aroma and flavor. Some hops do double duty.

The closest analogue for what hops are to beer is what grapes are to wine, though you wouldn't ferment hops as you would grapes. But like grapes, hops carry with them terroir in a way that barley doesn't. There are hundreds of hop varieties out there with new ones constantly being bred. The earliest record of cultivated hops dates back to eighth-century Germany, but hops thrive in many temperate climates between the 47th and 49th parallels—that is, approximately the border between Canada and the United States of America. Today hops are divided into three broad categories based on regions: New World hops, from North America, which are known for their bold flavors; Old World hops, from Europe, which are known for their balance; and Oceania hops, including New Zealand and Australia, which are known for their tropical fruit notes. Until Prohibition, hops were a major crop in the United States, and to this day the country produces almost 44,000 pounds of hops, mostly grown on farms in the Pacific Northwest. The United States is second only to Germany in hops production and is trailed by China, where it is used mostly for domestic beers.

Depending on the type, hops can summon flavors ranging from coffee and chocolate to pine and citrus. To say that only hops bring bitterness gives short shrift to a variety of factors that can add to bitterness, or perceived bitterness. This includes how deeply a malt is roasted, as well as the chemical and mineral makeup of the water used.

While all beers have some element of bitterness, no beer better embodies the possibilities of hops than India Pale Ale. IPAs, as they are widely known, are one of the most innately hop-forward styles there are. The story of how IPAs came to be—and came to be so resolutely bitter—is bound in Colonial history. In the nineteenth century, the British functionaries who ruled India were thirsty. The local moonshine, arrak (which was made by fermenting raw palm juice and by all accounts tasted horrible), was—and still is—often toxic. And much of the pale beer English brewers sent on the six-month journey from England to India went bad before it arrived. Brewers like Hodgson and Bell's eventually realized hops not only provided a pleasing kick but also helped to ensure the beer's survival. As the British Empire continued to flourish into the late nineteenth century, so too did the beer brewed to slake the thirst of its colonial rulers.

In the intervening years, much has changed. The British colonial rule in India is gone, but sadly, for

years, IPAs were maligned. Happily—hoppily—in the past twenty years, as craft brewing has grown, bitterness in general, and IPAs in particular, are seeing a resurgence.

As with anything, it seems, there is an impulse to go to extremes. There are IPAs today with far too much bitterness. But for me, bitterness remains the architecture in which flavors can flourish. Like a house, it can be ornamental, but it must have a solid foundation.

As a brewer, it's also just fun to play around. The combination of hops, and how they can be treated, is inexhaustible. It's one of the great experimental sandboxes of brewing. Hops provide endless variety and the ability to conjure flavors seemingly out of thin air. Combining them is like the crazy alchemy of a spice-blender. A good example is Falco, Evil Twin's classic IPA.

I first made Falco in 2013, in the aftermath of what is now known as the Great 2008 Hops Shortage. One of the unfortunate side effects of the rehabilitation of IPAs is that the demand for hops has nearly outstripped the supply. During the shortage, two of my favorite hops, Citra and Centennial, were prohibitively expensive and impossible to get. With Falco, I wanted to make a beer that showcased the ingenuity of hops farmers. Whereas I might normally use Centennial Type, a hop blend made rare by the shortage, to make an IPA, with Falco I relied on Falconer's Flight, a citrusy blend made of more common Northwest hops, which did well as an improvised substitute. It was as if we had all run out of orange paint, so a few canny farmers decided to mix red and yellow. The result was a bitter, but well balanced, IPA with floral and citrus notes. Does it taste just like an IPA made of Citra and Centennial hops? I don't know—and frankly, I don't care. It just tastes good.

DANIEL Early November in 2006. A clear day, blue sky, and crisp air. Barren landscape blurring past the train window, what few trees there were had already lost their leaves. I had just moved to Copenhagen from London to run the pastry department at René Redzepi's lauded restaurant, Noma. After three years in England—both at Fergus Henderson's St. John as senior chef de partie and at Heston Blumenthal's The Fat Duck where I was in charge of the pastry mise en place,—I had, of course, heard of the gastronomic revolution happening in Copenhagen. So when I got the gig through my friend Matt Orlando, I signed a contract for a year there without hesitation. But as I sat on the train from the airport in Copenhagen, zooming past signs with Klingon-like vowels—like ø, with which I would later become very familiar—and listening to chatter I couldn't parse, I realized how alone I was. It wasn't panic that overtook me, but the excitement that greets a new voyage.

Quickly after I had settled into my apartment in Valby, a working-class suburb, I established a routine. Cooks are lucky that way. Their lives are dictated by the demands of the kitchen, broken down into mise en place, service, and cleanup. I didn't have too much free time to fill. Get up at 9 a.m., ride my Long John bike or take the train a half hour into the city, grab a chokoladebolle fresh from the bakery on the corner, and head into the kitchen at Noma. When I'd get off, around 1 a.m., I'd reverse that commute, crash, and repeat the next day.

I was alone but not unhappy. I was busy at Noma as well as with organizing Foodball, an annual invitational 5-aside football tournament that I started in 2008. Restaurants versus restaurants, which turned into a fun charity event, and also helped me to get acquainted with all of the wonderful characters of the city—chefs and waiters alike. Soon, I developed a community of friends, teammates, and colleagues. One guy who became all three was Matt Orlando. I first met Matt, a handsome kid from San Diego, at The Fat Duck when he was in the butcher department. We were an odd pair, an American and a Canadian in an English kitchen, before kitchen work turned into a global poker game. Matt had moved to Copenhagen in 2004 to be a sous-chef at Noma. While there he met his wife, Julie Bergstrøm, who also worked at the restaurant. (They would later open the Copenhagen restaurant, Amass, just hours after Luksus opened, in 2013.)

It was Matt who awoke me to the wonders of bitter bread. One day, when our rare days off overlapped, he asked me to join him and Julie at a place called Toldbod Bodega for smørrebrød. An open-faced sandwich, smørrebrød is to Denmark what heroes are to America—that is, a flag in edible form. Unlike, say, a cheesesteak, there are few restrictions as to what can go on a smørrebrød, but typically, you'll find smoked fish like mackerel and herring as well as rich fish curries, cold cuts, and cheeses. There are two things that make smørrebrød smørrebrød: the smør and the brød. Smør, or butter, is often whipped and spread on like a thick

blanket. The proper application is achieved when one's teeth leave a mark in its tracks, hence the term smør land, or tooth butter. Smørrebrød lives and dies on the brød served—inky dark, dense, studded with seed, and, to my palate, bracingly bitter. It is called rugbrød and it changed my world.

With my first bite of this dense bread came jarring flavors: sourness, earthiness, and beneath it all, bitterness. My first thought was, "Why would anyone make bread that tastes like this?" My second thought was, "Why wouldn't everyone make bread that tastes like this?" For the last sixty years, our North American palates have become accustomed to virginally white breads made for longevity and made soft, sweet, and pillowy through highly processed industrial ingredients. What got lost was flavor. Sandwich bread had become nothing but edible envelopes.

Compared to the cumulus of white sliced bread to which I had become accustomed, rugbrød is a block of earth. It actually resembles soil, thanks to the sunflower and flax seeds baked on top and within. Whereas most industrial bread uses processed flours and loads of sugar, this dough relies on rye (rug in Danish) and malt flour, which gives it its signature bitterness. Studded as it is with seeds and whole grain, the result is a seemingly austere blend of flavors, at once bitter and warm. But when combined with the fatty rich flavors of the fish curries or smoked herring that often accompany it and a thick slather of butter, it was like snuggling up next to a spiky pillow—and I loved it.

Over the three years I lived in Copenhagen, even as my circle of friends grew and the place started to feel more like home, that smørrebrød and the crystal-clear sense memory of rugbrød reminded me of my first few days in the new city. Now that those days are over, I find the flavors, and the memories of the many hours spent over smørrebrød with Matt and Julie, even more comforting. They are, after all, bittersweet.

Because it was so important a welcome to me in Denmark—and because, frankly, it's damn tasty—rugbrød never comes off the menu at Tørst. Dense, hearty, and at once comforting and unexpected, it's the perfect bar snack. At Tørst, the fight for bitter is still uphill. We as a society do not look upon bitterness kindly. When's the last time you heard someone described as bitter in a good way? The reasons for our recoil are well founded: evolutionarily, bitter isn't just a flavor, it's a warning. On a chemical level, what we call bitterness is caused by often-toxic compounds. Bitter is a plant's way of saying "stay away" to would-be munchers.

But when developed and tempered, bitterness can function as a powerful invitation to a meal. One of our most popular salads at Tørst is the highly bitter dandelion and mustard green salad we get from Eagle Street Rooftop Farm, the local farm run by Annie Novak. Dandelion greens, or more accurately dandelion chicories, are themselves pleasingly bitter greens. The salad embodies the lesser-known, but no less important, quality of bitter as a digestion aid and appetite enhancer. The salad is like an alarm clock for your senses, telling your body that it's time to eat.

As I said earlier, bitter is chemically a "no trespassing" sign; but what would adventure look like without a little rule breaking? Good behavior to bad—the proportion on which I model bitterness in what I cook. A healthy dose of bending the rules a bit makes living within the law's confines much sweeter. Too much, reckless, or unchecked bitterness can cause visceral repulsion. But without it, a dish can feel muddled—a dissolute scrum of flavors without structure. In that way, it's not so different than beer. In fact, it's not different at all.

This balance between bitter and sweet is best embodied in our malt desserts. In terms of beer, bitterness is the result of hops. During the fermentation process, malt breaks down into maltose, a sugar that gives beer what sweetness it has. But when malt isn't fermented, the flavor is instead bitter, like chewing on cacao nibs. In otherwise sweet desserts, I take full advantage of malt's delicate bitterness. If a slice of rugbrød and a dandelion salad initiates the diner into bitterness, a dessert like a parsnip parfait with malt and cranberry closes the circle. The dessert's main star is of course the parsnip, an unjustly overlooked taproot. Cooked in milk, the parsnip yields a not-too-sweet parfait. The vivacity of the dish, however, is the malt crumble, which gooses up the dessert's flavors—flavors I would never have developed had I not been lucky enough to know Matt, and experience the wonders of rugbrød, that Danish winter a decade ago.

MAKES 5
INDIVIDUAL LOAVES

Starter:
300 g buttermilk
225 g water
75 g yogurt
25 g yeast

10 g sugar

Seed Soak:
575 g steel-cut (porridge) oats
260 g flax seeds
225 g sunflower seeds
60 g kosher salt
200 g buttermilk

120 g Starter
75 g yogurt
75 g beer, preferably IPA
600 g tepid water

SAISON + RUGBRØD, SEASONAL GREENS SALAD, HOUSE VINAIGRETTE

SUGGESTION: SAISON DU PONT, BRASSERIE DUPONT

I'm Danish. Rugbrød is my patrimony. And I have to say: Daniel makes a terrific loaf. Rugbrød is dense and intensely flavored. A thick blanket of whipped butter, with its sweet fat, balances out the bread's nutty, bitter notes. In Denmark one typically drinks a Pilsner with smørrebrød. But here I've chosen a Belgian farmhouse-style ale called saison. Historically, saisons were brewed during the winter to be drunk during the summer by thirsty farmhands. They are crisp, moderately bitter, top-fermented beers made strong to last for months in the bottle without spoiling. In the bottle they undergo a secondary fermentation, which yields a complex constellation of flavors: fruity, herbal, bitter, for sure, but with a balanced, long finish. There's enough going on in a saison—particularly one from the Brasserie Dupont, an actual working farm in Tourpes, Belgium—in terms of aromas. Theirs has banana, citrus (the result of a chemical compound called esters) and herbal notes, like clove and ginger, to make it a worthy companion to my precious rugbrød.

— JEPPE

Rugbrød:
375 g rye flour
35 g malt flour
262 g tipo "00" flour
240 g tepid water
125 g beer, preferably IPA
45 g yeast

Make the starter:
In a large bowl, whisk together all the starter ingredients. Move the bowl to a baking sheet in case the starter bubbles over. Let sit, uncovered, for 2 hours or until the froth subsides. Store in the refrigerator until needed. [Note: A starter can last for years, if regularly fed. So you can make this starter whenever you feel the urge.]

Make the seed soak:
In a large baking pan, mix evenly together the oats, flax seeds, sunflower seeds, and salt. In a medium bowl, whisk together the buttermilk, starter, yogurt, and beer. The consistency of the mixture should be kefir-esque. Gently combine the wet ingredients with the dry ingredients, pour in the tepid water, and mix well. Store covered in the refrigerator for at least 3 and up to 6 days.

Make the rugbrød:
Preheat the oven to 215°F/100°C/Gas Mark ¼.

In a large bowl, whisk together the rye flour and malt flour until smooth and completely and evenly incorporated. Now, whisk in the tipo "00" flour until incorporated. (If the mixture is not well incorporated, there will be lumps of malt in the final product.) In another bowl, whisk together the tepid water, beer, and yeast.

In the bowl of a stand mixer fitted with the paddle attachment, combine the yeasty beer mixture, the soaked seeds, and the flour mixture. Pulse the mixer on low speed to slowly incorporate all of the ingredients. Mix on low speed until uniformly combined, about 2 minutes.

Coat the insides of five 1-pound loaf pans with cooking spray. Divide the dough into fifths. Working each section of the dough back and forth in your hands, form a compact football shape, squishing out air bubbles. Distribute into pans.

Use the back of your hand (wear latex gloves so the dough doesn't stick to your hands) to press the dough evenly on top and flatten the dough into an even brick in the loaf pan. The dough should be about 1 inch/2.5 cm below the rim. Sprinkle 50 g flax seeds evenly over the bread.

Here comes the baking: Bake at 215°F/100°C/Gas Mark ¼ for 3 minutes, splashing water on the floor of the oven several times to add steam. Leaving the bread in the oven, increase the temperature to 410°F/210°C/Gas Mark 6 and bake for 10 minutes. Then reduce the temperature to 320°F/160°C/Gas Mark 3 and bake for another 50 minutes.

Remove the bread from the oven. Working quickly, invert the loaves onto a baking sheet and return to the oven for 50 minutes. When done, the loaves should sound dull and hollow when tapped with the palm of your hand and the seeds should be golden brown.

Remove the bread from the oven and allow to cool, uncovered, at room temperature for 2 hours on the baking sheet.

To serve, cut the bread into ⅛-inch/3 mm slices and serve with Yogurt-Touched Whipped Butter (see page 251).

NOTE: Wrapped in plastic and stored in the refrigerator, rugbrød can last 1 week; stored in the freezer, it can last for several months.

SEASONAL GREENS SALAD, RYE CRUMBLE

SERVES 4

60 g clarified butter
60 g rye bread, coarsely grated
Maldon salt
200 g dandelion and mustard greens
House Vinaigrette (Pantry page 251)

In a sauté pan, melt the clarified butter over medium heat. Fry the rye bread crumbs, stirring until browned and fragrant. Using a slotted spoon, transfer the crumbs to a tray lined with paper towels. Salt lightly.

Wash and pat the greens dry; trim into thirds. In a large bowl, toss the greens with the vinaigrette and sprinkle with salt. Divide the greens across 4 bowls and top each with rye crumble.

Food & Beer

SERVES 6

Gjetøst:
50 g gjetøst
200 g fresh cow's milk ricotta
30 g hot water
Fresh lemon juice
Maldon salt

Pork Mince:
20 g grapeseed oil
750 g ground (minced) pork
90 g minced shallots
15 g minced garlic
15 g minced fresh ginger
5 g urfa biber chile
4 g paprika

100 g tomato paste
    (double concentrate purée)
50 g white miso
45 g sherry vinegar
10 g Worcestershire sauce
Fresh lemon juice
Maldon salt

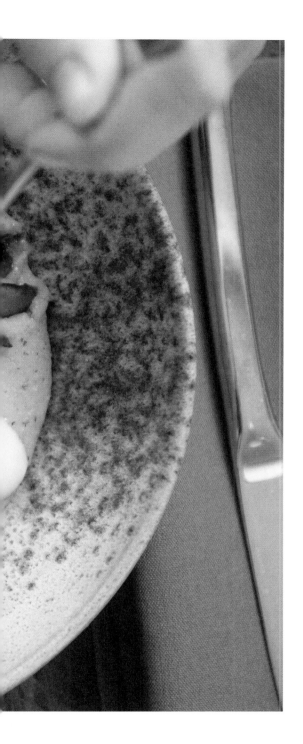

INDIA PALE ALE
+ SAGAMITÉ, PORK MINCE,
GJETØST

SUGGESTION: FALCO, EVIL TWIN

A light but sturdy IPA like Falco can hold its own against some pretty strong, rich flavors. I've always wanted to do a classic polenta Bolognese, but with a Tørst touch. When my friends at the Québecois collective, Société-Orignale, sent down some sagamité, a type of freshly milled unsifted cornmeal, I knew I had my chance. Sagamité isn't polenta per se, but it tastes like the best polenta you've ever had—just as rich, but with a more intense, fresher flavor. The pork mince is a Mangalitsa blend with a third made up of smoky bacon that we get from a New Jersey farm, Møsefund (gotta love the Ø). The gjetøst (a sweet, firm, golden-brown cheese, popular in Norway, traditionally made with goat's milk) adds a creamy luxuriousness. Not many beers could stand up to, or effectively cut through, the volume of so many rich ingredients, but Falco does it beautifully.

— DANIEL

Sagamité:
1050 g Vegetable Stock
    (Pantry page 248)
165 g sagamité
Kosher salt
15 g butter

Roasted Maitake Mushrooms:
160 g maitake mushrooms
Olive oil
Butter
Maldon salt
Fresh lemon juice

Make the gjetøst:
Cut the gjetøst into small pieces. In a food processor, combine the gjetøst and ricotta and blend until smooth but not too runny. Add hot water as needed, until the consistency is slightly thinner than sour cream. Season to taste with lemon juice and salt until the mixture tastes bright. Cover and refrigerate for at least 1 hour and up to 2 days.

Make the pork mince:
Heat a large heavy skillet over medium-high heat with just enough grapeseed oil to coat the bottom. Sprinkle half of the pork over the surface of the pan and cook, stirring occasionally, until lightly browned, about 4 minutes. Use a slotted spoon to move the meat to a colander set over a rimmed baking sheet. Repeat with the remaining pork.

Return half of the rendered fat from the baking sheet to the skillet and set over medium-high heat. Add the shallots and cook until slightly browned, about 3 minutes. Add the garlic, then the ginger, and fry until all three are nicely browned, a further 4 minutes. Reduce the heat to medium, add another splash of oil, the urfa biber, and paprika and cook, stirring, for about 30 seconds. Add the tomato paste and stir frequently as it cooks. Continue to cook until the mixture slightly darkens to a rusty hue, about 2 minutes. Add the miso and stir until it is fully integrated with the tomato paste. Deglaze the pan with the vinegar and Worcestershire sauce. Return the pork to the pan and cook for 1 minute, mixing thoroughly. Adjust the seasoning with lemon juice and salt. Serve immediately or refrigerate until needed.

Make the sagamité:
In a medium pot, heat the vegetable stock over medium heat until it reaches about 140°F/60°C. Start pouring the sagamité into the pot and whisk well to incorporate and ensure that no lumps form. Add a good pinch of kosher salt. Increase the heat to medium-high and whisk constantly until bubbles break the surface and the sagamité has thickened, about 6 minutes. Remove from the heat. Whisk in the butter until fully emulsified. Serve immediately or refrigerate until needed.

Make the roasted maitake mushrooms:
Gently pull the maitakes to find where the stem and cap would like to split; pull or cut them apart. Without cutting off the entire base, trim the base roots off, leaving the piece above intact.

Just before serving, warm a medium sauté pan over high heat. Add a good splash of olive oil and cook the mushrooms on the flat side until well browned; flip and add a large spoonful of butter. Continue to cook for another minute on high heat. Add a good pinch of salt. Check if the mushrooms are cooked through and if not keep rolling them around the hot pan until they are. Add a splash of lemon juice and remove the mushrooms from the pan onto a tray lined with paper towels. Season once again before serving.

Assemble the dish:
Divide the hot sagamité across 6 large bowls. Reheat the pork mixture, if needed, and divide over the sagamité. Add the maitake mushroom on top of the sagamité, then add a dollop of gjestøst.

FUNKY

JEPPE   How do you fit a barnyard into a bottle? Just ask the Trappist monks at the Abbaye Notre Dame d'Orval in southern Belgium. Those dudes make one of the funkiest beers on earth. Uncork a bottle of Orval and it's like sliding open the door to a horse-barn discotheque. Yeah, it's a barn, but it's also a party. The aromas of hay and horse blankets, perhaps some clover or field flowers, plus a sharp hard-to-define tartness, waft from the bottle. This is the funk. Can you feel it?

The secret to the monk's beer isn't Jesus, but rather a family of yeasts called Brettanomyces. Bretts, as they are also called, account for much of what is described as funky in beer. They are the slightly more domesticated cousins of some of the truly wild yeasts that waft in to make other beers like the famous lambics (see SOUR, page 76). But where lambics turn sour, Brett beers turn funky. They are hard to handle and unpredictable, but still domesticated, yeasts. That means one has to physically add Brett to beer, as opposed to letting the wild yeast of lambics simply waft in. The results are therefore slightly more predictable though no less exciting. If lambics are wolves, Brett beers are rescue dogs: not entirely wild but not entirely house-trained. And when it comes to inviting lambics or Bretts to the table, a lambic is often too stridently sour to pair with food whereas a Brett is a faithful companion.

As you might guess, Brett and I have a lot in common. So much so that I've taken the unusual step at Evil Twin Brewing of basing a series of beers, called Femme Fatales, on 100 percent Brettanomyces fermentation. Because you never know what you'll get with a Brett fermentation, this is sort of like going all in on a bet. But the payoff can be huge.

Exactly how funky a Brett is primarily depends on when the yeast is added to the beer and what specific strain of Brett yeast is used. One reason Orval is so funky is that the Brett is added once the beer is already in the bottle. Once the bottle is closed, it's a free-for-all as the Brettanomyces digest any residual sugars in the beer, yielding both funky flavors and CO_2. As in most additives in brewing, the later you add something in the fermentation process, the heavier an impression they make on the beer. In the case of a Brett beer like Orval, it's impossible to know the character the Brett will take until you open a bottle. It's like a magic trick: two bottles from the same fermentation can taste wildly different a few years apart. The flavors can be floral and fruity all the way to musty and earthy and it changes over time. But there is one thing that is guaranteed: It will be funky.

DANIEL "Hmmm, that's funky," can be said in a good way—or a bad way, depending on the tone of voice and the context. This particular and imprecise usage isn't one I'm interested in. Instead, I want to talk about meat funk, a technical term to describe the flavors that comes from aging a piece of meat in a carefully controlled environment. Vintners have their noble rot; chefs, dry-aging.

Taste a freshly butchered ribeye steak versus one left to age for twenty-eight or forty-two days and you'll immediately understand what this funk is. The taste of the aged meat is mellower, the mouthfeel is buttery, and there's a sweetness to it. These powers combined equal meat funk. Over time, as water evaporates from the meat and fat, and mold—the good kind—forms a barrier on the exterior of the meat, the meat undergoes a quiet transformation. Enzymes break proteins down into amino acids that deliver wallops of flavor. Carbohydrates melt and resolve into sugar, and the connective tissue that renders steak chewy is broken down. Like sour, funk is a function of time, but with the addition of control and isolation.

I came to New York on an O-1 Visa, the so-called "outstanding ability" visa. When I flew down through Nova Scotia, the border guard said the first time he saw one of those was when George Harrison came through. In June 2009, I left Noma to become the head of research and development at David Chang's Momofuku Test Kitchen. I had met Dave at the first "Cook It Raw," an annual conclave of chefs, in Copenhagen. Many chefs have test kitchens and each runs his or hers in a different way. Ferran Adrià huddles with his brother, Albert, in a secret location. René had his Nordic Food Lab. David Chang turned the ground floor of a building on East 10th Street in New York City into his. The idea was that I would solve questions he posed. How could we capture umami? How do you make koji, an inoculated rice product? What about rice paper? What's the deal with fermentation? It was Chang's idea that we not be seen in public so we drew the blinds and worked by fluorescent light.

I was alone in there for three months until another chef, Dan Felder, joined. All day, every day, Dan and I tested recipes, experimented with new techniques, explored new products. It was the first—and only—"regular" job I had. We were in at 9 a.m. and out by 6 p.m., so I could, for once, hang out with normal people. I joined a ball hockey team. I got to know the city.

At the time Chang had Ssam, Noodle Bar, and Ko. Each restaurant had its own chef responsible for his own menu. Naturally, each chef was reticent to adopt a dish from another chef, me included. Quickly after joining the test kitchen, I realized there was little chance of the recipes I had developed ever getting on the menus at any Momofuku, and I don't blame the chefs either. If someone told me I had to use another chef's recipe, I'd be very skeptical. So there was a lot of, "Nice dish, Dan," and eye-rolls; it was a poignant introduction to New York's restaurant scene. I had come from the very collaborative culture of European restaurants where we shared everything; but in New York, it was every chef for himself.

My time at Momofuku were a silencing act, a hibernation. In that windowless kitchen for three years, I metamorphosed. Knowing my recipes would never see the light of day—literally—I began to cook for myself. I thought hard about the balance of flavors. I meditated on methodology. I studied soy sauces and seaweeds. I became obsessed with texture. In isolation, I learned to visualize recipes in my head, down to the gram; and upon testing, they'd actually work!

With only time as my audience, no idea was too ridiculous to try. During those years, I learned to hone that process of experimentation; and take a silly idea seriously. When confronted with a new product, don't panic. Simply apply processes with which you are already familiar. See familiar products in new ways. Treat byproducts as products. The overlooked and misunderstood parts became the most important ones for me. Instead of mustard greens, what of mustard flowers? Instead of chicken thighs what about chicken oysters? When I emerged from that experience, I was a different chef. There's no way I could have helped it. I had gotten funky.

BELGIAN STRONG ALE + DRY-AGED RIBEYE, PICKLED RAMPS

SUGGESTION: TRAPPIST ROCHEFORT 8, BRASSERIE DE ROCHEFORT

Isolation and maturation, naturally, give rise to intense flavors. This is as true of a ribeye as it is of Daniel. So how does one support those brash flavors? To push back and even out the intense funky richness of the ribeye, you need a beer with substantial body and a robust ABV (alcohol by volume). Belgian Strong Ale is an ideal candidate, since the style offers formidable heft—the dark-roasted flavors of its malt and outer edges of fruity notes, which come from the yeasts. It's also no coincidence that these strong ales are often made in the Trappist abbeys that dot Belgium. The monks at the Abbaye Notre-Dame de Saint-Remy, for instance, where Rochefort is brewed, divide their time into equal parts work, prayer, and rest. This beer, the No. 8, was originally brewed for New Year's celebrations, but, since 1960, has been made year round. It's hefty and complex, with a 9.2% ABV. Like all beers from the abbey this one is bottle-conditioned, so the yeast is left to its own devices once the beer is bottled. This means that the longer it sits alone and undisturbed, the better it becomes. And thankfully, just like the ribeye and just like Daniel, there's no bitterness. Just a complexity and hard-earned balance.

— JEPPE

SERVES 6

30 g butter (plus more as
   needed)
1 bone-in ribeye steak with
   cap (sometimes called a
   tomahawk steak),
   aged 40 days
3 bay leaves
3 thyme sprigs
240 g Pickled Ramps
   (Pantry page 250)

Preheat the oven to 355°F/180°C/Gas Mark 4.

Preheat the oven to 355°F/180°C/Gas Mark 4.

In small sauté pan, melt 30 g butter over medium heat and cook until the solids brown and the butter smells nutty. Strain and set aside to cool.

Using a very sharp knife, separate the meat from its bone and cut away any dry bits of aged, overly funky meat. Remove the fat cap from the ribeye. Put the cap in a vacuum bag along with 10 g of the brown butter, 1 bay leaf, and 1 thyme sprig. In another vacuum bag, pack the ribeye with the remaining brown butter, and the bay leaves and thyme. Vacuum-seal each. Cook the ribeye in a water bath set to 128°F/54°C for 35 minutes and the cap in the same bath for 50 minutes. Let the meat rest for 10 minutes. Leave out if you'll eat it right away or shock in an ice bath and keep refrigerated if you want to eat it later.

If you've stored your meat, let it temper for 90 minutes on the counter. Meanwhile preheat the oven to 355°F/180°C/Gas Mark 4.

When you're ready for service, remove the meat and fat cap from their bags. In a heavy pan set over medium-high heat, render the fat from the beef cap. Move the pan to the oven and cook until medium, about 5 minutes. [We like the cap cooked more than our other meats as it is full of fat, which takes on a very special character as it heats up.]

Meanwhile, use the same pan to roast all sides of the ribeye. On the final side, add a good pat of butter and some thyme sprigs. Baste the meat aggressively with the butter as it browns. Remove the meat before the butter burns. Transfer the meat to a baking sheet and roast with the cap until just warmed through (remember, the meat has already been cooked in the bath, you are just warming it to serve at this point).

Let the ribeye and cap rest for 10 minutes in a warm spot and then slice into 6 slices from each piece across the grain. Serve on warmed plates with a few pieces of pickled ramps.

BRETT-FERMENTED BEER + CONFITED DUCK SANDWICH

SUGGESTION: ORVAL, ORVAL BREWERY

Opening a bottle of Orval is like inviting a very opinionated friend over to a dinner party. Regardless of how interesting he or she is, you have to pick the company carefully. You don't want a wallflower but you also don't want another alpha. I try to temper Bretts—not just Orval but also Jeppe's Femme Fatales, which uses Brett as its primary fermentation—with bold but soft flavors. Our duck confit sandwich, for instance, has lush texture and flavor, thanks to the fattiness of the protein and the richness of the confit that fills in the gaps of a Brett-forward beer. Basically, you want a cushioning agent that won't be overwhelmed but also won't be competitive. [I wouldn't kick a pâté de campagne out of my bed at this point.] Of course, even within the sandwich, the softness of the duck is mitigated by the tang of our pickles and the crunch of the crusty bread. And that's what you want: interesting internal monologues that make for compelling dialogues, which, in turn, make for many interesting bites.

— DANIEL

MAKES 4

Duck Confit:
25 g black peppercorns
12 g Sichuan peppercorns
25 g juniper berries
18 g star anise
10 g cinnamon stick
750 g coarse salt
25 g demerara sugar
8 Peking duck legs
2000 g rendered duck fat

Duck Sandwich Dressing:
80 g House Vinaigrette
    (Pantry page 251)
60 g sour cream
50 g Mayonnaise
    (Pantry page 250)
15 g Hot Sauce
    (Pantry page 250)

Confited Duck Sandwich:
Maldon salt
80 g mixed greens, such as
    young arugula (rocket)
    or mustard greens
400 g duck confit meat
4 ciabatta rolls
80 g Sandwich Dressing
80 g Pickled Kirby Cucumber
    (Pantry page 249)
80 g Pickled Green Cabbage
    (Pantry page 249)

Make the duck confit:

In a blender, pulse the black and Sichuan peppercorns, juniper berries, star anise, and cinnamon stick to a medium-coarse texture. Remove from the blender and transfer to a mixing bowl, then combine evenly with the salt and sugar. This is your cure. In a nonreactive container, gently toss the duck legs in about one-third of the cure. Sprinkle another third on the bottom of a baking pan. Arrange the duck legs snugly, but not overlapping, in the baking pan, and cover with the remaining cure. Cover and refrigerate for 12 hours.

Preheat the oven to 160°F/72°C.

Remove and brush off the excess cure and wash the duck in cool water until clean. Place the duck legs in a Dutch oven with a lid or a roasting pan. Gently melt the duck fat in a saucepan over low heat and pour over the duck legs. Cover with a lid or aluminum foil and cook in the oven for 12 to 14 hours, until tender and falling off the bone. Remove from the oven and let cool until you can comfortably handle the meat.

To prepare the duck, pull off the skin and pick the meat from the bones (discard the fatty bits of skin, bone, and cartilage).

Make the duck sandwich dressing:

Whisk together all of the dressing ingredients. Cover and refrigerate for at least 1 hour.

Make the sandwiches:

In a bowl, lightly salt the mixed greens and set aside. In a medium pot, warm the duck meat gently over medium heat, stirring with a spoon, for about 5 minutes. The duck will likely stick to the bottom of the pan and crisp up; these bits are very tasty.

Split the ciabatta rolls and toast in a 355°F/180°C oven until slightly crisped and warm throughout, about 5 minutes. Assemble the sandwiches by spreading the duck dressing evenly on each side of each roll. Pile on the duck, cucumber and cabbage pickles, and some greens. Serve immediately.

SWEET

JEPPE   Flavor wise, beer is a ménage à trois. Hops are cautious, careful, and impart a bitter flavor. Yeast, as we'll soon find out, is mercurial and dynamic. And malt is the sweetheart.

Malt actually refers not to the grain itself— often barley, as wheat, oat, and rye can also be used—but to the process by which it is dried, allowed to germinate, and dried again. This process is called malting. Malts contain maltose, a sugar, so it is no mystery why malt is the source for sweetness—and alcohol—in beer. As opposed to sugar's use in baking, through the fermentation process, sugar goes through a chemical transformation. When I give beer tastings, I channel my former school teacher self to explain, "Yeast is a living creature that eats the sugars in the malt as it stews in the wort. It pees out alcohol and farts out CO_2." (You can see why I was so popular at my school.) Naturally, the higher the sugar content in the wort, the higher the alcohol by volume (ABV) one can end up with since there is more to pee out. These two levels—the sugar before fermentation, and the sugar afterwards—are called the "original gravity" and the "final gravity," respectively. They are among the most important measurements to a

brewer because they allow one to calculate the ABV. Since yeast can only digest a finite amount of sugar before they're "full," the higher the original gravity, the higher the final gravity and the more residual sugars are left in the beer.

Since there are no dessert beers like there are dessert wines, there isn't a context in which beer can, or should, cavort in unbridled sweetness. Even if there were, I wouldn't make an entirely sweet beer, because it would be unbalanced. Daniel and I share the approach that sweetness is a beast best kept leashed. But, as it is integral to the brewing process, the importance of sugar shouldn't be underestimated. There would be no alcohol if there were no sugars to feed the yeast.

Of all the common styles, stouts are the most "malt-forward." Imperial Stouts, which are usually over 8% ABV, are nearly double the ABV of standard stouts, and are therefore even more malt-forward. Stouts are dark beers, made dark because of the deep roast of the malt used. That roast is what carries the rich notes of, for example, coffee and chocolate that make stouts so fun to drink. And it's the residual sugar that steers the flavors away from bitterness.

So jazzed am I on the style, and so popular is it, that one of the very first beers I ever made when I started Evil Twin Brewing was an Imperial Stout. It's called Even More Jesus and I guess you could say it's the beer that put me on the map. In 2011, I had just quit teaching and was looking to increase my portfolio of beers. Not having a brewery of my own, I was emailing back and forth with my American importer and friend, Brian Ewing, about contract brewing. I knew the secret of the stout is the mixture of malts, so I had the idea to combine eight different malts together to create the stout. Obviously that was going to be more expensive. As we approached breweries, one after the other, they came back with quotes of increasing financial untenability. "Jesus!" I wrote to Brian. He replied, "Well, we just got another quote. It's even more." "Even more, Jesus!" I replied. But Brian said he didn't care how much it cost. He was going to get this beer made and it was going to be excellent. "Even More Jesus" became our rallying cry. We would never sacrifice quality for price.

Even More Jesus has gone on to be one of our most popular beers. It alone has spawned Double Barrel Jesus, in which the stout is aged in rye and bourbon barrels for twelve months; Even More Jesus Port, aged in port barrels; and Una Mas Jesus, an Imperial Stout I made at the Companyia Cervesera del Montseny in Spain. One of the surprising developments is that those stouts, it turns out, have deep and rich enough flavors to accommodate the most insane additions. Over the years, I've added everything from beef jerky to cola nut to the beer, admittedly with mixed results. That cola nut experiment exploded, turning my kitchen into a stout-covered wasteland. Maria was not amused. But whenever I tell Brian about a new crazy idea, he rolls his eyes and says, "Even more, Jesus." And yet—we always find a way.

DANIEL   Signs of our national sugary obsession are abundant: Unnaturally bright cereal, floating like tiny life preservers in a sea of milk, greet our tongues like a reveille; the line that forms at dawn at Peter Pan, the doughnut shop near the restaurant, with its trays full of still-warm donuts, sugary glaze still glossy; the perplexing charm of cheese danishes and the unending parade of pains au chocolat that issues from bakeries and delis alike. Man craves sweetness. But me? I've never been a fan.

Those might seem strange words coming from someone who has spent years in the pastry world, a

discipline held by the four holy pillars of flour, dairy, eggs, and, most of all, sugar. But, it was James "Jocky" Petrie, the wonderfully crazy Scottish pastry chef with whom I worked at The Fat Duck, who taught me to be wary of sweet seductions. He saw sweetness as a lion tamer does his lions. For him it was an element that must be tempered rather than turbocharged. Jocky knew the best desserts lived in the no-man's-land between savory and sweet. That's why he hired savory cooks like me who didn't think solely in terms of sweetness as a trained pastry chef might.

Unfortunately, the temptation for many savory chefs, perhaps giddy at the chance, is to churn out cloyingly sweet desserts. Sugar can be a braggart, a bully, and a boor. Charming, to be sure, seductive to the point of addictive, sweetness is the kind of dinner party guest who takes up all the oxygen in the room. You can't get a word in edgewise. Try an inexpertly sweetened panna cotta or treacly pot de crème, for instance, and you'll taste how overwhelming the flavor can be. Of course, that doesn't mean sugar in its myriad forms shouldn't be invited. One important function sweetness serves is to signal to the diner where she is in the geography of her meal. Desserts, with their ramping up of sweetness, signal a winding down of a dining experience. But I want my desserts to be in the same neighborhood as the dishes that form the main body. There's nothing more jarring than travelling from a well-balanced layered dish like lamb with roast turnip and pickled spring onions to a head-bobbing, pupil-dilating sweet dessert. It's like walking from one restaurant into another without so much as getting up from your seat. Neat trick but not much fun.

When used wisely, sweetness is a versatile element. Time and time again, I lean on the sweetness imbued by caramelized onions in roasted vegetable purées, like sunchoke and rutabaga, to provide a subtle rejoinder to the deep-roasted char flavors of the vegetables. In the sunchoke, for example, the onions soften and deepen the flavor.

Conversely, in conventionally sweet desserts, I prefer to err on the side of under-sweetened. My rule of thumb is that one should taste savory first and sweetness second, but, ideally, at the same time. The goal is to find that moment of effortless equilibrium between the sweet and savory that is at once peaceful and unexpected.

That's one reason I love ices so ardently: They occupy the perfect nexus between savory and sweet. Especially when the base is savory. At Tørst, we've made ices with cranberry, juniper, wintergreen, and sorrel. My favorite, perhaps, is the pine ice.

All along the East Coast in early spring, as spruce and fir trees start to bud, they produce light green shoots. It's a lot of work to clip them, but thankfully, in Evan Strusinki, I have a loyal friend and forager. It's important to harvest the shoots in this small window, when they have all of the pine's essential oils but none of the astringency the needles develop later in life. They happen to make a tremendous ice. Though we use sweet cream and sugar, the sweetness is mitigated in a few key ways. The lowered temperature of the ice, around 7°F/-14°C, tamps down the sugar while the natural acidity of the pine—or whatever other savory base it might be—trims sweetness's sails.

If controlling sweetness was one chief lesson learned from pastry, the other was the importance of precision. In fact, these two lessons go hand in hand. Once one realizes the power of sugar, one must wield it carefully and accurately. One of the most useful tools a chef concerned with sugar can own is a handheld refractometer. It sounds fancy and laboratorial, but it's actually a very convenient, and easy-to-use, way to measure the level of sugar in a liquid solution, thus the level of sweetness a dessert will have. The level of sugar in a liquid is measured in a unit called Brix, named after the nineteenth-century German engineer, Adolf Ferdinand Wenceslaus Brix. Anything above thirty Brix is going to read as SWEET in all caps. Any underlying flavor will be subservient to that sweetness. In our sorbet we keep the Brix at around twenty-four.

In baked desserts, which are the true domain of pastry, that particular tool isn't applicable. But, as in ices, I rely not only on limiting the addition of sugar, but also in the introduction of naturally tart or herbal flavors to cut the sweetness. In Denmark, flødeboller—the chocolate-covered Italian meringue puffs similar to Whippets I had as a kid—are ubiquitous and admittedly delicious, but they're deadly sweet. As a child, I loved Whippets, but my wise mother would limit me to one or two, because otherwise I'd run around hyperactively for hours.

To any Dane, flødeboller are like a little chocolate-covered embassy of home. At Tørst, I wanted that comforting crowd-pleasing feeling, but I knew I'd have to find a way to maintain the DNA of the treat while taming some of its sweetness. Instead of using traditional meringue, I folded in a purée of pea and mint. Mint and chocolate are so obvious a combination they need not be explained, as are peas and mint, which have been served together for years in dishes like English pea soup with mint. Why hadn't anyone combined all three? The vegetal flavors of the peas, the sharp acidity of the mint, and the slight bitterness of the dark chocolate form an alliance, which reins in the sugar that one needs to make the meringue. Oh, it's sweet, as flødebolle should be, but it's also a taut, well-balanced treat. (We also serve a flødebolle as a petit four at Luksus.)

But before it seems like I'm on an anti-sweet tirade, let me just say: I grew up eating tenaciously sweet Maple Leaf Creme cookies by Dare in the 1980s; I am not above succumbing to a little sugar shock. Who is? No one, as I learned with Noma's infamous chocolate brownie.

When I worked with René Redzepi, the warehouse Noma occupied in Copenhagen's Christianshavn also housed a few other companies, such as the consulate for the Faroe Islands. Part of the agreement René had struck with the landlord was that we would also provide lunches at the office café. The remit was sandwiches and something sweet, so I made a brownie recipe that would serve its purpose during lunch and still be very good on its own. The café made for a wonderfully schizophrenic kitchen. Some days we would simultaneously be plating two desserts for Michelin inspectors while preparing a ham sandwich and a brownie for a paper salesman. That brownie, though, became legendary, both among the office workers and the staff at Noma, where we'd sometimes serve it at staff meal. The brownie is like an Autobahn of sugar but made with quality ingredients. The best brownie is half-baked. You only cook it nine minutes. Even out of the oven, it stays obscenely gooey, and that's the secret. There are some feints at balance: granules of salt, for instance, and hazelnuts. But here, I thought of the balance differently. It wasn't internal but holistic. For many of the folks who worked in that block of offices, their lunch hour, that brownie, was perhaps the only moment of sweetness they enjoyed before they returned to work.

MAKES 30 FLØDEBOLLER

Strawberry Butter Cookie:
150 g butter, diced
100 g sugar
12 g strawberry powder
205 g all-purpose (plain) flour

1 g baking powder
1 g Maldon salt
30 g egg yolks

Simple Syrup:
350 g water
50 g sugar

Mint Syrup:
55 g fresh mint leaves
200 g Simple Syrup

Mint Pea Liquid:
190 g Mint Syrup
70 g frozen peas

IMPERIAL STOUT + PEA MINT FLØDEBOLLER, STRAWBERRY BUTTER COOKIE

SUGGESTION: EVEN MORE JESUS, EVIL TWIN BREWING

Make the cookies:
Let the butter stand at room temperature for 20 minutes to soften slightly. In a stand mixer fitted with the paddle attachment, beat the sugar and butter together on low speed. Scrape the sides several times. Once incorporated, scrape again, add the strawberry powder, and mix on low until incorporated.

In another bowl, whisk together the flour, baking powder, and salt. Add the flour mixture one half at a time to the butter-sugar mixture and work on low speed until mealy, about 1 minute. With the mixer running, add the yolks, one at a time.

Divide the dough into 3 equal portions. Place each portion between 2 sheets of parchment paper and, using a rolling pin, roll into a sheet ⅛ inch/3 mm thick. Freeze for at least 3 hours and up to 1 week.

Remove the dough from the freezer and use a Matfer #30 (30 mm/1¼-inch) ring cutter to punch the frozen sheets into discs. If you punch the cookies quite close together you should have about 90 pieces. Alas, you may not reroll the dough. Keep the discs frozen in layers separated by sheets of parchment, in a covered container, until ready to bake.

To make the flødeboller, preheat the oven to 320°F/160°C/Gas Mark 3.

Remove the frozen cookie rounds and place on a heavy baking sheet. Bake the cookies until lightly browned, 11 to 13 minutes. Remove and let cool on the baking sheet. Once cool, transfer the cookies to a baking sheet lined with a wire cooling rack.

Meringue:
135 g Mint Pea Liquid
12 g sugar
25 g egg white powder
12 g pea powder

Meringue Syrup:
85 g sugar
90 g glucose
60 g water

Coating Chocolate:
500 g 64% dark chocolate
65 g powdered cocoa butter

Make the simple syrup:
In a small saucepan, combine the water and sugar and bring to a boil until the sugar is completely dissolved. Remove from the heat and refrigerate or cool over an ice bath.

Make the mint syrup:
In a large pot of boiling water, blanch the mint for 45 seconds. Remove with a slotted spoon and transfer to an ice bath. Drain the mint and squeeze out as much water as possible.

Blend with the cooled simple syrup for 25 seconds. Pass through a chinois into a bowl, pressing through with the back of a ladle.

Make the mint pea liquid:
Measure out 190 g of the mint syrup and transfer to a blender. (Set the remaining mint syrup aside.) Add the frozen peas to the blender and blend for 90 seconds. Pass the mixture through a chinois into a bowl, pressing through with the back of a ladle. Set aside.

Make the meringue:
In the bowl of a stand mixer, combine all the meringue ingredients, and holding the whisk attachment with your hand, use it to roughly combine the ingredients. Attach the whisk to the mixer and whip on medium-high speed until the meringue rises significantly, about 5 minutes. If the volume doesn't expand much, increase the speed to high and continue to whip until it does.

Make the meringue syrup:
In a 1-quart heavy-bottomed saucepan, combine all the meringue syrup ingredients. Set the pan over medium-low heat and cook until the syrup reaches 237°F/114°C. Let stand for a few seconds.

Pour a small dollop of the hot syrup into the meringue. With the motor running, whisk the ingredients for 5 seconds, then add a second dollop of hot syrup. Repeat once more. Now add the rest of the syrup in a steady stream. Continue whisking on medium speed until the meringue is at room temperature, about 10 minutes.

Fit a piping bag with a #10 INOX tip (10 mm). Fill with the meringue and pipe onto the strawberry butter cookies, still on the cooling rack. Keeping the tip low, pipe until the meringue comes just to the edge of the cookie. Raise the tip and repeat creating a 2-inch/5 cm-high ribbed cylinder of meringue. To get the perfect peak, stop squeezing

the piping bag, and quickly lift the tip up and away from the meringue at a 45-degree angle. Trial and error is needed to get the shapes perfect. This takes practice.

Refrigerate the meringue cookies on the rack for several hours and allow them to firm up.

Make the coating chocolate:
Combine the chocolate and cocoa butter in a metal bowl set over a small pot of water over medium-low heat. Stirring occasionally, melt the chocolate completely. Remove the bowl to a towel-lined cake pan (to ensure that the bowl doesn't contact the surface) and set aside in a cool part of the kitchen. Stir every 10 minutes with a wooden spoon until the chocolate has cooled to 86°F/30°C. Return the bowl to the double boiler set up. Over medium-low heat, stir constantly to bring the temperature up to 91°F/33°C. Work quickly once the chocolate is tempered.

Assemble the flødeboller:
Remove the meringue cookies from the refrigerator. Using a sauce dispenser, pour the chocolate over the cookies and, with two small offset spatulas, transfer carefully from the wire-lined baking sheet to a parchment-lined baking sheet. Return to the refrigerator to allow the chocolate to set for 1 hour. Serve cool.

Food & Beer

VANILLA & PINE ICE SWIRL

SERVES 4

Vanilla Ice:
550 g milk
75 g heavy (double) cream
40 g trimoline
35 g granulated sugar
25 g corn maltodextrin
15 g milk powder
0.5 g vanilla seeds
1 bronze-strength gelatin sheet
1.7 g sorbet stabilizer

Chocolate Crumble:
150 g butter

16 g olive oil
30 g demerara sugar
260 g tipo "00" flour
70 g cocoa powder
20 g malt powder
2 g Maldon salt

Pine Ice:
460 g milk
105 g pine or spruce shoots
25 g trimoline
25 g heavy (double) cream
25 g corn maltodextrin
20 g yogurt
15 g granulated sugar

2 g fresh lemon juice
3 g sorbet stabilizer
1¼ bronze-strength gelatin sheets

Blueberry Purée:
150 blueberries
15 g demerara sugar
15 g water
8 g sweet potato vinegar

To Assemble:
120 g Vanilla Ice
120 g Pine Ice
40 g Chocolate Crumble
20 g Blueberry Purée

Make the vanilla ice:
In a blender, combine 300 g of the milk with the cream, trimoline, sugar, maltodextrin, milk powder, and vanilla and blend for 30 seconds. Pass through a chinois into a bowl and set aside.

Bloom the gelatin in cold water; drain and blot on paper towels. In a saucepan, warm the remaining milk over medium heat and whisk in the sorbet stabilizer to thicken. Ensure that no lumps form. When thickened, remove from the heat and whisk in the gelatin to melt. Whisk a little of the vanilla ice base into the stabilized milk. Whisk the stabilized milk back into the vanilla ice base. Transfer to a Pacojet container and freeze.

Make the chocolate crumble:
Temper the butter on the counter for 1 hour. Preheat the oven to 320°F/160°C/Gas Mark 3.

In a stand mixer fitted with the paddle attachment, beat the butter, olive oil, and demerara sugar until combined. In a separate bowl, whisk together the flour, cocoa powder, malt powder, and salt. Add half the flour mixture to the butter mixture and beat on low speed for 1 minute. Add the remaining flour mixture and beat on low speed until the mixture is a mealy consistency. Transfer the dough to a baking sheet and spread it out evenly without compacting. Bake until dry, about 25 minutes. Cool in the pan; then freeze in a to-go container. Once frozen, pulse in the food processor until you get a texture similar to instant coffee. Transfer to a container, cover, and freeze until serving.

Make the pine ice:
In a blender, combine 200 g of the milk with the pine shoots, trimoline, cream, maltodextrin, yogurt, sugar, and lemon juice and blend for 15 seconds. Pass through a chinois into a bowl and set aside.

Bloom the gelatin in cold water; drain and blot on paper towels. In a saucepan, warm the remaining milk over medium heat and whisk in the sorbet stabilizer to thicken. Ensure that no lumps form. When thickened, remove from the heat and whisk in the gelatin to melt. Whisk a little of the pine base into the stabilized milk. Stir the stabilized milk back into the base. Transfer to a Pacojet container and freeze.

Make the blueberry purée:
In a small saucepot, combine the purée ingredients and cook over medium-low heat, stirring occasionally, until the berries release some juice, about 15 minutes. Transfer to a blender and purée on medium-high speed until smooth, about 10 seconds. Pass through a chinois into a bowl, cover, and refrigerate until cold.

Assemble the dessert:
Using a spoon, in a frozen metal canister, swirl half of the vanilla ice and half of the pine ice.

Line 4 chilled plates with a spoonful of chocolate crumble. Add a large dot of blueberry purée to the middle of the plate. Scoop non-uniform shapes of the swirled ices into the bowl. Add more chocolate crumble on top.

NOMA BROWNIES

MAKES 30

250 g blanched
    peeled hazelnuts
Cooking spray
500 g butter, diced
450 g 40% milk chocolate
450 g 64% dark chocolate
660 g tipo "00" flour
20 g baking powder
6 g Maldon salt
1000 g sugar
8 eggs
4 egg yolks

Preheat the oven to 320°F/160°C/Gas Mark 3.

Spread the hazelnuts on a rimmed baking sheet and toast until golden. Remove from the oven and let cool.

Leave the oven on and increase the temperature to 340°F/170°C/Gas Mark 3. Line 2 baking pans with parchment paper and coat with cooking spray.

Place the butter in a heatproof bowl along with both chocolates. Add 1 inch/2.5 cm of water to a saucepot and place the bowl on top. Be sure that the water does not touch the bottom of the bowl. Bring the water to a bare simmer over low heat and melt the chocolate with the butter, stirring every few minutes.

Meanwhile, in a separate bowl, whisk together the flour, baking powder, and salt.

When the chocolate has almost completely melted, combine the sugar, whole eggs, and egg yolks in a stand mixer fitted with the whisk attachment. Whip on high speed until quite airy, about 8 minutes.

Stop the mixer and switch from the whisk to the paddle attachment. With the mixer running on low speed (important!), pour in the melted chocolate and butter mixture. Mix until just combined and uniform in color. Add half of the flour mixture and mix on low speed until homogenous. Repeat with the remaining flour. Fold in the hazelnuts.

Use a spatula to gently move the brownie batter into the baking pans and even out their thickness. Bake until a cake tester inserted in the middle of the brownies comes out clean, about 9 minutes. Let cool before cutting into 3-inch/7.5 cm squares.

EARTHY

JEPPE   Terroir is a word uttered in reverence and shrouded in mysticism. Oenophiles and gourmets use it to describe a relationship to the peculiar soil that sprouted it, but its significance runs deeper: How high up the mountainside was the particular lot on which the grapes were grown? From what direction came the wind, and at what hour the shade? These are questions routinely asked of a glass of wine; being able to answer them somehow signifies a noble connection to the earth. Beer, pretty much, has remained separate from terroir-isme. But of course beer comes from the earth too. There are fields of barley, farms of hops, and aquifers full of water, and all these are from the earth. Clearly the relationship is different. The distance is farther between the barley and the beer than between the grape and wine. And few beers can boast the geographical singularity of wine. Many, if not all, beers contain ingredients of mixed origins.

But terroir exists in beer in wonderful ways. On a molecular level, any beer that uses wild yeast like lambics or Bretts relies on the microflora present in the ambient environment. I suppose this is less terroir and more aireoir. Hops, as discussed in BITTER (page 36), display characteristics depend-ing on their cultivation. But moving from molecules to the meta, beer captures time, place, and community in a way wine can't. Over the years, I've made countless one-off beers like Mission Gose, The Porthole, and Russian Roulette. Each one reflects a moment in time and many reflect a collaboration. They are both the souvenirs and the reason for cherished time spent among friends. Because a beer can be conceived, brewed, and bottled in a couple of weeks, it's a process friendly to spontaneity and experimentation.

When Luksus first opened, Daniel and I spent a lot of time together, brainstorming what we wanted to do. Everything was possible. One of our ideas was to create a symmetrical meal in which flavors transfer from the glass to the plate. For example, Daniel, a champion of the beet, had been working on a beet and licorice dessert. So I wanted to start the meal with a beet and licorice beer. I had never tasted a beet beer before—and I haven't since. For the idea to work, it was important that the earthiness of the beets was clear. They are, perhaps, the vegetable most capable of producing strong and tasty earthiness. At first, we considered using a Brett-fermented beer, which can yield a somewhat

69   *Food & Beer*

beet-y funkiness. But here the funkiness of the Brett was stepping on the earthiness of the beets. Instead, we went with a pulled-back, low-key Berliner Weisse, a tart style that, like an old friendly dog, you can rely on to play well with puppies.

We had no idea how to get the beets into the beer, so we tried everything. We threw a couple of roasted beets into the wort. We poured in beet juice. Nothing seemed to bring out the earthiness we wanted. Finally, we tried beet powder, and it was exactly what we needed. The result was perfect.

Daniel and I were both really excited for Luksus One. We bought a huge tub of beet powder and headed down to Westbrook Brewery near Charleston, South Carolina, to see my friend, and owner Ed Westbrook. We made the beer over a long weekend in March 2014. But when we got back to New York, Ed called with some bad news. According to Department of the Treasury, one of the many bureaucracies involved in beer, new beer formulas need to be registered with the Alcohol and Tobacco Tax and Trade Bureau, import, and export of beer. We had forgotten to register this one so there was no way we could sell it in the United States. Saddled with 5,000 bottles of Luksus One, we decided to cut our losses and offload the beer in Europe and other export markets. Though it lacks the shocking deep red color of Luksus One, and some of the soil-y notes, Evil Twin's Joey Pepper, a Belgian pale ale named after our dashing bartender, still has a vibrant earthiness that, if you find a bottle in Europe, you'll immediately recognize. Now, there are a number of breweries experimenting with vegetable beers. As for Luksus One, it had its time and place. Sadly, that was long ago and far away.

DANIEL   As Jeppe notes, everything we eat comes from the earth. For a chef, the idea of terroir applies not just to what I cook but to who I am. Every summer, my brothers and I would visit my maternal grandmother in her modest farmhouse in Bathurst, New Brunswick, a seaport on the Baie de Chaleur on the eastern edge of Canada. She was a taciturn, though loving woman who wouldn't put up with any mischief. She had grown up in the area, raised six kids, and knew how best to use the area's natural bounty. Most of my memories as a young boy are either of her farm fields, the evergreen forest surrounding it, or of early mornings in her warm kitchen, which stretched the length of the entire house.

I wish I could say the thing I remember most about my grandmother's cooking was the fiddlehead ferns. But really what I remember is waking up early and her fixing me a bowl of corn flakes, sprinkled with the perfect amount of sugar. I'd slurp away while she drank her coffee. I never wanted anyone else to make me cereal after that. I still don't. But the fiddleheads were a close second.

In early spring, for a few weeks, the forest floor is overtaken with young ferns. It is a frond flash mob. In fact, New Brunswick is famous for its fiddleheads—the fiddlehead capital, Tide Head, is an hour up the coast—and these ferns, peeking above the soil for a few precious weeks, explain why. Sent out on lazy morning sorties, my brothers and I would snip them close to the ground, picking only the greenest and most tender to bring back into the kitchen. Taking them from us with a quiet approval, my grandmother would quickly rinse them, add a thick pat of butter to a pan and immediately sauté the fronds. After a few minutes, we'd all dig in. The fiddleheads at that point weren't that far removed from the forest floor and they tasted like it too—fungal and vegetal, grassy but not bitter, earthy but not musty. I don't know what I treasured more: the time spent in the forest, talking with my grandmother as the fiddleheads hissed in the pan, or the taste itself. But I've carried that memory with me for close to thirty years.

There's an Italian man I met in Copenhagen named Andrea Petrini. Petrini's name engenders awestruck nods in the culinary world, but blank stares from most everyone else. Andy, as he's known, was a journalist for a number of French and Italian newspapers. He also helps select the San Pellegrino's World's 50 Best Restaurants. But what makes him remarkable are the absolutely insane dinners he throws called Gelinaz. The dinners, which occur maybe once a year, gather the chefs from San Pellegrino's list for an evening somewhere in the world. There have been Gelinaz dinners in Ghent, Tuscany, Copenhagen, at hotels and monasteries and, of course, restaurants. I still don't understand how he cajoles very busy men and women into flying across the world for one meal but he does. If Andy asks you to dinner, you say yes.

In April 2014, just eight months after we opened, Andy organized a Gelinaz dinner for Wylie Dufresne, the chef of wd~50 who was going to close his New York restaurant after more than ten years. The idea was that twenty-six chefs from around the world would pay tribute to Wylie by riffing on classic dishes from his restaurant. The whole affair was very secretive. A few weeks before the event, I got an email out of the blue from Andy. "Hey," he asked, "do you want to help out? René Redzepi and Ben Shewry need a place to do their mise en place. Could they use your kitchen at Luksus?" I had no idea what he was talking about, but of course I said yes. Shortly after, as if the first feint was a test, I got another email asking me whether I'd like to cook in the dinner. Again, befuddled, I said yes. Or rather, I shouted "Awesome! Yes!" and wrote, "I'd love to." When I looked at the email chain I saw the names of the top chefs in the world. Alex Atala, Magnus Nilsson, Petter Nilsson, René Redzepi, Daniel Patterson, Inaki Aizpitarte, and Daniel Boulud. The list went on and on.

I shot an email back asking Petrini where the chefs were going to eat for the one extra day they'd be in town. Chefs have to eat too, you know. This could be my one chance to cook for these guys. Who knows when they'd ever be in the same room again? Soon it was settled. The best chefs in the world would be having lunch at Tørst on Monday, April 7 at 1 p.m. Now the only question was: what to serve them. What does a chef serve for the most important lunch of his life?

Every chef has a best-of-the-best compendium. Heston has Sounds of the Sea, a seafood course served with an iPod-stuffed conch shell. There's the razor clam parsley gel and horseradish snow at Noma, and the bone marrow at St. John. But we had been open only eight months. We were still trying to figure out where the salt goes in the pantry! The one thing I knew is that I wanted to bring something unexpected, to juke these chefs from their comfortable lexicon of flavors and technique. Each of them possessed virtuosic talent and flawless technique. If they didn't they wouldn't be there. And if I didn't I wouldn't either. But for my peers, my friends, my fellow chefs, I wanted to show where I came from, so I brought them a taste of Bathurst from those summer mornings at my grandmother's farm.

That Monday, Luksus was a madhouse. René Redzepi of Noma was prepping in our tiny upstairs kitchen. Ben Shewry of Attica and Petter Nilsson from Spritmuseum were sardined in there, too. Meanwhile, I had to prepare lunch for thirty-two people. So I gently asked those guys to go to the basement prep kitchen and set out to start plating the fiddleheads. Though I loved my grandmother's recipe, I couldn't just do a sauté. We pickled the fiddleheads with roasted garlic, fish sauce, and a ham broth the day before, and I served them with a touch of the pickling liquid at the bottom of the bowl. This was my first statement of who I was as a chef—a declaration of who I was and where I came from.

BIÈRE DE GARDE + PICKLED FIDDLEHEAD FERNS

SUGGESTION: AVANT GARDE ALE, THE LOST ABBEY

When Daniel first told me the story of harvesting fiddleheads, I immediately started thinking of bière de garde. Bière de garde is a French style also known as a farmhouse ale. Farmhouse ales are sort of idiosyncratic beers once made in the French farmhouses in the Pas-de-Calais. The style can vary wildly one from to the other, as one might expect from so democratic a style, but generally they are highly effervescent, well-balanced beers, with a relatively low ABV (alcohol by volume). Daniel's pickled fiddleheads are complicated scrolls that have an intense earthiness, acidic snap, and hammy broth. They need a strong yet not overly aggressive beer. Bière de garde, with its mild sweetness and subdued hops, plays off the sharp flavors while providing supportive echoes of the slightly earthy flavors. This one actually comes from Southern California where my friend Tomme Arthur runs The Lost Abbey. It starts with a touch of maltiness, fades into steady hops, and finishes with green apples.

— JEPPE

SERVES 4

500 g fiddlehead ferns
20 g garlic, thinly sliced
5 g olive oil
30 g demerara sugar
120 g apple cider vinegar
20 g fish sauce
400 g Ham Broth (Pantry
    page 247)
3 g dried bird's eye chiles
50 g Cracovia spicy Polish
    mustard

Clean the fiddlehead ferns by slicing off the darkened, oxidized end of the stem and scraping away any blackened leaves from the scroll. As you work, keep the fiddleheads in a large bowl of cold water so they do not wilt. Once finished, give them a good shake to allow any dirt to fall to the bottom of the bowl. Rinse in cold water twice more to ensure that they are well cleaned.

In a large pot of rapidly boiling water, blanch the fiddlehead ferns for 45 seconds and then shock with an ice bath. Remove from the icy water and lay out on a towel-lined tray. Then transfer to a nonreactive 2-quart container with a lid while you prepare the pickling liquid.

In a heavy 2-quart pot, roast the garlic with olive oil until golden. Add the sugar and allow it to caramelize slightly. Deglaze the pot with the vinegar and fish sauce. Next add the ham broth and

bring to a boil. Skim away the impurities with a ladle, then add the dried chiles. Simmer for 10 minutes until aromatic and slightly spicy.

Strain the liquid into a bowl (discard the chile and garlic). Whisk the mustard into the liquid and pour over the ferns while still very hot. Cool completely, cover, and refrigerate for up to 1 week.

To serve, simply place a few ferns in a bowl with some of the pickling liquid.

Food & Beer

BEET BEER
+ LICORICE-CURED TROUT ON RYE RUGBRØD

SUGGESTION: LUKSUS ONE, EVIL TWIN BREWING

Beets are omnipresent in my cooking. We roast, dehydrate, smoke, juice, slice, and make them into sorbets, as well as incorporate them into sauces and marinades. We use beets in every station of the kitchen in as many ways we can. Though Jeppe's and my master plan for a beet and licorice bookend at Luksus didn't pan out, I used the licorice and beet combination at Tørst when creating one of our smørrebrøds. Both beet and licorice can be unpleasantly intense flavors when not pulled back and balanced. Here the addition of the silky, smoked trout and the bitter, seed-studded rugbrød achieve a nice equilibrium.

— DANIEL

SERVES 4

Licorice-Cured Trout:
250 g coarse salt,
    plus more as needed
20 g demerara sugar
8 g licorice powder
3 g grated lemon zest
3 g dill, chopped
200 g trout fillets

Pickled-Beet Dressing:
125 g Pickled Beets
    (Pantry page 248), chopped
80 g sour cream
75 g Mayonnaise
    (Pantry page 250)
2 g dill, chopped
Fresh lemon juice
Maldon salt

To Aseemble:
12 (¼-inch/6 mm-thick)
    slices Rugbrød (page 42)
120 g Pickled Beet Dressing
36 slices Licorice-Cured Trout

Make the cured trout:
Mix the first 5 trout ingredients together. Place the trout fillets on a tray lined with parchment paper, skin side down. Pack the salt mixture on the flesh of each fillet to well cover. Cure the fish for 1 hour in the refrigerator. Rinse well and slice into ¼-inch/6 mm-thick slices, lengthwise on a bias. Sandwich the slices between sheets of parchment paper and refrigerate until needed.

Make the pickled-beet dressing:
While the trout is curing, combine the pickled beets, sour cream, mayonnaise, and dill in a bowl. Season to taste with lemon juice and salt.

Assemble the dish:
When ready to serve, preheat the oven to 355°F/180°C/Gas Mark 4. Bring the trout to room temperature. Toast the rye bread until lightly golden around the edges, looking at the interior seeds for color, about 5 minutes.
    Divide the pickled beet dressing evenly across the toasts and top each with 3 slices of cured trout.

Food & Beer

SOUR

JEPPE   There are many beers with sour elements, but a so-called "sour beer," which by the way is not a style but a general description of beers with sour elements, is a rapidly expanding universe of its own. Everybody, including me, wants to make a sour beer these days. At Evil Twin, we lean toward styles such as Berliner Weisse and Gose, which are given their sourness by the presence of lactic acid bacteria. However, one of the oldest and most interesting of all beers is a style that originated in Belgium called lambic. Lambic draws its sourness from the wild yeast used in its fermentation. It's by far the most unpredictable of beers and, therefore, one of the most exciting.

Many people say that lambic is the beer that most resembles wine, and it's often compared with a dry crisp white wine. I don't see it that way. While lambics are complex, multilayered, and subtle, I'm a brewer, and therefore don't want a beer that tastes like wine. I want a beer that tastes like beer: rich, wild, and interesting. For me, that's a lambic.

The lambic style hails from Pajottenland, a region in western Belgium through which the Senne river flows. What makes lambic sour is also what makes it exciting and wild. Unlike any other

beer—but not unlike sourdough bread—lambics are fermented with wild yeast in a beautifully haphazard way.

Brewers are notoriously punctilious about keeping their fermentation systems closed. Generally, they want control over what bacteria make it into the wort, introducing specialized cultures to fine-tune the fermentation. But with lambic, they just dump the wort in a koelschip (essentially a giant open bathtub), throw the windows and doors open, and let whatever yeasts are in the air make their way inside. People say it's the air of the Senne that makes Pajottenland lambics so special. I'm not sure the microflora is so different in, say, Brooklyn, but it is true that lambic is the only beer with a real terroir.

As in sourdough, the yeast eats up the maltose, the sugar from the malt, and expels CO_2 and alcohol. After the wort undergoes its first wild fermentation, it then goes into oak or chestnut barrels for anywhere between one and four years to develop richness and depth. In the barrel, the beer picks up a host of flavors, from the tartness imbued by the yeast, to tannins from the barrel, to funk, and even fruit. The longer a lambic stays in barrel, the more sour it tends to be. Some people say it's like drinking a barnyard, with horse-blanket flavors and hints of wet hay. The first time I had one I almost spit it out, but over time I've grown to adore the style.

Americans, for reasons that are practical as well as deeply ingrained in the American spirit of ingenuity, have cottoned on to lambics. It's a risky beer that welcomes experimentation. Recently, I collaborated with Prairie Artisan Ales in Oklahoma for a lambic we called Coolship Truck. We had no idea if it would work out or not, what microflora would find its way in, or how that would affect the beer. But it turned out really well, with just the right amount of barnyard funk over a balanced body of sour fruit and slight florals.

As in all beer, but especially with beers that accompany food, balance is important. An out-of-whack sourness in a lambic will overwhelm other wonderful flavors that deserve their due.

Traditionally, the way brewers have mitigated the sourness is by combining oude (or old) lambics, which are barrel-aged for two to three years, with less sour jong (or young) ones, then left to ferment for six months to a year. This blend of oude and jong is called a gueuze. There's some debate about where the term comes from, but many agree it derives from Geuzenstraat, home of the first lambic brewery in Brussels. Not only does blending of the old and the new standardize the product—much the same way a champagne house will blend vintages— but it also allows the brewer to create a complex, well-rounded beer.

The other method of counterweighting the beer's intense sourness is with the addition of fruit. Cherries (kriek) and raspberries (framboise) are the most traditional, added after the first fermentation and spawning a second. Ten years ago I collaborated with Cantillon, one of the most lauded Belgian lambic makers, for a blueberry lambic. These days people are doing strawberry lambics, cassis lambics, and even grape lambics.

Presently, we're in the wild west of lambic making. Brewers all over the globe are letting in the wild yeast and calling their beer a lambic. Legally, of course, a lambic can't be made outside of Pajottenland, but this is a whole new world.

DANIEL Sourness, as anyone who has unwittingly taken a swig from a carton of spoilt milk knows, can be an overwhelming, immediate, and unpleasant sensation. But when used wisely and with purpose, it can be a loyal and selfless flavor in your culinary repertoire. Supportive and surprising, sour is everywhere in my food. I think of sourness as the sustain pedal that carries and elongates the notes of other flavors.

For instance, one of the first snacks we offered at Tørst was a plate of radishes accompanied by a creamy sorrel dip. It's a simple starter but with complex flavors. We served the radishes raw, sliced in such a way as to bear the weight of the dip, and sprinkled with housemade celery salt. Just as fries are vehicles for ketchup, one of the noblest roles a crudité can play is to ferry dip to your mouth.

Sorrel has a bright, pleasantly bitter flavor, made sharp by the oxalic acid in its leaves. When cooked, sorrel loses its brightness and slumps, becoming much like spinach. But when left raw, the taste is sharp, bitter, and bracing. For me, sourness is sorrel's perfect complement. It is the rumbling percussion under those herbal, bright top notes. Sour can be aggressive and astringent, but, to me, that's not sour at its best. It's a flavor best served gentle.

Of all the ways to deliver sourness, dairy is still my favorite, for it cloaks its tang in creaminess. Man has been souring milk since at least 10,000 B.C., or rather, man has used soured milk since that time. The sour occurs naturally with time, as lactic acid bacteria (LAB) transforms milk's sweet lactose into lactic acid. Cultured milk products like buttermilk, yogurt, fromage blanc, and quark, each add their own tone of sourness. Buttermilk, for instance, is slightly sweeter than plain yogurt. Fromage blanc, with its higher fat content, has a sourness and a richness, though goat cheese is the creamiest iteration of sour. But the tang abides.

At Tørst, I usually blend the souring elements together. I don't want someone to come in, taste the dip, and be able to pinpoint the sourness as, for instance, yogurt. Instead, I want the flavors to be a little disorienting. When your mind is a little unsure, it can be more easily opened. We do a variety of dips according to the season, as well as vary the vegetables according to availability. We make Radishes, Sorrel Dip (page 84) in the spring, and Roasted Cauliflower, Treviso (a slightly bitter variety of radicchio) Dip (page 89) in the fall. Roasted Beets, Almond Dip (page 87) is served throughout the year. Each relationship—of the ingredients in the dip, as well as between the dip and what is to be dipped—needs its own fine-tuning. Since roasted almonds aren't naturally as bright as herbs, I add some vinegar and pickled pepper to up the acidity.

Since Treviso is quite bitter, mayonnaise mellows the dip. For brightness, I always add a splash of lemon juice, and ask my chefs before they plate a dish, "Did you add the salt? How does it taste? Did you add the lemon juice? Taste it again." The importance of each can't be overestimated. Regardless of the particulars, the goal is always to highlight the winning qualities of sourness.

But if you asked me what's the one thing we do at Tørst that champions sourness, the answer is easy: sourdough. Sourdough is where Tørst started. I knew it would be part of the menu even before we opened. If we were going to be serious about food at Tørst, there would be no ordering bread from another bakery. When you have a restaurant, you make the bread. End of story.

Sourdough embodies one of sourness's most unique qualities: its relationship to time. A pinch of sugar can add sweetness; a splash of lemon juice, acid. But only time can produce a true sour tang, as it takes time for bacteria and yeast to work, and those two do not like to be rushed. In my mind, that is what separates tartness or acidity from sourness. The time in which fermentation takes place adds dimension and depth to tartness until it emerges, after some time, as sour.

A few months before we opened the doors at Tørst, I began my starter. Also called "the mother dough," it is at the heart of what sourdough is, because it begins the fermentation process, which in time begets the tang. Making a starter was remarkably simple to do. One night I went to our basement kitchen and mixed some Brooklyn Bee honey, Mt. Marcy flour, and water in a bowl. I left it uncovered and when I arrived in the morning, the dough was swollen, fragrant, and alive. Three years later, we're still using the same starter and it's still considered young. Boudin Bakery in San Francisco has been using the same starter for their sourdough since 1849.

I always want to keep the sourness in bread balanced just as I do with my dips. A loaf of bread is, after all, a web of ratios: crust to crumb, fresh dough to mother dough, water to flour, sweetness to sourness. I wanted a beautifully crusted sourdough with a sourness that emerges as a slow release, hitting you on a delay. The trick is in the poolish, an overnight, pre-fermentation syrup made of beer, water, flour, and malt extract. The poolish appealed to me for a few reasons. First, using it imbues the dough with a handsome nut brown hue, like how squid ink dyes pasta dough. Secondly,

poolish yields a beautiful crust, which, to me, was one of the most important qualities. Over time, it also adds both depth and complexity. And lastly, since poolish contains malt, a key ingredient in beer, as well as beer itself, it neatly embodies how closely beer and food are related.

Today we serve the sourdough accompanied only by yogurt-touched whipped butter, which teases out the bread's own subtle sour qualities. It's a pillar of our menu. It arrives in a woven leather basket and after the first bite, the sourness arrives a few beats later. That flavor and tang sticks with you and keeps you coming back.

LAMBIC + FLANK STEAK SALAD, PICKLED OYSTER MUSHROOMS

SUGGESTION: OUDE GEUZE, 3 FONTEINEN

Let's be frank—there are some extremely sour lambics I just wouldn't want to drink with food. Cantillon makes tremendous lambics, but they stand on their own. That's no knock on them but it would be like trying to pair a digestif with an entrée. Some players are meant for monologues. But there are a whole bunch of lambics, especially the slightly floral and complex ones from breweries like 3 Fonteinen that accompany food extremely well.

The barnyard smell of a lambic immediately brings to mind how well it goes with the flavors of a well-seared piece of meat. The sweetness caused by the Maillard reaction in seared flank steak, accentuated by the sugars in the marinade, plus the grounded earthiness of the mushrooms, complement perfectly the sour effervescence of the beer. The pairing isn't traditional. In Pajottenland, you'll probably enjoy a lambic with a mild cheese. Sweet and sour are a classic combination and here you'll see why. Note that you'll wind up with more mushroom pickle than you'll need for this recipe—hardly a terrible thing as it's a great pickle to have on hand and ready in your fridge.

— DANIEL

SERVES 4

Oyster Mushroom Pickle:
450 g apple cider vinegar
275 g sherry vinegar
275 g water
35 g honey
5 g star anise
5 g black peppercorns
Olive oil
2000 g oyster mushrooms, cleaned and divided into individual petals
Butter
Fresh lemon juice
Kosher salt

Marinated Flank Steak:
1000 g flank steak
50 g shallot, sliced
Olive oil
20 g garlic, sliced
20 g honey
130 g usukuchi soy sauce
105 g apple cider vinegar
10 g shiro-dashi shoyu
45 g Worcestershire sauce
4 g coriander seeds
3 g fennel seeds
2 g dried bird's eye chiles

Horseradish Vinaigrette:
100 g horseradish, grated
70 g white wine vinegar
55 g rice vinegar
15 g Lyle's Golden Syrup
5 g Dijon mustard
5 g caper pickling liquid
50 g olive oil

Flank Steak Salad:
600 g greens, such as ruby streak mustard greens, watercress, and dandelion
4 breakfast radishes, thinly sliced

Make the pickled mushrooms:
In a saucepan, combine the vinegars, water, honey, star anise, and black peppercorns and bring to a boil. Simmer for 10 minutes, then strain and cool.

In a wide heavy pan, heat a small amount of olive oil over high heat. Working in batches so as not to crowd the pan, add the mushrooms, and cook until browned. Add a pat of butter and brown further. Arrest the caramelization with a splash of lemon juice and season the mushrooms with salt. Transfer the mushrooms to a baking sheet lined with paper towels. Repeat this process until all the mushrooms are cooked.

Transfer the cooked mushrooms to a nonreactive storage vessel and cover with the cooled brine. Let stand at room temperature overnight. The mushrooms will hold up to 2 weeks, refrigerated.

Prepare the flank steak:
Clean the flank steak of its connective tissues using a very sharp knife and score lightly on both sides.

In a heavy pot, heat some olive oil over medium-high heat until very hot. Add the shallot and cook for 3 minutes, stirring occasionally. After some color forms, add the garlic. Stir frequently for 3 minutes until browned. Add the honey, cooking briefly until bubbles form, about 1 minute. Stir in the soy sauce, vinegar, shoyu, and Worcestershire sauce and bring to a simmer. Add the coriander and fennel seeds, and chiles and simmer for 10 minutes. Remove from the heat and let cool, uncovered. Strain through a chinois into a bowl, pushing on the solids with the back of a ladle.

Combine the steak and the marinade and vacuum-seal in a large vacuum bag. Refrigerate overnight.

Thirty minutes before serving, remove the flank steak from the refrigerator and brush off excess marinade. In a very hot pan, roast the steak to just above rare, 2 to 3 minutes per side. Remove from the heat and allow the meat to rest for 15 minutes.

Make the horseradish vinaigrette:
In a blender, combine all the ingredients except the olive oil. Blend for 10 seconds on high. Continue to blend for another 20 seconds while slowly drizzling in the oil. Strain through a chinois into a bowl, pushing on the solids with the back of a ladle. Transfer to an airtight container or squeeze bottle, and refrigerate for up to 1 week.

Assemble the salad:
While the steak rests, toss the greens, radishes, and pickled oyster mushrooms together. Season with the vinaigrette and toss to distribute.

Slice the steak across the grain, and on the bias, into ¼-inch-thick strips and toss in with the dressed salad. Divide evenly across 4 bowls, being sure to keep the greens, mushrooms, radishes, and steak evenly distributed.

SOURDOUGH

MAKES 6 (6 X 4-INCH)
INDIVIDUAL LOAVES

Poolish:
300 g bread flour
90 g IPA
12 g barley malt syrup
140 g tepid water

Bread:
450 g bread flour
33 g kosher salt
32 g fresh (cake) yeast
450 g warm water
Poolish (recipe above)
300 g sourdough starter
    (available commercially;
    King Arthur has one)
Cooking spray
100 g water
Yogurt-Touched Whipped Butter,
    for serving (Pantry page 251)

Make the poolish:
In a stand mixer fitted with the dough hook, combine all the ingredients and mix on low speed until a loose ball begins to form, about 5 minutes. Transfer the dough to a bowl and tie the whole thing loosely in a small, clear plastic storage bag. Let stand overnight in a temperate area (50° to 57°F/10° to 14°C). After 10 hours, the poolish should have formed between 3 and 5 small air bubbles on the surface of the dough. If it has many more bubbles than that, transfer the bowl to a refrigerator to slow down the yeast growth. If no bubbles are forming, transfer to a warmer area, up to 85°F/30°C.

Make the bread:
In a large bowl, whisk together the flour and salt. In another bowl, dissolve the yeast in the water by gently stirring. Transfer the poolish to a stand mixer fitted with a dough hook. Add the sourdough starter, followed by the yeasty water and the flour-salt mixture. Mix on a low speed until the dough is homogeneous, about 6 minutes. Transfer the dough to a container with a tight-fitting lid and allow to ferment and leaven for 2 days at room temperature.

On the third day, preheat the oven to 430°F/220°C/Gas Mark 7. Spray two heavy 18 x 13-inch/46 x 33 cm rimmed baking sheets with cooking spray. Using a bench scraper, divide the dough into 6 equal 5-inch/13 cm round loaves by scraping them out of the bowl and depositing them directly onto the baking sheet: You should be able to fit 3 loaves per sheet. Leave a few inches between the loaves. [If you have only one baking sheet, bake the bread in batches.]

Move the baking sheets into the oven. Just before closing the door, sprinkle the bottom of the oven with 100 g of water. (The steam will improve the color and the shine of the crust.) After 15 minutes lower the temperature to 410°F/210°C/Gas Mark 6. Bake for 10 minutes. The loaves should have a walnut brown crust and smell amazing. Remove from the oven, slice, taking care not to burn yourself, and serve immediately with whipped butter.

RADISHES, SORREL DIP
SERVES 8

100 g sorrel leaves, washed
   and thoroughly dried
450 g yogurt
150 g fresh goat cheese

125 g fromage blanc
10 g fresh lemon juice
Maldon salt
2 bunches radishes,
   cleaned with nice tops on
Celery Salt (Pantry page 250)

Combine the sorrel leaves with
the yogurt in a blender and
blend for 10 seconds. (Be careful: sorrel leaves, if blended too
much, will discolor and take on
a bitter flavor.)

AMERICAN-STYLE PALE ALE + SEASONAL VEGETABLES, DIPS

SUGGESTION: BIKINI BEER, EVIL TWIN BREWING

Before you taste Daniel's dips, they seem basic. That of course is by design. There's a delicate harmony of flavors in each, between the sourness, the herbal notes, and the vegetables, which can be earthy like beets or spicy like the radishes. What one wants is a mellow, easygoing beer that won't butt heads or battle wills with the already crowded stage. Light in terms of alcohol, but with a backbone, American-Style Pale Ales like Evil Twin's Bikini Beer, at 2.7% ABV, are expansive enough to accommodate the range of flavors but not so assertive that they clash. As opposed to the English pale ales from which they sprang, American-style pale ales are generally cleaner and hoppier (though they are less hoppy than an Indian pale ale). But the most important characteristic to look for—I suppose not only in beer but in life—is a keen sense of balance. The beer must keep its equilibrium amidst a bustle of disparate flavors. An American-style pale ale's bitterness cuts the earthiness of the various vegetables but doesn't overpower their subtle charm. Its crispness should complement the rich sourness of the creamy dips instead of cutting through it completely.

— JEPPE

In a deep bowl, whisk the goat cheese with the reserved sorrel base until smooth. Fold in the fromage blanc and whisk until smooth. Season with lemon juice and salt as needed. Cut the large radishes in half. Sprinkle with celery salt. Serve the dip in a small, shallow dish alongside the radishes.

SERVES 8

Roasted Beets:
4 bunches mixed beets or 4 large
    red beets (beetroot)

Almond Dip:
70 g blanched, peeled,
    and sliced almonds

100 g yogurt, plus more
    as needed
25 g roasted garlic
6 g Pickled Hot
    Peppers liquid
    (Pantry page 249)
6 g sherry vinegar
20 g fromage blanc
15 g shallot, minced

5 g fresh lemon juice,
    plus more as needed
2 g honey
2 g dill, chopped
Maldon salt
Celery Salt (Pantry page 250)

Roast the beets:
Preheat the oven to 395°F/200°C/Gas Mark 6.

Clean the beets and remove the greens and any dirt. Cover each with foil to completely enclose. Roast the beets on a baking sheet in the oven until the beets are fork-tender, about 2 hours. Transfer to a wire cooling rack and allow to cool completely.

Leave the oven on but reduce the temperature to 215°F/100°C/Gas Mark ¼.

Using a kitchen towel, peel off the beet skins by wiping them forcefully. Then insert and twist a small paring knife into the flesh of the beet to break them into smaller pieces. Repeat until each beet yields 10 to 12 irregularly shaped ¼-inch/6 mm chunks. Return the beets to a baking sheet and place in the oven to dehydrate. After 1½ hours, the beets should be dry to the touch and slightly shriveled and intensified in flavor. Transfer to a wire cooling rack and set aside.

Make the almond dip:
While the beets are roasting (at 395°F/200°C), spread the almonds on a baking sheet and place in the oven until they turn the color of peanut butter,

about 6 minutes. (Ideally, though, the almonds should be roasted at 320°F/160°C for 10 to 12 minutes.) Let cool in the pan on a wire rack. Measure out 15 g of the almonds, roughly chop, and set aside.

In a blender, combine the remaining almonds, the yogurt, garlic, pickled pepper liquid, and vinegar. Blend until very smooth and transfer to a bowl. Add the remaining base ingredients; then fold in the reserved chopped almonds.

Using a rubber spatula, fold in the fromage blanc, shallot, lemon juice, honey, and dill into the purée. Adjust the seasoning with lemon juice and salt. A small amount of additional yogurt may be used to thin the dip if needed. Cover and refrigerate until plating.

Assemble the dish:
About 45 minutes before serving, while the beets are drying in the oven, remove the almond dip from the refrigerator and bring to room temperature, about 20 minutes. Place the warm beets on a serving plate and lightly sprinkle with celery salt. Serve the beets with the almond dip.

SERVES 8

Cauliflower:
50 g olive oil
15 g ground turmeric
3 g cayenne pepper
2 medium heads cauliflower
    (300 g each)
Maldon salt
Celery Salt (Pantry page 250)

Dip Base:
85 g Treviso radicchio, cut
    into 2-inch/5 cm pieces
15 g olive oil
35 g yogurt
30 g buttermilk

Treviso Dip:
50 g heavy (double) cream
70 g Dip Base
70 g Mayonnaise
    (Pantry page 250)
45 g fromage blanc
8 g lemon juice, plus more
    as needed
50 g Kirby Cucumber Pickles
    (Pantry page 249), brunoised
Maldon salt

Make the cauliflower:
Preheat the oven to 465°F/240°C/Gas Mark 8.
Place 2 baking sheets on a middle rack in the oven.

In a small bowl, whisk together the olive oil, turmeric, and cayenne. Set aside.

Trim the cauliflower of core and leaves, and cut into bite-size florets. Rinse well and pat dry. In a large bowl, toss the cauliflower with the spiced oil mixture and a sprinkle of Maldon salt.

Arrange the florets on the preheated sheets in a single layer. Roast until nicely charred (they should still have a nice bite), about 5 minutes. Remove from the oven and transfer to the refrigerator to cool completely.

Make the dip base:
Rinse the Treviso and set aside in a small bowl.

Heat a 6-quart Dutch oven over high heat until very hot. Add the oil and immediately add the Treviso and sauté for 20 seconds. You want char, but the leaves should still have good life. Transfer the Treviso to a baking sheet to cool slightly. When the radicchio is still warm, but no longer hot, transfer to a blender and add the yogurt and buttermilk. Blend on high speed until smooth. Pass through a chinois into a bowl, pushing on the solids with the back of a ladle.

Make the Treviso dip:
In a medium bowl, whip the cream to medium peaks. Cover and refrigerate.

Measure the dip base into a medium bowl. Whisk in the mayonnaise, fromage blanc, and lemon juice until incorporated. Gently fold in the whipped cream followed by the cucumber pickles. Adjust the seasoning for salt and lemon juice to taste. Set aside.

Assemble the dish:
Bring the cauliflower to room temperature before serving. Sprinkle with celery salt and serve with the Treviso dip.

SMOKY

JEPPE   Growing up in Denmark, where smoked herring is as common as bologna sandwiches in the States, I always associated smoked flavors with an intense fatty fishiness. But when I came to the States for university, I arrived in the cradle of 'cue. Arkansas, like many places in the U.S., has a strong barbecue tradition. There are numerous sauces: vinegar-based, tomato-based, mustard-based. There are various cuts of meat and types of animal: whole hog, pork shoulder, ribs. As a nineteen-year-old weaned on smoked fish, it blew my mind. I traipsed across the state, hitting up every joint I could. The appeal of slow-and-low cooking, of tender meat imbued with smoke, was irresistible and indelible. A year later, when I returned to Denmark, I brought back with me a bottle of Colgin Liquid Smoke, an ingredient popular during the days of home meat curing. I put it on everything: lasagna, pasta Bolognese, even smoked herring.

Since those days, I've become obsessed with smoked things. In 2014, I finally got a Big Green Egg, a schmancy smoker, about the same time I befriended Joe Carroll, owner of Fette Sau, Brooklyn's best barbecue joint. Smoking a brisket, watching the fragrant hickory smoke waft up from the

Egg, and knowing that meat is lowly and slowly on its way to tenderness, is my retreat. Churchill once said a man should have a hobby far removed from his daily work. He had landscape painting; I have smoking.

But when you have beer in your blood, as I do, it's inevitable that all thoughts and hobbies eventually lead to the brewery. Smoked beers have a long tradition. In fact, in the early days of brewing, all beers were smoked, since the only way to dry out the barley was over an open flame. The malted barley then carried into the beer intense campfire smokiness, not unlike how some Scotch bears the flavors of smoldering peat.

Today, only one quaint town, Bamberg, located in Bohemia, keeps the smoked beer tradition alive with a style of beers called Rauchbier (rauch is German for smoke). I love a good Rauchbier, and one of my favorites is made at a brewery called Brauerei Heller, one of the most famous producers of the style. Rauchbiers are on the extremely smoky end of the spectrum. It's not like you're wandering through the woods and through the pines and catch a few whiffs of a distant campfire. With a Rauchbier, you are the campfire. That's great when you want to get as close to drinking firewood as possible, but it's hard when you want to have dinner, too.

Happily, more and more beer makers are discovering that modulated smoke can add a depth of flavor and unexpected heartiness while still producing a drinkable brew. There are as many ways to add smokiness to beer as there are things to burn. The most common way is to add it using smoked malt. The smoke flavor can also be added with leftover yeast from a smoked beer, since those little guys carry flavors from their past lives. Or, similar to whiskey, smokiness can be achieved via charred barrel aging.

Among my favorite examples of balanced smoke use is Brauerei Heller's Aecht Schlenkerla Helles Lagerbier. Though Heller's Rauchbier made them famous, their Helles Lagerbier is its more pleasant, mellower cousin. The lager is fermented with yeast left over from the brewery's Rauchbier and is brewed in the same copper kettles, resulting in subtly smoky, light-bodied lager.

But the inspiration for The Cowboy, Evil Twin Brewing's smoked Pilsner, has nothing to do with Bamberg. It has more to do with the bold flavors of the Marlboro Man. A few years ago, while I was visiting my friend Aaron Porter of The Trappist, one of the country's best beer bars, in Oakland, California, I happened to notice his wedding picture. There was Aaron, in a tuxedo and a cowboy bolo, smiling. Turns out Aaron had always wanted to be a cowboy. We started wondering what beer cowboys like to drink. A quick Google search was not promising. The light Pilsners and lagers that dominated the American market for the last sixty years, spoiling the reputation of beer, had, by dint of marketing brilliance, become the chosen beverage on the range. As a gift to Aaron, and his idealized cowboy, I wanted to change that. Using fifteen percent smoked malt and a Pilsner base, I brewed The Cowboy to prove to all the beer snobs that not all Pilsners need to be watery wastes and not all smoked beers must be charcoal pits. Aaron, not all dreams must be given up.

DANIEL   For an American, the first thing you think about when you hear the word "smoky" is barbecue. I grew up in Canada and if you've never had Canadian barbecue, don't. (Even Montreal's smoked meat has more to do with Eastern European peasant traditions than anything south of the Mason-Dixon line.) In Nova Scotia, smoke was the flavor we most closely associated with fish. The coastlines of Eastern Canada are lined with smokehouses full of salmon, mackerel, and herring. As a kid, one of the earliest memories I have is my mother buying smoked mackerel for my brothers and me. Smoked mackerel has an intense, fatty flavor, and we'd eat it alone or on bread. Growing up surrounded by the flavors of smoked fish is a history Jeppe and I, and many peoples of that parallel, share.

Because I don't have a barbecue tradition to draw upon, at Luksus and Tørst I use smoke more as a flavor element than a cooking method. I apply it more often to fish and vegetables than to rich, fatty meats like brisket. Nevertheless, there are plenty of other intense flavors for the smoke to augment. A good example is kedgeree, one of our best-selling dishes. Kedgeree, like khaki trousers, grew out of British colonialism. It's essentially a mellowed-out curry to which Victorian colonists added egg and fish and called breakfast. In its earliest incarnations, the fish was fresh, but the contemporary English execution is to use smoked fish. At Tørst, we use smoked trout and smoked whitefish from our friends at Acme Smoked Fish, one of the last remaining fish-smoking facilities in the five boroughs of New York. The dish is a nod to the time I spent at Fergus Henderson's St. John, in London. That restaurant's building used to be a smokehouse and still serves some of the best kedgeree I've ever had, though they use the even more intense smoked eel. Regardless, even with the more mellow trout, the smokiness lends a mouthwatering depth to the dish. Kedgeree is by far the most balls-to-the-wall thing Victorians ever ate.

Smoke adds heft to protein, and also functions as an effective counterpunch to other intense flavors, as with our whitefish æbleskiver. The first time I encountered æbleskiver, in Denmark, I was intrigued. Resembling ping pong balls of fried dough, they are like pancakes that made it to Edwin Abbott's Sphereland. Though traditionally sweet, at Tørst we make savory æbleskiver reminiscent of Japanese takoyaki (a Japanese street snack). Into the rich dough, made with melted butter,

cream, and egg yolks, we fold the smoked fish.
When they're well executed, they're like tiny planet
flavor bombs. To ground that flavor, we serve the
æbleskivers with a smoked-hay gribiche of sorts.
While traditional gribiche relies on hard-boiled egg
whites, I don't like them, so they aren't used in my
cooking. I first encountered hay-smoking at Noma,
where René smoked quails eggs and served them on
top of mounds of hay, thus conjuring campfire
flavors. Here, the smoked hay reigns in the fluffy,
fishy dough, which otherwise might traverse to
decadent lands.

SMOKED PILSNER
+ KEDGEREE, ÆBLESKIVER, HAY GRIBICHE

SUGGESTION: THE COWBOY, EVIL TWIN BREWING

Our bodies are attuned to process smoke with alarm bells. It is such a specific flavor that to try to put it out, by pairing contrasting flavors, would be futile. Instead, we think that smoke in the higher, lighter registers of flavor—the sort that comes through in smoked fish or a smoked Pilsner as opposed to barbecue or a smoked stout—is best served by finding a similarly weighted flavor in its mate. Were we dealing with a Rauchbier, or some other very intensely smoky brew, Daniel might rightly suggest a thick-cut bacon sandwich. And if Daniel were steeped in the hickory-smoked brisket universe, Jeppe might choose a dark German lager like a Dunkel to cut that rich spicy flavor. But we both have chosen of our own accord a beer and a dish of subtle smokiness; they deserve each other.

— JEPPE AND DANIEL

KEDGEREE
SERVES 4

Olive oil
75 g shallot, minced
12 g garlic, minced
12 g fresh ginger, minced
8 g curry powder
250 g jasmine rice
300 g water
300 g Roasted Chicken Stock
   (Pantry page 247)
120 g smoked trout,
   meat picked
20 g jalapeño pepper, minced
10 g flat-leaf parsley
Fresh lemon juice
Maldon salt
4 eggs

Heat a heavy pot over medium heat. Add some oil and sauté the shallots until slightly softened, about 1 minute. Add the garlic and ginger and sauté an additional 2 minutes. Add another splash of oil and then the curry powder. Toast for 30 seconds or until highly aromatic. Add the rice and cook for 1 minute to toast the rice slightly. Add the water and chicken stock. Bring to a boil, reduce to a simmer, cover, and cook for 20 minutes. Fold in the smoked trout, jalapeño, and parsley. Season to taste with lemon juice and salt.

While the rice cooks, bring a small pot of water to a boil. Gently drop in the eggs and immediately turn down to a simmer. Cook for 5 minutes and test an egg by shocking it in ice water and then cracking it open. The white should be set but the yolk very runny. (Eat or discard.) Cook the other eggs for an additional 30 seconds if needed. Remove and plunge the eggs into ice water to arrest the cooking. Gently crack the egg's shells and peel in a bowl of cool water. Bring the eggs to room temperature by running under hot water.

To serve, divide the rice mixture across 4 serving bowls. Split each egg quickly to keep as much of the yolk intact as possible. Top each bowl with the split egg and a sprinkle of Maldon salt over the egg.

ÆBLESKIVER WITH
ROASTED HAY GRIBICHE
SERVES 8

Hay Cream:
100 g hay
500 g heavy (double) cream
Fresh lemon juice
Maldon salt

Roasted Hay Gribiche:
100 g Mayonnaise
   (Pantry page 250)
20 g Pickled Kirby Cucumbers
   (Pantry page 249), brunoised
50 g Hay Cream
10 g shallots, brunoised
5 g capers
2 g chives, minced
2 g tarragon, minced
1 g chervil, minced
1 g flat-leaf parsley, minced
Fresh lemon juice
Maldon salt

Æbleskiver Filling:
250 g smoked whitefish
40 g Pickled Celery
   (Pantry page 249), chopped
5 g chervil, chopped

Æbleskiver:
185 g egg yolks
240 g heavy (double) cream
250 g all-purpose (plain) flour
5 g kosher salt
2 g ground cardamom
225 g egg whites
135 g butter, melted
100 g clarified butter

Make the hay cream:
Preheat the oven to 355°F/180°C/Gas Mark 4.

Spread the hay on a baking sheet and roast until fragrant, about 20 minutes. Transfer the hay to a small container that seems too small; it should be some work to get all the hay inside. While the hay is still warm, pour in the cream, close the lid, and refrigerate for 24 hours. Strain the hay cream through a chinois into a bowl (discard the hay). Freeze the cream or use immediately.

Make the roasted hay gribiche:
In a bowl, combine the mayonnaise, pickles, hay cream, shallots, capers, chives, tarragon, chervil, and parsley, seasoning to taste with lemon juice and salt. Refrigerate for at least 1 hour.

Make the æbleskiver filling:
Pick through the whitefish for bones and break the flesh into smaller pieces without shredding. Gently combine the fish with the pickled celery and chervil.

Make the æbleskiver:
In a large bowl, whisk the egg yolks and cream together until homogeneous. In a separate bowl, combine the flour, salt, and cardamom. Whisk the flour mixture into the cream mixture in two additions. It should be smooth after each addition. In a third bowl, whisk the egg whites to medium-stiff peaks.

Whisk the melted butter into the batter in two additions, incorporating until the dough becomes a homogenous mass each time. One half at a time, add the egg whites to the dough. The first addition can be quite aggressively mixed, but the subsequent addition should be much more gentle so as to preserve the light texture of the finished dough. (While being gentle, also be sure there are no egg white spots remaining.) Transfer the batter to a large piping bag and let come to room temperature. Tie off the open end of the piping bag with a rubber band to ensure it is sealed. Cut off the excess of the bag with sharp scissors, leaving about 3/4 inch/2 cm.

Heat an æbleskiver pan over medium-high heat for 1 minute. Brush each mold with a liberal amount of clarified butter. Cut the corner off the piping bag 1 inch/3 cm from the end tip, and pipe enough batter into each mold to come just up to the rim. Cook until lightly browned. When moved with a cake tester, the edge should come away from the mold. Using a metal cake tester, rotate the æbleskiver in their molds 90 degrees. This should result in half a sphere sticking out of the mold while the still-liquid batter spills into the bottom.

Working quickly, use a small spoon to place a marble–size amount of the æbleskiver filling into the center of each æbleskiver. Using the cake tester, rotate each æbleskiver another 90 degrees again to form a complete sphere. Continue cooking until the tester comes out from the center slightly hot. Remove the æbleskiver by lifting it with the tester. Place on a plate lined with paper towels.

Serve immediately with a dollop of gribiche on the side.

COMMON ÆBLESKIVER PROBLEMS
I don't have an æbleskiver pan!
Get one.
My æbleskiver stick to the pan when I try to rotate them!
Your pan may have been too cold when you added the batter.
The æbleskiver collapse after the first rotation!

They weren't cooked enough.
But the color was right!
Yeah, but maybe your pan was too hot.
My æbleskiver are weird and spotty.
Your pan might be too dry. Turn down the heat a little and add more clarified butter.
I can't pronounce the word "æbleskiver."
Don't worry about it. Just eat!

TART

JEPPE   Welcome to Flavortown, Beer Edition. On the south side, in the grassy lowlands, you'll find flavors like Earthy and Funky. To the west in brightly colored houses resting on high ground are Sweet, Fruity, and its racy neighbor, Spicy. Alone and mumbling sits Bitter and way out on the outskirts, in their weird ménage, live the feuding brothers, Sour and Tart.

Perhaps more than any other of the flavor families we've discussed, Sour and Tart are the most closely related. The main distinction I draw between the two is the source of their tang. Sour is the donkey son of Bitter and Funky. It is, as Daniel writes of sourdough, a product of time. The same is true in beer. The sour flavors that develop in lambics do so gradually, as the wild yeasts do their digesting work. Sourness can be bracing, but it's often a soft, round flavor. It can be a punch, but more like a looping overhand right.

Tart, on the other hand, is a sharp jab. When I think of what beer embodies tartness, my mind turns to Berliner Weisse. In that style, and in many of the other tart beers, the sharp flavors are a product of lactic acid bacteria. (The sour flavors in lambics, for instance, come from yeast; the bitter

flavors in IPAs come from acids associated with hops.) Like yeast, lactic acid bacteria (LAB) acts on carbohydrates to cause fermentation. But instead of alcohol and CO_2, the LAB converts the carbohydrates into lactic acid. It's the same thing that caused my muscles to burn when I was running. That idea alone, that the same process that happens in my body as happens in the wort, is enough to get me excited about lactic-acid–fermented beers.

Lactic acid yields a crisp tartness, distinct from a diffuse sourness or sharp bitterness. This tart nature is largely what defines Berliner Weisse, a wheat beer with relatively low ABV and a high effervescence. Though Berliner Weisse has been around for centuries, it didn't flourish until the late nineteenth century. Generally speaking, Berliner Weisses are accommodating beers. Traditionally, they were infused with syrups like woodruff and raspberry to mask imperfections, but as it turns out, they offer a clean, crisp background for other fruit as well. A couple of breweries in Florida have recently been experimenting with citrus infusions and calling the style Florida Weisse. At Evil Twin, along with stouts, a tart Berliner Weisse is one of my workhorses, lending itself as nimble backdrop for everything from cilantro (Biere Blanca) to blue-berries (Justin Blabaer; see FRUITY page 60).

DANIEL   Every Christmas, my mother, Arlene, hosted a three-day extravaganza at our house on Beckfoot Drive in Dartmouth, Nova Scotia. The kickoff was always at 8 p.m. on Christmas Eve. She would spend the day in the kitchen, and when night fell and my brothers and I would finally get in from playing hockey, she'd place a fragrant meat pie, topped with a golden crust, in the center of the table. Next to it were always mashed potatoes, but it played a distant second to the main event. Above all, my favorite was her cranberry sauce, served alongside the pie. When it came to the sauce, my mother always erred on the side of tartness. Mom's wise intuition was that the tartness was something to be celebrated—not muted. It is bracing and refreshing, and perhaps one of the reasons why tart sorbets are often used as palate cleansers. It's also one of the reasons that tart cranberry sauce worked so well with the meat pie. Every family with French-Canadian blood probably has their own version of meat pie, the Acadian meat pie so famously eaten in the Maritimes. My mother used chicken and pork. My godmother used minced rabbit. My aunts—Carmel, Bernie, and Marvel—each had her own variation. Each was rich and comforting and benefited from the sharp tartness of cranberry sauce. So we'd eat, and eat, and eat, until we could barely move.

And yet, I always saved a bit of room for dessert—my mother's rhubarb crisp. Behind our house grew a rhubarb patch, thick and unruly, which my mother would hack at with a chef's knife. Rhubarb, like cranberries, is both tart and acidic, and, just as with cranberry sauce, Mom was wise to let that tartness shine. My brothers and I would attack it like it was an enemy alien—a delicious enemy alien.

Then, near midnight, we'd all pile in the car and drive to Midnight Mass at Saint Peter's, our church. We'd return, sleepy and full, but excited. And before heading off to bed we were allowed to open one present each—mine was usually something Boston Celtics related. And, if we were extra lucky, we'd get another scoop of the custard.

BERLINER WEISSE + MEAT & CHEESE PLATE

SUGGESTION: NOMADER WEISSE, EVIL TWIN BREWING

Our meat and cheese plate is one of the most frequently ordered items at Tørst. It's also one of the easiest to prepare, which is great when the bar gets busy. My goal is just to provide the necessary elements for the perfect bite. Using American-cured meats, we have three different styles: a saucisson sec, cacciatore, and country ham. Each has varying levels of salt, smokiness, and spice. We serve three styles of cheese too: an English Cheddar, a washed rind cheese, and a blue. My favorites are Mrs. Quicke's Cheddar from Neal's Yard; a washed rind cheese called Dorset from Consider Bardwell Farm in Vermont; and a creamy, not funky, blue called

Chiriboga from Bavaria. We serve the meat and cheese plate with pickles to cut through the fattiness, a few olives whose briny saltiness complement the richness of the cheese, and of course our Danish rye bread. All this means is that you need a beer pliable enough to work with any of the many combinations a guest might create. Berliner Weisse, with a lactic tartness that cuts through the meat's fattiness and complements the acid of the pickles, is just the thing.

— DANIEL

SERVES 4

5 slices saussiçon sec
5 slices cacciatore
4 slices mildly smoky
    country ham
1 chunk cheddar cheese, such
    as Mrs. Quicke's Cheddar
1 chunk creamy blue cheese
1 chunk washed-rind cheese
25 g Pickled Kirby Cucumber
    (Pantry page 249)
25 g Pickled Carrots
    (Pantry page 248)
25 g Pickled Cauliflower
    (Pantry page 248)
25 g Mixed olives, such
    as Niçoise, Kalamata,
    and Castelvetrano

Place slices of meat and cheese on a plate. Add the pickles and olives. You know what? You got yourself a meat-and-cheese plate! Eat with slices of warm rugbrød.

BELGIAN DUBBEL
+ ARLENE'S MEAT PIE, CRANBERRY SAUCE, RHUBARB CRISP

SUGGESTION: WESTMALLE DUBBEL, WESTMALLE ABBEY

Unfortunately, I never got a chance to try Arlene's meat pie with a side of cranberry sauce or her rhubarb crisp, best eaten in a state of Christmas Eve excitation. But when presented with the sort of tartness Daniel describes, a Belgian dubbel is the perfect foil. The modern dubbel is a product of the Westmalle Brewery, at one of the six Belgian Trappist monasteries. A dubbel is less alcoholic than a tripel (and more than the rare beer, a singel).

It has a beautifully dark body—at 7% ABV, it's no wimp—but thanks to the yeast, a proprietary strain of which is used at the monastery, it has notes of ripe banana and raisin. Now, if it had a lingering sweet finish, the pairing wouldn't work as well. But this particular beer's dry finish means that it keeps pace with the quick-moving tart flavors and harmoniously ends in unison.

— JEPPE

ARLENE'S MEAT PIE,
CRANBERRY SAUCE
SERVES 8

Cranberry Sauce:
650 g fresh cranberries
125 g demerara sugar
90 g orange juice
15 g orange peel, cut into strips
8 g cinnamon stick
3 g star anise

Dough:
850 g all-purpose (plain) flour
4 g baking powder
2 g salt
250 g lard
200 g vegetable shortening
10 g rice vinegar
160 g water
1 egg

Filling:
1 (3 lb/1500 g) chicken
1 (3 lb/1500 g) boneless
    pork shoulder
150 g onion, cut into eighths
100 g celery, chopped into
    3-inch/7.5 cm pieces
6 fresh bay leaves
4000 g Vegetable Stock
    (Pantry page 248)
Olive oil
125 g onion, diced
15 g butter
15 g all-purpose (plain) flour
2 g summer savory, chopped
Kosher salt

To Assemble:
All-purpose (plain) flour
1 egg, beaten
5 g milk
Cranberry Sauce

Make the cranberry sauce:
In a saucepan, combine all of the ingredients and cook over low heat for 35 minutes, stirring occasionally. Fish out the orange peel, cinnamon stick, and star anise and discard. Beat with a spoon to help a few cranberries break up. Cool. Refrigerate until needed for up to 1 week.

Make the dough:
In a bowl, whisk together the flour, baking powder, and salt. Using a pastry blender, cut the lard and shortening into the flour until a mealy texture is formed. In a separate bowl, combine the vinegar and water. Mix the liquid into the flour mixture. When most of the liquid is absorbed, add the egg and gently bring the dough together with your hands. Divide it in half, pack each half into a ball, and flatten into loose discs. Wrap well in plastic wrap (cling film) and refrigerator for 1 hour.

Make the filling:
While the pie dough chills, remove the giblets and any large fatty bits of skin from the cavity of the chicken. Move the chicken and the pork shoulder to a pressure cooker. Combine the onion eighths, celery, and bay leaves and add, along with the vegetable stock, to the pressure cooker. Over medium heat, bring to high pressure and cook for a further 40 minutes. Let stand for another 10 minutes, and then release any residual pressure. Cool the meat in its liquid. Once cool, remove the chick-

en, discard the skin and pick the meat from the bones. Pick the pork shoulder meat. Set aside 400 g of chicken meat and 450 g of torn shoulder meat. Freeze the rest for another use. Strain and reserve the cooking liquid; measure out 200 g and freeze the rest.

In a wide pot, heat a bit of oil over medium heat. Add the diced onion and cook until soft and without taking on any color. Melt in the butter, then add the flour. Cook over medium heat for 1 minute, stirring constantly to coat the onion well. Stir in the reserved cooking liquid in 3 installments, fully stirring the flour into the liquid on each addition. Add the reserved chicken and pork. Cook over low heat for 10 minutes to thicken. Add the savory, cook for 1 minute, then season with salt and cool.

Assemble the pie:
Preheat the oven to 345°F/175°C/Gas Mark 4.

Let the dough temper at room temperature for 10 minutes. Using a lightly floured rolling pin, roll each disc into a 14-inch/36 cm round about ⅓ inch/8 mm thick. Lay one round in a 10-inch/25 cm pie dish and press gently against the bottom and sides of the dish. Rest both the pie dish lined with dough and the remaining dough round, covered, in the refrigerator for 1 hour.

Remove from the refrigerator and fill the pie dish with the meat filling. Cover with the other round of dough and crimp the edges together with your fingers or a fork. Whisk together the egg and milk. Brush the crust all over and bake for about 50 minutes until hot through and deep golden brown.

Cut pie into 8 equal pieces. Add one warm piece to a plate and serve with a generous dollop of cranberry sauce.

RHUBARB CRISP, CUSTARD
SERVES 6

Custard:
185 g egg yolks
120 g granulated sugar
750 g milk
250 g heavy (double) cream
40 g milk powder

Topping:
115 g butter
100 g brown sugar
70 g all-purpose (plain) flour
50 g rolled oats

Filling:
150 g powdered (icing) sugar
15 g all-purpose (plain) flour
1000 g rhubarb, cut into
    1-inch/2.5 cm pieces
5 g fresh lemon juice

Make the custard:
In a medium bowl, combine the egg yolks and granulated sugar. In a deep-sided pot, combine the milk, cream, and milk powder. Whisk over medium heat and bring to 122°F/50°C, at which point the milk powder will begin to dissolve. Stir some of the warm milk mixture into the egg mixture and whisk to incorporate fully. Then add the egg mixture back into the pot and continue to cook, now stirring constantly with a heatproof spatula, until the custard reaches 149°F/65°C. Strain immediately into a bowl set over an ice bath and refrigerate until completely cool.

Make the topping:
Preheat the oven to 330°F/165°C/Gas Mark 3.
    Temper the butter to room temperature.
    In a large bowl, use a spoon to beat the brown sugar into the butter. In a separate bowl, stir together the flour and oats. Mix the oat and flour mixture into the sugar and butter. Set aside.

Make the filling:
In a large bowl, stir together the powdered sugar and flour. Add rhubarb and stir until coated, then add the lemon juice. Arrange the rhubarb in a (12 x 8-inch/30 x 46 cm) baking dish. Spread the topping evenly over the fruit. Bake until the top is golden, about 40 minutes.
    Serve warm with a generous spoonful of room temperature custard on the side.

SPICY

JEPPE   In Danish, stærk means spicy, as in hot; and krydret means spicy, as in richly spiced. In English, no such differentiation exists. Spicy is ambiguous. When you think about it, "spicy" dishes should imply krydret, with only a handful also stærk. However, when beer is described as spicy, it usually refers to heat.

When a beer is spicy, that heat often comes from the yeast. Belgian saisons, ales, reds, and browns are famous for the heat brought on by yeast. Some heat can also result from varieties of hops—Hallertau, one of the four Noble Hops, is notably spicy. (A noble hop, like the seven noble grapes, are among the oldest and most respected varietals.) But hops often manifest spiciness in aroma more than a flavor.

Within the Evil Twin universe, when I want a spicy beer, I'm not content with tasting notes; I want the real thing, goddammit! Why have notes of white pepper when you can actually just add white pepper? That's exactly what I did with a Belgian pale ale called Joey Pepper, named after Tørst's own bartender. Anyone who knows Joey knows he's a guy with strong opinions about beer. In his honor, while collaborating with Sante Adairius

Rustic Ales, a craft brewery out in Capitola, California, we added a healthy dose of white pepper during boil. The result is spicy, but like Joey, nice.

For Spicy Nachos (page 112), nice wouldn't just do. Our friend Ed Westbrook, of the Westbrook Brewing Company in South Carolina, has been nicknamed "Spicy Nachos" by his wife Morgan. But when two guys who make beer get together and there's a joke—or in this case, a nickname—that joke inevitably becomes a beer. Chile beer, to which actual chiles are added, has a solid history. It's not historic, like a kriek lambic, but it's not a gimmicky arriviste, like a cotton candy beer, which pops up from time to time. We wanted to mimic that corn-y, spicy, almost crunchy flavor that draws someone toward a plate of nachos. To this beer, we added fresh jalapeños and corn just after fermentation, to capture the nachos' maize spirit.

The beer exploded—both literally and figuratively. In the process of making it, we had some bottling issues, but those road bumps aside, the beer proved extremely popular. After we fixed the bottling problem, we re-released it, changing the name to Firewater to avoid painful memories.

In general, the danger with spicy beers is never that there's not enough heat but that there's too much. Spicy, as in hot, is one of those flavors that seem to court machismo. Perhaps because there's an actual scale to measure it—the Scoville scale—man has been obsessed with proving how tough he is by tasting insanely hot peppers. Ghost peppers exist for no other reason except for boasting.

Unfortunately, this maximist machoness frequently carries over into brewing, where many "spicy" beers verge on the undrinkable. The question shouldn't be how spicy can we make the beer but rather, how spicy do you want it to be? A chile beer isn't an exemption from the necessity of a well-balanced drink. This is doubly true when you want to pair a chile beer with food.

DANIEL   I never had much use for heat in food. That element in cooking grows more important the closer one gets to the equator. I grew up on the 45th parallel and trained in kitchens mostly above the 55th. So, though I eat spicy food in my free time, mouth-burning heat was rarely a tool in my culinary arsenal. Perhaps for that reason, when I think of spicy food, I think about spices, as opposed to heat, and naturally my mind turns toward Sunday. During the winter months, we have a Sunday Roast at Tørst. It's a habit I picked up while living in London and going to the pub on Sunday afternoon, but also one that harkens back to weekends of my youth. On Sundays, like in many households, our family would gather over a big piece of roasted meat. Sometimes it was pork loin or beef sirloin; occasionally it was duck. At Tørst we have featured a lot of different cuts and varieties of meat, but the key to success lies in the marinade.

Alluringly, for an inveterate fiddler, a marinade involves seemingly countless options. Aside from deciding on which spices to include, there are also the questions ranging from, how concentrated the marinade should be, to when to add spices, and how long the protein should rest in the liquid. Do I add 1 gram of black peppercorns every hour, allowing a small amount to steep in over time, or add 10 grams for 1 minute, providing a blast of flavor but only momentarily?

My first exposure to the world of spices came through the Hong Kong–born, Canada-raised chef Susur Lee. I was thirty-one, working as an entremetier—a lowly position in the kitchen brigade—at Susur's flagship restaurant in Toronto. What I remember most vividly are the huge stockpots, burbling all day. Inside these steel colossi, Susur made his richly flavored stocks, abundant in spices I had never heard of, like Chinese cinnamon and tsaoko fruit. These, as well as many others, were the key to much of his stocks' flavor, and he zealously guarded its exact ingredients and proportions. There was just one woman devoted solely to the spice mixes for his curry, but even after she finished her job, he'd sneak in and add a few more.

In the kitchen at both Tørst and Luksus, we have shelves full of spices. But you'll rarely see them in the food. The beauty of a marinade is that the spices have long been at work, using the liquid to exert their influence onto the meat. This is the advantage of spicing a poaching liquid or brine— it's the pleasure of a long game.

GERMAN-STYLE PILSNER
+ SUNDAY ROAST, PORK SANDWICH

SUGGESTION: LOW LIFE, EVIL TWIN BREWING

Sunday is the day of rest, a time to relax, let our kids run around, and just hang. I love stopping by Tørst on a wintry Sunday, just as the team is pulling the pork out of the oven. The fragrant spices fill the air, wafting from the kitchen into the bar area. Rather than trying to go eye-to-eye with those flavors with spiced Gose or an herbal Belgian ale, a German Pilsner is a suitably relaxed foil for the roast. Pilsners in the States are often dismissed, and sometimes rightly, as watery, domestic. (Hello, Pavement fans!) But when done well, using high-quality hops and sufficiently hearty ABV, the golden lager is a well-balanced mix of hop-forward bitterness and a crisp clean body. Alternating bites of the roast with the Pilsner is comfort and refreshment incarnate.

— JEPPE

SUNDAY ROAST
SERVES 6, WITH LEFTOVERS
FOR SANDWICHES

Pork Brine:
120 g coarse salt
80 g muscovado sugar
4000 g water
2 g whole cloves
3 g star anise
4 g Sichuan peppercorns
4 g cinnamon stick
10 g coriander seeds
12 g black peppercorns

Pork:
5000 g boneless pork
    shoulder
Kosher salt
Freshly cracked black pepper

Green Sauce:
125 g liquid from Pickled
    Ramps (Pantry page 250)
50 g arugula (rocket) leaves
10 g chives, cut into 1-inch/
    2.5 cm pieces
30 g flat-leaf parsley, stemmed
5 g tarragon leaves, roughly
    picked
5 g Vietnamese mint leaves,
    roughly picked
2 g chervil leaves, picked
10 g capers, minced
15 g garlic, minced
55 g olive oil

Roast Vegetables:
100 g Marble Pot potatoes
20 g olive oil
Maldon salt
50 g baby carrots
20 g cippolini onions
120 g Pickled Red Cabbage
    (Pantry page 248), to serve

Brine the pork:
In a medium stockpot, combine the salt, muscovado sugar, and water. Bring to a boil, add the spices, then lower the heat and simmer for 10 minutes. Strain and cool. Pour the cold brine over the pork. Cover tightly in a nonreactive container and refrigerate for 4 days.

Cook the pork:
Preheat the oven to 135°F/56°C.

Drain the pork thoroughly and pat dry. Move the pork to a shallow baking pan. Salt liberally and season with freshly cracked pepper. Cook, uncovered, for 10 to 12 hours. If your oven has a steam function, turn it on to its lowest setting. Otherwise, place a shallow pan of water on the floor of the oven during cooking.

Remove the meat (and the shallow water pan) from the oven and turn the oven to 375°F/190°C/Gas Mark 5. Drain off any liquids and fats that have collected in the pan. Return the meat to the oven for another 15 minutes, or until crisped. Let meat rest 20 minutes before carving.

Make the green sauce:
While meat is roasting, in a blender, combine the pickle liquid, arugula, and all the picked herbs and blend. Transfer to a medium bowl and add the minced capers.

Now sauté the chopped garlic in the olive oil in the pan until golden. Pour the hot oil and garlic on top of the capers and blended herb mixture. Whisk to incorporate. Season with salt. Let stand for 2 hours, at room temperature.

Roast the vegetables:
Preheat the oven to 375°F/190°C/Gas Mark 5.

Arrange the potatoes on a rimmed baking sheet and sprinkle with the olive oil and salt. Roast for 20 minutes or until golden and just cooked through.

Meanwhile, in a pot of boiling salted water, blanch the baby carrots for 2 minutes. Remove and set aside. Peel and quarter the cippolini onions.

As the potatoes are cooking, sauté the onions and carrots in a very hot pan with a splash of olive oil.

In a medium bowl, toss the roasted vegetables with the green sauce. Season with salt.

Assemble the dish:
To serve, slice the meat across the grain. Accompany with the sauced vegetables. Add a spoonful of pickled red cabbage to the plate. Enjoy.

PORK SANDWICH
SERVES 4

Pork Sandwich Dressing:
10 g Pickled Beets
    (Pantry page 248)
75 g Mayonnaise
    (Pantry page 250)
25 g sour cream
20g fromage blanc
5 g spicy Polish mustard,
    preferably Cracovia brand
1 g fresh tarragon leaves
1 g fresh mint leaves
Maldon salt
Fresh lemon juice

Pork Sandwich:
4 ciabatta rolls
160 g Pork Sandwich Dressing
500 g roasted pork shoulder
    (leftover from Sunday Roast,
    page 109)
120 g Pickled Red Cabbage
    (Pantry page 248)
80 g dandelion greens
20 g red onion, thinly sliced
20 g House Vinaigrette
    (Pantry page 251)
Kosher salt
100 g Pickled Beets
    (Pantry page 248)

Make the pork sandwich dressing:
In a bowl, fold together the pickled beets, mayonnaise, sour cream, fromage blanc, mustard, tarragon, and mint. Season as needed with salt and lemon juice. Cover and refrigerate for at least 2 hours to thicken.

Make the pork sandwich:
Meanwhile, partially freeze the pork for 90 minutes. Remove and shave into very thin slices. Let temper in the refrigerator for 30 minutes.

To assemble the sandwiches, split the rolls and toast slightly. Divide the pork dressing evenly across the 8 halves. Divide the shaved pork across the bottom halves, fluffing as you separate the layers. Divide the pickled red cabbage equally among the bottom halves. Quickly toss the dandelion and red onion in the vinaigrette, and season with salt if needed. Add to bottom halves. Close the sandwiches by gingerly placing the other half of ciabatta atop the rest of the layered ingredients. Slice in half on a bias.

CHILE BEER + SPICY NACHOS "DANI Y DANI"

SUGGESTION: FIREWATER, EVIL TWIN BREWING

We don't normally serve spicy nachos at Tørst, but an exceptional beer calls for an exception. There really was no question that a beer this specific and this absurd deserved to be paired with actual spicy nachos. These nachos are a collaboration with my girlfriend, the beautiful Daniela Soto-Innes. Dani is from Mexico City but lives in Brooklyn, and is a the chef de cuisine at Enrique Olvera's restaurant Cosme. We met right before Cosme opened. Truth be told, Dani doesn't make spicy nachos often either. But, as two chefs, we love to cook together for ourselves on our rare days off. The secret to these nachos is Dani's chorizo and the refried beans with avocado leaf. Enjoy!

— DANIEL

SERVES A PARTY

Daniela's Chorizo:
60 g guajillo chile, rinsed
60 g ancho chile, rinsed
Grapeseed oil
150 g white onion, diced small
30 g garlic, sliced
200 g distilled white vinegar
2 g cumin seeds
2 g coriander seeds
40 g smoked paprika
20 g salt
4 g ground cinnamon
3 g fresh Mexican oregano
3 g black pepper
2 fresh bay leaves
1000 g pork shoulder (40% fat),
    coarsely ground

Refried Beans:
200 g dried black beans
Olive oil
200 g yellow onion, peeled
    and quartered
15 g garlic, peeled and lightly
    crushed
5 g thyme sprigs
4 g fresh bay leaves

Water, Roasted Chicken Stock
    (Pantry page 247), or Vegeta-
    ble Stock (Pantry page 248)
50 g lard, bacon drippings,
    olive oil, or flavorful fat of
    your choice
2 g avocado leaf
Kosher salt
Fresh lemon juice

Chorizo Mixture:
Olive oil
100 g yellow onion, minced
Daniela's Chorizo
115 g sambal oelek
Kosher salt

Salsa:
10 g red pearl onions, sliced
175 g avocado, diced large
50 g heirloom tomatoes,
    diced small
50 g tomatillos, sliced
20 g Pickled Jalapeños
    (Pantry page 249), sliced into
    ¼-inch/6 mm rings

15 g fresh lime juice
Kosher salt

Chips:
2000 g peanut (groundnut) oil
250 g corn tortillas, cut into
    6 wedges each
Kosher salt

Spicy Nachos:
Chips
200 g Chorizo Mixture
150 g Refried Beans
150 g grated well-aged
    cheddar cheese, such as
    Prairie Breeze
60 g sour cream
Salsa
50 g cilantro (coriander),
    coarsely chopped

Make the chorizo:
Place the chiles in a medium saucepan and cover with water. Bring to a simmer over medium-high heat and cook for 5 minutes. Drain and cool. Cut the chiles open, remove the seeds and ribs, and discard.

Coat the bottom of a large heavy pan with grapeseed oil and heat over high heat until almost smoking. Add the white onion and cook, stirring frequently, until browned, about 5 minutes. Add the garlic and cook for another 5 minutes. Add the chiles, cook for 2 minutes, and deglaze the pan with the vinegar. Transfer to a blender and purée until smooth, about 1 minute.

In a small skillet, toast the cumin and coriander seeds over medium heat, stirring often, until fragrant, about 5 minutes. Cool the seeds and then grind in a spice grinder. Add the paprika, salt, cinnamon, oregano, black pepper, and bay leaf to the grinder and process for 1 minute. Add the spices to the puréed chiles and let cool.

In a bowl, thoroughly combine the chile-spice mixture with the pork. Cover and cure in the refrigerator for 4 days.

Make the refried beans:
The day before the chorizo finishes curing, soak the beans overnight in 3 times as much (by volume) cold water.

Drain the beans. Heat a heavy pot over medium heat. Add some olive oil, roast all sides of the yellow onion quarters until golden, about 6 minutes total. Add the garlic and cook a further 4 minutes, until the garlic smells sweet. Add the drained beans, thyme, and bay leaves. Cover the beans by 2 times as much (by volume) cold water, chicken stock, or vegetable stock. Bring to a boil, reduce to a simmer, cover, and cook until very tender, about 2 hours. While still warm, drain the beans, reserving their cooking liquid.

Heat a heavy pot over medium heat and add the lard. Heat until nearly smoking and add the avocado leaf. Cook 1 minute or so until it gives off a nutty aroma. Add the beans and fry for another 5 minutes, stirring constantly. Add 300 g of the reserved cooking liquid and use an immersion blender to blend once again until smooth. Season with salt and a splash of lemon juice. Set aside until needed.

Make the chorizo mixture:
In a wide, heavy pan, heat a bit of olive oil over medium-high heat. Add the onion and fry until golden. Add the chorizo and fry until cooked through, about 5 minutes. Using a slotted spoon, move the chorizo and onion to a bowl. Stir in the sambal oelek and season with salt. Allow to cool.

Make the salsa:
Soak the onion slices in ice water for 30 minutes to lessen their bite. Drain very well and mix with the avocado, tomatoes, jalapeño, and lime juice. Season to taste with salt.

Make the chips:
In a heavy pot, heat the oil to 355°F/180°C. Fry the tortilla wedges in small batches until golden and crunchy, about 90 seconds. Lift out of the oil with a wire-mesh spider and drain on paper towels. Season with salt immediately, before they cool.

Make the spicy nachos:
Preheat the oven to 375°F/190°C/Gas Mark 5.

Line a 18-by-13-inch/46 x 33 cm rimmed baking sheet with chips, top with the chorizo mixture, the refried beans, and cheddar. Bake until the cheese is melted and golden, 8 to 10 minutes. Remove the nachos from the oven and add the sour cream liberally. Top with salsa and cilantro. Serve immediately.

Food & Beer

FRUITY

JEPPE When it comes to beer flavors, spicy and fruity weirdly have a lot in common—they both underscore the wild and wide possibilities of brewing. Both heat spice and herbal spiciness can come from certain strains of yeasts as well as certain hop varietals, two of the three legs on which brewing stands. But spiciness can also come directly from spices that one adds to the beer. Beer contains the possibility for both indirect suggestion of a flavor— the result of chemical compouds produced during fermentation—as well as the addition of the actual flavor itself; the latter is the result of being able to add pretty much whatever you want whenever you want to add it.

Similarly, fruitiness in beers largely comes from hops—especially from hops from Oceania with notes of pineapple and tropical fruit—or from the esters (flavor compounds) released during fermentation. Esters are a product of yeast, the shape of the fermentation vessel, and the temperature of the wort. But as with spiciness, I think adding other ingredients is more fun.

The reputation of fruit beer has long been maligned as cloying kiddie beer, geared toward adults who never graduated from the juice-box fantasy of kindergarten beverages. Some of the disaffection is warranted: on the crummy end of fruit beers, instead of actual fruit, some brewers use sugary syrups, which result in beers that taste like spiked sodas. But as the science fiction writer Theodore Sturgeon argued in what is now called Sturgeon's law, "90 percent of everything is crap." You shouldn't dismiss fruit beer because a lot of it stinks—a lot of everything stinks.

There is a long history of brewers adding fruit of some kind to rein in the sharper, tarter, or more sour flavors of a style. Fruit in beer is especially common in lambics. For centuries, the old breweries of Pajottenland like Cantillon and Brouwerij 3 Fonteinen have offered kriek, a lambic where cherries are added after fermentation, and framboise, a lambic with raspberries. Because of the intensely sour character of the base brew, the sweetness produced by the fruit doesn't drag these beers too far to the sweet side.

One of the first beers I ever made was a fruit beer collaboration with Cantillon. I had met Jean van Roy, the fifth-generation owner of Cantillon, during some of my earliest beer pilgrimages. When we opened Ølbutikken, he was one of our earliest supporters, sending us bottles of his ultra-rare releases. In 2005, we decided to collaborate on a beer. I'm a lover of blueberries, and I have been ever since I was a little boy. So I thought why not make a blueberry lambic? After all, since there was a tradition of adding fruit, the addition of blueberry was only an incremental expansion, not a radical experiment.

It was, to say the least, an educational experience. I drove from Copenhagen to Anderlecht, the neighborhood of Brussels that is home to Cantillon, with the trunk of my Ford Mondeo filled with organic blueberries. Jean met me at the door with a huge, slightly quizzical smile. We did a test run, mixing in the fresh blueberries with 150 liters of his lambic. But the batch was unsuccessful: The skin of the blueberries spoiled the beer. One hundred fifty liters of beer might not seem like that much, but to me, ruining it felt like the end of the world. Jean was really nice about it though, and encouraged me to try again. A year later we did another batch, this time using frozen blueberries, and that made all the difference. Since the membrane of the skin was broken, the juicy flesh of the berries could interact with the wort. Today, Cantillon Blåbær Lambik is considered one of the best beers of all time. Highly sought after and incredibly rare, a bottle sells for up to $350 on the secondary market. The success of the Blåbær Lambik just shows that beer is as agnostic about process as I am. I didn't follow a plan and I certainly didn't follow convention. And yet, we made a tremendous brew. In beer, there is no snobbery.

Sourness is one of the flavors fruit can balance out. For many fruit beers, Berliner Weisse works as a wonderfully tart counterpoint to the fruity flavors. (See TART page 98 for more.)

Historically, various sweeteners like woodruff or raspberry syrup were added to mitigate uneven acidity in the style. Today, due to the standardization of the brewing process, there's no need for fruity masking agents, but the fruit flavors make a lovely complement to the tart beer. So when I decided to make the follow-up to the Cantillon Blåbær Lambik under the Evil Twin label, I chose a Berliner Weisse as a base. I was working with Ed from Westbrook Brewing on a blueberry beer. The year was 2011. Justin Bieber was at the height of his stardom, and no longer a boy. It just so happens that Bieber was in the news, and blåbær, the Danish word for blueberry, was on my mind. Thus was

born Evil Twin's Justin Blåbær. And if you happen to glance at the bottle label and think you see a familiar face, yes, that's me on the label, giving the "Blue Steel." I don't know how (or where) Ed found this picture, but it dates from when, as young men, my brother and I worked as runway models.

DANIEL   Meat is available year round. Vegetables come and go, but there are so many that their seasons overlap. Fruit, on the other hand, generally has a short growing season. Fruit allows a chef to mark where he is in the year, and the excitement of using fruit in the kitchen is inexorably tied to time. When New Jersey strawberries appear at the farmers' market, bright red fruit set against the green cardboard boxes, it takes willpower not to buy them all. When blueberries are at their best, little matte orbs of white-tinged inky blue, every chef has—and should have—the impulse to buy as many bushels as he or she can, and figure out their use later. Ditto with peaches and plums, gooseberries and raspberries, figs and currants, sour cherries and blackberries. Fruit inspires frenzy.

The challenge of such bounty is what to do with the glut, knowing the eventual dearth is coming. At Tørst, as it is with many kitchens, my philosophy is use as much as you can right away—and preserve the rest. Since most fruit, unlike vegetables, is meant to be eaten raw, it needs little, if any, manipulation as long as it is ripe. My job is to be a subtle encourager of its flavor. I can do that either by heightening fruit's innate qualities, or offsetting it with complementary flavors. I try not to mess around too much.

As far as preserving goes, there are jams, cordials, and ices, just to name a few ways. Some fruit, like plums, respond well to hanging out in salt. Others—like sour cherries—need a little more finesse to keep them delectable through time.

In any case, one must never trample on summer fruit's greatest asset: the spirit of summer the season carries in its flesh. In the cold of winter, fruit can serve as a reminder of long, hazy, summer days filled with juicy peaches or succulent blackberries—the best encapsulation of a perfect day.

FRUIT-INFUSED BERLINER WEISSE + MACERATED STRAWBERRIES, ROSEHIP VINEGAR MERINGUE

SUGGESTION: JUSTIN BLÅBÆR, EVIL TWIN BREWING

You won't find fruit salad on the menu at Tørst—but we're still fans. Like everything at Tørst, caution must be used. For instance, the sweetness of Daniel's macerated strawberry dessert is balanced by its tart vinegar meringues, and the sweetness of Jeppe's Justin Blåbær by a tart Berliner Weisse.

You often read about certain berries pairing well with the dark richness of stouts or porters. And we're not opposed to that. But just as hard as it is to appreciate stained glass windows at night, so too is it difficult to appreciate the lighter notes of fruit against the inky heft of a stout. Lighter beers that are more tart or sour, like a fruited Berliner Weisse or a lambic, buoy the flavors.

— JEPPE AND DANIEL

SERVES 4

Vinegar Meringue:
100 g egg whites
8 g powdered egg whites
145 g sugar
65 g water
30 g rosehip vinegar

Macerated Strawberries:
800 g strawberries, fresh and
    the best you've ever tasted
75 g demerara sugar
10 g rosehip vinegar

Chantilly:
300 g heavy (double) cream
1 vanilla pod, split and seeds
    scraped out

Make the vinegar meringue:
In a stand mixer, using a whisk attachment by hand, gently bring the egg whites and egg white powder together.

In a small pot, combine the granulated sugar and water. Bring to a boil over medium heat, stirring with a spoon until the sugar is dissolved. Cook until the syrup reaches 250°F/121°C. But as soon as it hits 230°F/110°C, attach the whisk to the mixer and start whipping on medium speed. While the syrup cooks, watch the egg whites. They should reach medium peaks by the time the syrup is ready. (If they are aerating slowly, increase the speed slightly.)

Once the syrup reaches its goal temperature, turn off the heat, and swirl the pot for a few seconds to calm the syrup. Reduce the speed of the mixer to medium-low and pour 1 tablespoon of syrup into the whites. Whip for 5 seconds. Repeat this twice more. After the third addition of syrup has been incorporated, slowly stream the remainder in. Let the meringue whip on medium-low speed until just warm to the touch, about 8 minutes. Add half the vinegar, making sure the first amount is fully incorporated, then adding the rext.

Using a large offset spatula, spread the meringue evenly across 3 dehydrator sheets in layers about ¼-inch/6 mm thick. Do not worry about getting it perfectly smooth, you won't, and those variations will show that you made your meringue by hand. Dehydrate at 135°F/57°C for 12 hours.

The best way we've found to lift off the meringues is to position yourself at the edge of a table with squared sides. Lay a sheet of parchment paper on the table and gently pull the dehydrator sheets off the table at an angle and down toward the ground, causing the meringue to lift from the sheet. This should result in a sheet of meringue slowly advancing toward you while the dehydrator sheet drops away. Keep your hand under the meringue, as it is fragile and will break as you pull the sheet out from under it. When you have about a third of the sheet lifted, rotate 90 degrees to break off and repeat. Keep the meringue in a very dry place, with silica or dessicant packs if you have them.

Macerate the strawberries:
In a bowl, combine the strawberries, demerara sugar, and vinegar and let stand for 45 minutes at room temperature.

Make the chantilly:
In a chilled medium bowl, whip the cream lightly until thickened. Add the vanilla seeds and continue to whip until soft peaks form.

Assemble the dish:
Divide the strawberries across 4 bowls with a good spoonful of their juices. Top with a generous dollop of whipped cream and cover in shards of rosehip vinegar meringue.

Food & Beer

TASTY

JEPPE   So far, Daniel and I have showcased various elements of flavors that we think constitute important bridges between the kitchen and the keg. We've touched on everything from hop varietals (page 38) to lactic acid fermentation (page 78), to Brix (page 61), to beets (page 69). In each of the preceding chapters, we've focused on the most germane characteristics of each ingredient that we felt embodied those flavors. But, now that we're at the end of our journey of flavor, it occurs to us that sometimes the flavor most present is just plain tasty, fuck it. "Tasty, fuck it," is what one says when the logic of the particular deliciousness of a particular item proves elusive. One can't say with certainty whether it stems from, say, SOUR (page 77) or FRUITY (page 117) or some combination of the flavors; or maybe it isn't just the flavors but the accumulation of memories and flavors. Anyway, that's what these recipes and beers have in common. They're not meant to go with each other and aren't offered as pairings. They're just plain tasty and sometimes that's enough.

Jolly Pumpkin Baudelaire iO Saison
On April 1, 2010, April Fools' Day, Melvin, my second son, was born. Shortly after we returned from the hospital, I sat on my couch holding this little perfect boy in my arms. His tiny face with glistening brown eyes peered out at mine. I looked at the clock: 1:30 a.m. I thought, what should I do to celebrate this moment? With Melvin cradled in my arm, I dug out a bottle of Jolly Pumpkin Baudelaire iO Saison that my friend JP had sent me from his Dexter, Michigan, brewery. Melvin had dozed off. His three-year-old brother, Elliot, was fast asleep. Maria was by my side, holding Melvin, and the beer was in a glass in front of me. I took a sip. This, I thought, is the most perfectly balanced beer I remember having since the first time I had an Orval. This, I thought, is the reason I got interested in drinking craft beer to begin with, nearly fifteen years before. I drank the Saison, I looked at Melvin. And I promised to him that someday, I will take him to Dexter when he's old enough to experience maybe the greatest brewery in the world.

Girardin Gueuze Black Label

In the early 2000s, at the start of my pilgrimages to Belgium, I invited myself to the Girardin Brewery, on the outskirts of Brussels. Girardin—founded in 1845, and one of the most esteemed producers of lambics—is run by the fourth generation of the Girardin family. I had long been curious how they made their beer, and decided to go see for myself. The brewery is a charming brick building with a modern addition. Through the windows, I could see large copper kettles used for brewing. Peering through the gates made me feel like Charlie in the Chocolate Factory.

It turned out Girardin didn't give public tours, but they seemed so surprised that I had driven all the way from Copenhagen that they agreed to let me see the brewery. The gates creaked open and I was allowed inside. Open before me were hundreds of years of history; the traditional methods of beer making were alive and continued uninterrupted. Instantly, witnessing this process connected what I was doing with my homebrews with a much older tradition, which made my brewing projects take on a more serious weight. At Girardin, the brewers let me taste one-or-two week-old baby lambics, which are only rarely tasted and never sold. Barely fermented, they tasted sweet like grainy orange juice! Every time I open a bottle from Girardin, I'm reminded of that wonderful day a decade ago. This gueuze, in particular, blends younger lambics than are normally used, which makes it probably the most balanced of all oude gueuzes.

Rodenbach Grand Cru

They say the first cut is the deepest. Well, the same is true for Flanders Red Ale. The first time I had one it was this Rodenbach Grand Cru. Rodenbach is an old brewery in West Flanders famous for their Red Ales. The history of the brewery is entwined with the history of the country. Pedro Rodenbach, who founded the brewery, was instrumental in the Belgian revolution of 1830. His brother, Constantijn, wrote the national anthem. Pedro's grandson, Eugene, traveled to England to study the barrel-aging then used for English porters. Today, Rodenbach still uses these large oak casks, called foeders. Red Ales, which take their carmine color from special red malt, are usually aged in oak barrels and fermented using lactic acid bacteria, which give it a sour tang. This particular beer is aged for two years in the barrel, which gives it an almost wine-like depth. I remember

thinking, "This takes like sweet 'n' sour sauce!" It blew me away; I was in love.

DANIEL   It took a good couple months before Tørst regulars began to order Welsh rarebit. Most people think it's some sort of heavy rabbit stew or something. It's not: It's cheese and beer on bread—no rabbit in sight—and when done right, is absolutely irresistible: creamy, funky, and sweet. The cheese and beer—and a few other piquant ingredients—are whisked together to make a Mornay sauce, cooled, and then smeared on toast before being broiled. Despite its relatively straightforward preparation, people get it wrong more often than they get it right—even in England, its native land.

The first time I was exposed to it was when I was living in London, where the Welsh rarebit, made with sharp English cheddar and Guinness, was one of the most popular and celebrated English pub snacks. When we opened Tørst, there wasn't even a question whether or not we'd offer a Welsh rarebit at the bar. At the time, no one in New York—save for April Bloomfield's John Dory Oyster Bar—was making a legit Welsh rarebit. It isn't just a slice of melted cheese on bread (that's blasphemy). Since Tørst is located in Greenpoint, Brooklyn, home of a substantial Polish community, I use Polish rye bread from the New Warsaw bakery next door. I also use Prairie Breeze, a sharp cheddar from Milton Creamery in Wisconsin and pair the sandwich with Even More Jesus, Jeppe's famous stout. It's a shout-out to Fergus, St. John, and the tradition of English pubs. But mostly it's tasty.

WELSH RAREBIT

SERVES 6 AS A SNACK

50 g butter
50 g all-purpose (plain) flour
135 g stout beer, such as Even
    More Jesus
375 g heavy (double) cream
3 g mustard powder
1 g cayenne pepper
30 g aged cheddar cheese,
    grated
1 loaf Polish rye
Worcestershire sauce

In a heavy-bottomed pot, melt the butter over medium heat. Once melted, whisk in the flour, and cook until the color shifts slightly darker, about 4 minutes. Add half the stout, making sure the beer is fully incorporated into the roux before adding the rest. Add half the cream, making sure it is fully incorporated into the mixture before adding the rest. Whisk in the mustard and cayenne to incorporate fully with no lumps. Cook until the mixture thickens nicely, 5 to 7 minutes. Be careful not to burn the bottom of the pan. Reduce the heat to medium-low and slowly add the cheddar, whisking after each addition. Be mindful of the heat: if the cheese begins to separate from the roux, cut the flame entirely. Let the rarebit mixture cool completely.

Slice the bread 1¼-inch/3cm thick and toast until golden. Let cool and top each slice with 75 g of rarebit mixture. Use an offset spatula to spread the mixture evenly over the top of bread.

Broil (grill) until bubbling and slightly darkened. Drizzle Worcestershire sauce over the hot rarebit, slice into 5 pieces, and serve immediately.

A PROPER TOMATO SANDWICH

A tomato sandwich from my mother's kitchen was a thing of beauty and polish. Multigrain bread, toasted a golden brown. Butter and mayonnaise generously spread over the still-warm bread melting into glistening dew. Tomatoes, sliced with a razor-sharp knife were so fresh it was almost as if they had been stunned and were living still. Once, when I was young, I was visiting a friend and his mother made us tomato sandwiches that lacked all of the above things. I ate the sandwich, but as soon as I got home, I asked my mom to make me one of her tomato sandwiches—the one I was used to. And only when it arrived—so precise, so perfect—were my mind and spirit soothed.

SERVES 4

300 g heirloom tomatoes
8 slices multigrain bread
80 g Mayonnaise
    (Pantry page 250)
20 g butter, at room
    temperature
Maldon salt
Freshly cracked black pepper

Cut the tomatoes into uniform ⅓-inch/8 mm-thick slices. Toast the bread on both sides. Slather with mayonnaise and butter on half the bread slices. Top with slices of tomato to cover the surface of the bread. The tomato should not unduly hang over the edge of the bread, nor should there be large expanses of mayonnaise left exposed by lack of tomato.

This is a simple dish but you must take care. Salt liberally and add a few grinds of black pepper. Finish with a second slice of bread. Do not push down on the bread when it comes time to slice; use a very sharp knife. Exerting pressure at this late stage will ruin the careful work hitherto put forth. Eat with a very cold glass of milk.

FRIED CIPOLLINI ONIONS, TOMATO RELISH

The Bloomin' Onion, a one-pound onion appetizer-served at the Outback Steakhouse restaurant chain, is fried and cut into a beautiful blossom. It contains 2,000 calories— each one, worth it. At Tørst, I don't serve a Bloomin' Onion. But I did want to capture and recreate the deeply satisfying experience of eating one. My answer was to supercharge a cipolini, a naturally sweet small onion that looks like a flattened golf ball, and fry it. By cooking the onion in mushroom broth, we're able to amplify the sweet and earthy flavors. The onions are then quartered and fried, by a dedicated bloomologist, or as I like to call him, a cook. We serve it at the bar with a tomato relish, which just makes everything better but in particular this.

SERVES 6

250 g cipollini onions,
    peeled and halved
125 g Mushroom Stock
    (Pantry page 247)
Peanut (groundnut) oil
120 g Wondra flour
40 g Crisp Film
Kosher salt
Tomato Relish (Pantry page 251)

Fill a large pot halfway with water and bring to a boil. Reduce to a simmer. Place the onions and mushroom stock in a vacuum bag and vacuum-seal. Place the bag in the water and let simmer until the onions are tender, about 25 minutes. Remove the bag from the water and shock in an ice bath.

    Meanwhile, fill a heavy pot halfway with peanut oil and heat to 355°F/180°C.

    Drain the onions (discard the stock) and let any excess stock drip off. In a shallow pan, whisk together the Wondra flour and Crisp Film. Toss the drained onions in the flour mixture, shaking off the excess with a slotted spoon.

    Working in batches, fry the onions until crispy and slightly darker than gold. (Onions have a high water content, which is why they must be fried close to the point of burning.)

    Remove and blot the fried onions on paper towels. Salt immediately and aggressively. Serve hot alongside tomato relish.

PART II

LUKSUS

DANIEL   My dream was to open a restaurant of my own. It wasn't a matter of fame or glory. Certainly riches or a healthy work-life balance are not involved. But the shimmering goal—to manifest my personal vision with little external accommodation or concession to others—is irresistible. The devotion to self-expression might sound egotistical or abstract—and on some level, perhaps it is a bit of both—but it's also not confined to artists, or poets, or chefs. It's one of the most universal urges, animating the hearts of all freedom-loving peoples. The medium through which you express yourself,be it painting, cooking, writing, or building, isn't nearly as important as that you actually do it.

Yet pure self-expression is elusive. If achieved at all, it is done so only spottily and at the expense of others. For most of the time I'm Daniel Burns.* But there is a 225-square-foot sliver of land in Greenpoint, Brooklyn, where I can just be Daniel Burns, unasterisked. I can be ME. And that's the kitchen of Luksus.

By 2013, I had worked in kitchens for more than a decade. I had the good fortune to work with chefs, each of whom had a singular vision of what they wanted to achieve in the culinary landscape. From Susur Lee and René Redzepi, to Heston Blumenthal and David Chang, those guys had no intention of imitating anything that had been done before. They were creatively reckless, relentless, and restless. During the years I spent in their kitchens, I didn't absorb just technical aspects of their individual approaches. The most important takeaway was that the concept of originality and self-expression were held up as twinned ideals to which every chef should aspire. Eventually, that became an imperative.

After I left David Chang's test kitchen, I had some time to think about what to do next. Should I return to Denmark or England or back home to Canada? Should I become one of the roaming consulting chefs, a culinary ronin, adding my expertise to the projects of others? Even when I met Jeppe and we started discussing what would become Luksus, I was still undecided. What a terrifying prospect to be yourself! When you're finally given a stage and a spotlight, there are no excuses, no props to hide behind. Was my vision sufficiently developed and did I have the skills to execute it? I've seen more than a few chefs fall like Icarus did in the Greek legend when their visions outstripped their ability—or worse, when those visions themselves were hazy and embryonic.

In addition, there was the anxiety of influence. Because I had worked in the world's top kitchens, I had gleaned swaths of brilliant techniques and daring innovation. With those years spent carefully learning, I drew on my exposure and experience. Nevertheless, I resolved never to repeat verbatim what I had learned there. My mission was clear: make it new, make it mine.

As for my style, it had been taking shape gradually—less an evolution than erosion. When I was a young cook, just starting out, I had good intuition but little form. Over the years, through exposure to various elements, crags developed and fissures formed. By the time I was thirty-eight, I knew who I was, what I liked, and what I didn't. I was confident in my skills. But you never know a fighter until you see him in the ring. It was time to find out if I had what it took to run my own place.

We opened Luksus on July 16, 2013. It was then, and still is now, a small space without a sign, located through a pocket door in the back of Tørst. It seats only sixteen, and the upstairs kitchen is about the size of a large-ish New York closet. But it was my universe and, at first, it felt vast. I've never written fiction, but it felt like I was writing a story when creating my menu from scratch; I imagined a world (the restaurant) and then let the characters (courses) live in it. Before I could say what I wanted to say through food, I needed to create a language of flavor.

While at Noma, I had been initiated into the cult of pickling, where nearly every dish contained a pickled element. At Luksus I knew I wanted to use that funky acidity as a foundation. A few months before we opened, I began buying up all the produce that was in season—cauliflower, carrots, cucumbers, ramps, hot peppers, garlic scapes—and brining and storing them in the walk-in refrigerator. I felt giddy, like a kid who got a new toy.

From my time at The Fat Duck, I drew on the world of dairy. England may not be considered the world's most thrilling food culture, but it has amazing milk, butter, and cheese. Their Jersey and Guernsey cows yield famously rich, fatty milk that's bursting with barnyard flavor. My search for suppliers who could deliver on the highest form of dairy took me to Norwich, New York, where the Sunrise Family Farms churn out lush butter and Ithaca Milk makes an extra-tangy yogurt and fatty milk.

And from Momofuku, I drew on a tradition of fermentation. My years chasing umami in the dark solitude of the test kitchen were not for nothing, and my shelves quickly filled with shiro-dashi (a Japanese stock made with white miso), sweet potato vinegar, and lightly colored usukuchi soy. In every corner of the cramped basement kitchen, things fermented. In the corner sat some rice, bound to become a fermented rice called koji, and later to be mixed with barley, lentils, or cashews to make miso. Soy sauce aged in a bourbon barrel. A pork loin, surrounded in rice, was well on its way to hardening into pork katsuobushi, a riff on the Japanese traditional shaved, dried fish staple. Finally, I had a kitchen that mirrored my mind.

Once the world of Luksus flavors began to flourish, it was a question of figuring out which ones played well together. What would happen if I turned English peas into sorbet? What if I made ham broth into a chip? What techniques could I use to reveal a flavor in an innovative way or illuminate it from a new angle? What stories could I tell? I would learn as I told them.

We opened during a heat wave on July 16 with limited planning and even less equipment. It was just me and a young cook from Blue Hill, Dan Barber's restaurant in New York. The first months were hectic: though we were open just four days, from Wednesday through Saturday, it was a round-the-clock, no-days-off job. On the days we were open, we did everything, from prep to service to washing dishes. If a carrot came in from a farmer, I shepherded it from delivery to the plate, not particularly out of philosophical commitment to husbandry, but because there was no one else around. I'd spend my days off in the restaurant kitchen, trying new ideas and flavor combinations. But despite a grueling schedule, it was also among the most rewarding months of my life. Finally, I was serving the food that I had been dreaming about, and sharing it with others. And those "others" were responding favorably, partially because Tørst was already so busy, but also because the idea of Luksus was so unique, and we were full almost from day one. One day, Dave Pegoli walked in and soon became our sous-chef. Dave is a true-blue New Yorker, and an incredibly hard worker. In a kitchen like ours, you need people like Pegoli—who can happily switch tasks and learn new skills, with a tireless cheerfulness and attention to detail. Plus, as I learned from Jocky, the pastry chef with whom I first bonded at The Fat Duck, you need to genuinely like the people you spend your life with.

Running your own restaurant, as I came to discover, is an all-consuming endeavor. What you gain in freedom of expression, you lose in free time. It has challenged me in ways I hadn't even anticipated. Being Chef brings with it responsibilities to nurture talent, to support creativity, and still to insist on only the highest level of execution. With ambitions as high as ours, and a staff as small, the kitchen is in every way a crucible. Learning how to negotiate that—not only as a boss but also as a person—while maintaining a healthy community is, perhaps, even more important than turning out perfectly plated food, the real work of a kitchen.

Thankfully, as I refined my philosophy in the kitchen, there was spillover onto how I treated my staff. It's just logistically inconsistent to exalt balance and respect on the plate, but to ignore those values in yourself and with your colleagues. "If you are kind to kale, be kind to others" has been the follow-through from honing my culinary vision. Luksus has given me an opportunity to create cultures of flavor and a community of people, from our suppliers to our porters and cooks and, of course, our guests.

Perhaps it's a sign of the time, but we found out about our Michelin star from Eater, a food and restaurant website. It was October 1, 2014, a little over a year since we first opened. Though Jeppe and I had seen the list online, we didn't want to celebrate yet. But at 2 p.m., when we received a congratulatory call from a functionary at Michelin, the reality set in. The star itself is something grand. But what it symbolized—that this vision of flavor I had so assiduously worked towards was appreciated—meant more than any plaque. Finally instead of an asterisk, I had a star. I ran downstairs to tell the team; they looked up from their prep stations and grinned. We high-fived and hugged, but shortly after, we were back to work. Service was starting in just a few hours.

*Subject to the terms and conditions placed on one by the obligation for harmonious intercourse with one's fellows, not to mention the accommodation that must be given to financial and creative exigencies.

SNACKS

By the time guests arrive at Luksus, they've probably navigated the public transit system, dealt with a surly cab driver, or eked out a win after a hard-fought battle with city parking. Very likely, they've wandered along our block, perhaps entering the hair salon that's also called Luksus, before retreating to the street again. Finally, they'd find Tørst; but even upon entering, they were likely momentarily befuddled by the crowded bar scene, which doesn't exactly convey "fine dining." Resolute, they'd wander to the back of the bar, past the throngs, and then a door would slide open and they would find Luksus, the land of milk and honey—or, in our case, food and beer.

Every element of the Luksus experience is calibrated to create the opportunity for surprise and delight, to confound conventional notions of fine dining, and to communicate our thesis: fine dining can be welcoming, unexpected, informal, and delicious. Snacks, the first morsels guests at Luksus eat, are our first chance to communicate that on the plate.

In traditional fine dining, amuse-bouches, a fancy word for snacks, are often served with elaborate accoutrements—golden spoons, diminutive forks, hollowed-out eggs—and extensive instruction from the server. At Luksus, these bites are plucked off their slab of wood or slate and delivered into the mouth with one's hands, the original implement. Eating with your hands is a vestige of childhood, and because the snacks are small, comes across as playful, not savage. It's an easy way to dispel the nervousness and pretension that so often influence the fine-dining experience.

Beyond setting the mood, snacks act as the opening motifs of dinner at Luksus—attention-grabbing, like a catchy riff. Normally we serve about five snacks in quick succession, each its own burst of flavor. Were the snacks any larger, these intense, and densely layered flavor bombs, would bludgeon. But because they're quick hits, they instead awaken the senses and prepare the palate for the meal ahead.

LOBSTER RELISH, SEAWEED BISCUIT

SERVES 6

Seaweed Biscuit:
400 g butter, diced, at room
    temperature
70 g demerara sugar
50 g dulse powder
800 g all-purpose (plain) flour
200 g rye flour
8 g baking powder
225 g milk

Hazelnut Mayonnaise:
50 g blanched, peeled hazel-
    nuts, toasted and cooled
100 g Mayonnaise
    (Pantry page 250)
Kosher salt
Fresh lemon juice

Poached Lobster:
750 g live lobster
225 g champagne vinegar
155 g white wine vinegar
150 g water

125 g fennel, sliced
80 g shallot, sliced
30 g demerara sugar
25 g fresh ginger, sliced
20 g fresh horseradish, grated
15 g fresh bay leaves
10 g white peppercorns
10 g juniper berries
2 g dried bird's eye chiles

Lobster Relish:
Olive oil
2 g garlic, minced
1 g Fresno chiles, seeded and
    minced
100 g white daikon, brunoised
Fresh lemon juice
1 g tarragon, minced
1 g flat-leaf parsley, finely
    chopped
Kosher salt

PAIRING:

Evil Twin Brewing, Bikini Beer
(eviltwin.dk)

Evil Twin's Bikini Beer is the
first beer of the evening. Jeppe
makes this beer at Two Roads,
a brewery in Stratford, Connecticut. It's a baby IPA, only
2.7% ABV, compared to the
standard 5% to 7% of most
IPAs. It's very light, but still it
doesn't feel like you're drinking
water. Because the snacks have
so many flavors packed so
closely together, you don't want
an intrusive beer. Bikini has a
nice body hence the name but
it's clean and crisp.

Make the seaweed biscuit:
In a stand mixer fitted with the paddle attachment, beat together
the butter and demerara sugar on low speed. Add the dulse powder
and mix until evenly incorporated. In a separate bowl, whisk
together the flours and baking powder. Add the flour mixture to
the butter mixture and beat on low until mealy. Drizzle in the milk
until the dough just comes together. The dough will look very dry;
do not be alarmed if your instincts tell you it needs more liquid.
Do not overmix. Divide the dough in half. Roll each between 2
sheets of parchment to a ¼-inch/6 mm thickness. Transfer to a
baking sheet and freeze overnight.

The next day, let the sheets warm up on a counter for 5 minutes. Using a Matfer #40 (1½-inch/40 mm) ring cutter, punch out
discs. Return the discs to the freezer for 2 hours. Using an offset

spatula, lift the discs and place in a shallow airtight container with sheets of parchment between the layers. Cover and freeze.

Make the hazelnut mayonnaise:
Pulse the hazelnuts in a food processor until they resemble wet sand. At this point, the oil will start to emerge and the mixture will develop a sheen. Work in the mayonnaise in short pulses. If the mayonnaise shows sign of breaking, add 1 teaspoon cold water and continue to pulse. Once well mixed, season to taste with salt and lemon juice. Refrigerate until ready to serve.

Make the lobster:
Bring a large pot of water to a boil. Boil the lobster for 2 minutes, then shock in an ice bath. Remove the claws, knuckles, and tail. Split the tail in half and remove any roe and the digestive tract. Pick the meat from the knuckles and claws. Set aside in a nonreactive container while you make the poaching liquid.

In a saucepan, combine the vinegars, water, fennel, shallot, demerara sugar, ginger, and horseradish and bring to a boil. Add the bay leaves, peppercorns, juniper, and chiles and simmer for 10 minutes. Remove from the heat and let cool to 140°F/60°C. Strain over the lobster, cover, and refrigerate. Let marinate for at least 3 and up to 5 hours.

Make the lobster relish:
In a sauté pan, heat enough oil to just coat the pan until very hot. Add the garlic and cook until it starts to brown, about 10 seconds. Add the chiles and, after 10 seconds, add the daikon. Cook another 15 seconds. Splash with lemon juice and a pinch of salt. Transfer to a wide bowl and let cool on the counter to room temperature.

Chop the marinated lobster into small uniform pieces and set aside. Right before serving fold the lobster, tarragon, and parsley into the daikon mixture. Taste and season aggressively with more salt and lemon juice.

Assemble the dish:
Preheat the oven to 340°F/170°C/Gas Mark 3.

Bake the seaweed biscuits straight from the freezer until lightly browned at the edges and dry at the center, 10 to 12 minutes. Let cool.

Place a small dollop of hazelnut mayonnaise on each biscuit. Top with a heaping tablespoon of the lobster relish. Serve immediately.

KNÆKBRØD,
PICKLED MACKEREL

Knækbrød:
60 g rolled oats
130 g sunflower seeds
60 g flax seeds
160 g rye flour
70 g all-purpose (plain) flour
1 g Maldon salt
2 g baking powder
130 g water
60 g olive oil

Mackerel Pickle:
450 g water
110 g rice vinegar
75 g sweet potato vinegar
75 g fennel, sliced
50 g shallot, sliced

35 g celery, sliced
8 g coriander seeds
5 g juniper berries
1 g dried bird's eye chiles
1 g bay leaf
1 (1000 to 1250 g/ 2 to 3 lbs)
    whole mackerel, Spanish or
    Boston

Celery Gribiche:
50 g mayonnaise
15 g shallot, brunoised
15 g celery, brunoised
5 g capers, chopped
2 g dill, chopped
2 g chives, finely sliced
Maldon salt

Make the knækbrød:
Blitz the oats in a blender for a few seconds. Mix with the seeds, flours, salt, and baking powder. Mix the water and olive oil together and pour over the dry ingredients. Using your hands, just bring the dough together without excessive kneading. Divide the dough in half and roll each half out between 2 sheets of parchment to a ⅛-inch/3 mm thickness. Transfer to a baking sheet and freeze for 1 hour until firm.

Using a sharp knife, cut each sheet into 1-inch/2.5 cm-wide strips. Portion each long strip into 1½-inch/4 cm pieces. Store in a shallow airtight container with parchment between each layer in the freezer.

When ready to bake, preheat the oven to 340°F/170°C/Gas Mark 3.

Bake the knækbrød until lightly colored, about 12 minutes. Let cool on the counter to room temperature.

Make the mackerel pickle:

In a saucepan, combine the water, vinegars, fennel, shallot, and celery, and bring to a boil. Reduce the heat to a simmer, add the rest of the pickle ingredients, and simmer for 10 minutes. Let the pickling liquid cool to 122°F/50°C.

Meanwhile, clean, gut, and fillet the mackerel. If using a Spanish mackerel, take off the skin entirely. If using Boston mackerel, use a sharp knife and your hand to pull the thin, tough membrane off from the skin. Transfer the fillets to a nonreactive pan so they can sit side by side without any overlap or excessive space.

Pour the cooled pickling liquid over the fish and immediately refrigerate. Let pickle for 3 hours or until a nicely pronounced pickled flavor is reached.

Strain the pickling liquid and clean off any aromatics or spices that have clung to the flesh. Slice the fish on a slight bias to make pieces ¼-inch/6 mm thick and about the size of the knækbrød until you have 12 nice pieces. Set aside.

Make the celery gribiche:

In a bowl, combine all the gribiche ingredients, season with salt, and refrigerate for 30 minutes.

Assemble the dish:

Place a small teaspoon of celery gribiche on each knækbrød cracker and top with a slice of fish. Serve immediately.

FRIED OYSTER, CAULIFLOWER, CABBAGE

SERVES 8

Cauliflower Purée:
250 g cauliflower, cut into rough florets
500 g milk
5 g brown butter
Kosher salt

Oyster Pickle:
30 g usukuchi soy sauce
20 g verjus
15 g maguro shirodashi shoyu
10 g water
5 g honey
25 g shallots, sliced
10 g fresh ginger, sliced
3 g Fresno chile, sliced
2 g Chinese cinnamon stick (also known as cassia bark)
1 g black peppercorns
1 g star anise
1 g bay leaf
45 g fresh celery juice
8 large, briny oysters, such as Black Point

Cabbage:
Maldon salt
8 green cabbage leaves, preferably Arrowhead (conehead)

Oyster Fry:
80 g panko breadcrumbs, pulsed in food processor to
    resemble cornmeal
30 g quick-mixing flour
10 g Crisp Film
Peanut (groundnut) oil
Kosher salt

Make the cauliflower purée:
In a saucepan, combine the cauliflower and milk and cook over medium-low heat until tender. Drain the milk used for cooking the cauliflower (and sicard), and blend until smooth. Blend in the brown butter to finish. Pass through a chinois pushing on solids; season with salt and allow to cool.

Make the oyster pickles:
In a saucepan, combine the usukuchi soy sauce, verjus, maguro shirodashi shoyu, water, and honey and bring to a boil. Add the shallots, ginger, chile, cinnamon stick, peppercorns, star anise, and bay leaf and reduce the heat to a simmer. Simmer for 10 minutes, strain, and let the pickling liquid cool. Stir in the celery juice.

Shuck the oysters, rinse, check over for dirt and shell bits, and transfer to a small, lidded nonreactive container. Pour the cooled pickling liquid over the oysters and let marinate for 3 hours in the refrigerator.

Make the cabbage:
While the oysters marinate, blanch the cabbage leaves in salted boiling water for a few seconds. Strain and cool on a baking sheet lined with a clean kitchen towel. Once cool, use a Matfer #80 (3-inch /80 mm) ring cutter to cut out discs of the cabbage leaf, avoiding tears, wrinkles, and the tough center stem. Pat dry and set aside.

Fry the oysters:
Make the fry mix by whisking together the panko, flour, and Crisp Film.

In a medium wide, heavy pot, heat 1 inch/2.5 cm of oil to 365°F/185°C.

Meanwhile, let the oysters drip off their marinade briefly and coat in the fry mix well, patting gently on all sides.

Fry the oysters until golden, 20 to 30 seconds. Using a slotted spoon, remove oysters from the oil, drain on paper towels, and sprinkle with salt while hot.

Assemble the dish:
Sprinkle Maldon salt on each disc of cabbage, then top with a dollop of cauliflower purée and a fried oyster. Serve immediately, while the oysters are still warm.

FIRST SERVINGS

When developing a tasting menu, a chef considers what role each course is meant to play. Tasting menus are, for better or worse, the equivalent of an oratory where each course is a statement that adds up to a moving address. Our snacks are meant to set the mood and initiate the diners into the language of Luksus; our first course directs their focus to the quality of ingredients. The "first servings" are, as a whole, a subtler course than the snacks, usually showcasing a single ingredient, touched as lightly as possible.

Chefs talk a lot about showcasing individual ingredients, but more often they wind up over-manipulating them, as if a reconstituted radish is innately more radish-y than just one perfect radish au naturel. I suspect that in some cases there's a little bit of insecurity behind this, as if the chef wants the guest to know he or she really did do something to the ingredient on the plate. It's a fact that the lion's share of running a restaurant goes into the sourcing of quality products. The true job of a chef is to compose those products into a well-balanced polyphony, in which the voice of each rings out clearly.

While our first servings aim for more than just presenting an ingredient raw, the guiding philosophy is very much a minimalist one. These courses are more about juxtaposition of flavor than the chemical transformations of cooking. Proteins are often served raw or as close to raw as possible. Take, for example, the beef tartare: I never thought I would put tartare, especially beef tartare, on the menu; though tasty, it's sort of a culinary cliché. But I recognized there's no reason tartare must be served with raw shallots and egg yolks. My version uses the meat more as a textural island around which wild herbs and green almonds can coalesce. Each element on the plate bounces off the meat, illuminating something new about the ingredient.

The approach is the same with each of our first servings, whether it's the sweetness of a fresh scallop or the delicate flavor of barely cooked squid. In this course, my job is to be a facilitator of natural flavor, to act as a bridge between the ingredients and the guest. That's why the technique is administered lightly and gently, as a paleontologist might brush dirt from a fossil to better reveal its contours. As a chef the tendency is sometimes to shout one's point of view. But here, speaking quietly makes the most powerful statement.

BEEF TARTARE, RAZOR CLAM

PAIRING:

XX Bitter, De Ranke,
(www.deranke.be)

The XX Bitter from the Belgian
brewery De Ranke is a hop-
forward pale ale that, as the
name suggests, is robustly
bitter. Belgians, in general, are
more interested in yeast than
hops but this one started to turn
the tide. Made with Hallertau
and Brewer's Gold, the beer has
a clean profile with a touch of
sweetness and some grassy
notes that complement the
earthiness of the tartare. The
beer has a relatively high ABV
(6.2%) for the style, but with
flavors as robust as the beef, the
pickled ramps, and wild chives,
not to mention the sharp
herbaceous leaves, you want a
well-rounded beer that is as
assertive as this one.

SERVES 4

Almond Milk Vinaigrette:
20 g raw blanched almonds
115 g water
25 g Pickled Hot Peppers liquid (Pantry page 249)
6 g apple cider vinegar
5 g rice vinegar
2 g fresh lemon juice

Beef and Razor Clams:
150 g beef tenderloin, free of sinew and fat
3 razor clams
6 fresh green almonds
Olive oil
8 wild garlic chives
Kosher salt
Fresh lemon juice

To Assemble:
Maldon salt
6 Pickled Green Almonds (Pantry page 249), brunoised
20 stonecrop tips
20 ground ivy leaves
16 yarrow leaves or flowers
16 bittercress tips
16 mustard or arugula (rocket) flowers
40 g Almond Milk Vinaigrette
Cold-pressed rapeseed oil
4 Pickled Ramps (Pantry page 250)

Make the almond milk vinaigrette:
In a blender, combine the almonds and water and blend for 2 minutes until well incorporated. Strain through a chinois into a bowl, then strain again through a soup strainer or cheesecloth. Whisk in the vinegars and lemon juice. Set aside.

Prepare the beef and clams:
Using a sharp knife, scrape the beef with the grain using short sharp thrusts away from yourself. Chop through the scraped beef once perpendicular to your original cut, to ensure that there are no large chunks of meat. Portion into 4 (35 g) balls. Spread each ball to cover 6 x 4½-inch/15 x 11 cm squares of parchment paper. This can be done a few hours ahead and kept refrigerated.

One hour before serving, prepare the razor clams by running a small offset spatula along the seams of the shell. Open the shell and pull out the main muscle. It is solid and milk-white with a brown end known as the "foot." Discard the rest. Slice the clams on a slight bias ¼-inch/6 mm thick. Keep on ice.

Using a small knife, carefully pry the fresh green almond shells open and gently pull out the nut. Slice on a bias, creating ⅛-inch/3 mm-thick ovals the same size as the razor clam pieces.

In a smoking hot pan with just a few drops of olive oil, pan-roast the chives until slightly browned. Salt lightly and sprinkle with a few drops of lemon juice. Blot on a paper towel and set aside.

Assemble the dish:
Invert each parchment-coated meat over the left side of each of 4 plates and carefully peel the parchment off. Distribute the razor clam bits atop the meat. Salt aggressively. Scatter the pickled green almonds around the plate. Distribute the herb leaves evenly across the 4 portions. Cover the beef with a thin layer of vinaigrette and several drops of rapeseed oil. Arrange the ramps on the plate to the side of the beef and place the roasted garlic chives on top of tartare.

CHIPS

One of the techniques we developed at Tørst and Luksus that I have been most happy with is a process of chipification. The "chip" has taken on many flavors and is widely applicable. The most important thing for me with my tasting menus is to offer a variety of textures and temperatures throughout dinner to engage with our diners in terms of flavor, texture, and overall experience. For me, eating multiple courses with the same flavor, temperature, and texture gets boring and tiring.

When I worked at the Momofuku test kitchen, I was experimenting with ramen broth, to get the proper flavors of the right intensity. We were experimenting with dried ingredients, particularly with mushrooms. One day, what felt like the hundredth failed test, having tasted yet another underflavored broth I stared at the bottom of the chinois containing shiitake mushrooms. "If the broth doesn't have any flavor, then the remainder must," I thought to myself. I puréed it and spread it thinly on a nonstick baking sheet and stuck it in the dehydrator overnight. The next day I returned to find a beautifully wavy and texturally perfect shiitake chip—crispy and wafer-thin, with intense umami.

Having made a great-tasting chip at Momofuku, I set out to make one at Luksus, with an all-new technique. I experimented with tapioca as a thickening agent and expanded the world of flavors to be chipified. We had a lot of country ham scraps left over from the meat plates at Tørst and I wanted to make them into a broth, which I would purée, dehydrate, and then fry. To thicken the liquid, I used cooked tapioca pearls, which have a neutral flavor and are a potent thickener. The experiment proved successful, and the technique was born.

Since those days, we have made many different chips: caramelized onion, roasted chicken, sunchoke, and cabbage, just to name a few. Thickening with tapioca allows us to use any broth or purée to make a chip. Separately, we also make different "dusts" (dehydrated powders) to coat each chip to enhance and add contrast in flavors.

HAM CHIP

MAKES ABOUT 40

20 g olive oil
125 g cremini (chestnut) mush
  rooms, sliced
90 g shallots, sliced
1500 g Ham Broth
  (Pantry page 247)

200 g ham ends, diced
5 g coriander seeds
6 g tsaoko fruit
60 g usukuchi soy sauce
175 g tapioca pearls

In a heavy pot, heat the olive oil over medium-high heat. Add the mushrooms and sauté until browned, about 10 minutes. Add the shallots and continue to sauté until caramelized lightly, about another 10 minutes. Add the ham broth and ends and bring to a boil. Reduce the heat and simmer, skimming any impurities that collect on the surface. Add the coriander and tsaoko fruit. Simmer for 1 hour. Strain the ham broth (discard the solids) and return to a saucepan. Stir in the soy sauce and keep warm over a very low flame.

Meanwhile in a large pot of boiling water, cook the tapioca pearls. Stir frequently with a whisk to prevent clumping. When only a tiny dot of white remains in the center of the pearls, drain (discard the liquid). Measure out 900 g of the ham broth. Cool and freeze the remainder of the broth in a sealed container.

Transfer the tapioca and ham broth to a blender and puree. This may have to be done in several batches; each batch should have the same amount of broth and tapioca, so it comes out evenly. Pass through a chinois into a bowl and cool, stirring frequently to prevent a skin from forming. Measure out 95 g of the mixture and spread into an even layer on a 12 x 12-inch/30 x 30 cm dehydrator mat. Dehydrate for 12 hours at 135°F/57°C. Using an offset spatula, lift up the chips and store in a dry container in a dry space.

NANTUCKET BAY SCALLOP DULSE, UNI, SILVERBERRY

PAIRING:

Seson, Piccolo Birrificio
(www.piccololab.it)

Saisons belong to that idiosyncratic family of beers known as farmhouse ales, traditionally brewed in the French-speaking region of Belgium called Wallonia. As each farm is unique, so too is each saison. Over the years, they've coalesced into a style more or less defined as highly carbonated and very refreshing pale ales. This particular saison beer was produced by Lorenzo Bottoni, who has a small brewery in the tiny Ligurian town of Apricale; the brewery is called, fittingly, Piccolo Birrificio. The beer differs from traditional saisons in that it is brewed with coriander and chinotto, an Italian bitter orange that is often used in amari. That's what makes it pair so well with the natural sweetness of the scallops, the salinity of the dulse and uni, as well as the umami of the mushroom chip.

SERVES 4

Roasted Mushroom Chips:
Olive oil
375 g oyster mushrooms
75 g Vidalia or other sweet onion, sliced
15 g garlic, sliced
10 g fresh ginger, sliced
500 g Roasted Chicken Stock (Pantry page 247)
140 g tapioca pearls

Dulse Purée:
140 g rice vinegar
40 g sherry vinegar
40 g mirin
60 g water
8 g fresh horseradish juice
100 g dried dulse
100 g Vegetable Stock (Pantry page 248)

Maitake Uni Purée:
25 g olive oil
250 g maitake mushrooms, coarsely chopped
115 g cremini (chestnut) mushrooms, sliced
60 g Vidalia onion, sliced
5 g garlic, minced
25 g sherry vinegar
75 g uni
Kosher salt
Fresh lemon juice

Silverberry Vinaigrette:
325 g silverberries
65 g apple cider vinegar
20 g rice vinegar
8 g honey
5 g fresh lemon juice
55 g fresh celery juice
Maldon salt

Scallops and Black Trumpet–Dusted Chips:
15 g tapioca maltodextrine
10 g black trumpet powder
5 g mushroom powder
6 g vinegar powder
7 Nantucket Bay scallops
Peanut (groundnut) oil
4 large pieces Roasted Mushroom Chips (page 155)

Make the roasted mushroom chips:
In a rondeau, heat the olive oil over medium-high heat and pan-roast the oyster mushrooms in batches. Caramelize deeply without burning the bottom of the pot. Drain the mushrooms on a perforated pan.

Use the same pan to sauté the onion until lightly browned, about 5 minutes. Add the garlic and ginger and cook for another 5 minutes. Return the mushrooms to the pot along with the chicken stock. Bring to a boil and simmer for 15 minutes.

Meanwhile, bring a large pot of water to a boil and whisk in the tapioca pearls. Stir often with a whisk to avoid clumping. When the tapioca is cooked so that only a small dot of white remains in the center, drain the tapioca (discard the liquid).

Transfer the mushrooms with poaching liquid and the drained tapioca to a blender. Blend on high speed for 30 seconds. This may need to be done in several batches; aim to keep the amounts of each product even in each batch. Pass through a chinois into a bowl; mix the final batch with the rest thoroughly and cool. Stir frequently as this cools to prevent a skin from forming. Measure out 95 g of the cold mixture and spread evenly on a 12 x 12-inch/30 x 30 cm acetate, silicone, or dehydrator sheet. Dehydrate overnight at 135°F/57°C.

Using an offset spatula, gently lift the mushroom sheets and break into large rectangular "chips" about 6 x 4 inches/15 x 10 cm. Store in a dry airtight container.

Make the dulse purée:
Combine the vinegars, mirin, horseradish juice, and water in a vacuum bag and vacuum-seal with the dried dulse. Marinate in the bag for 3 days in the refrigerator. Drain any excess liquid and transfer the dulse mixture to a blender. Add the vegetable stock and purée until very smooth. Pass through a chinois into a bowl and refrigerate for up to 1 week.

Make the maitake uni purée:
Heat the olive oil in a heavy-bottomed pot over medium-high heat. Pan-roast the mushrooms in batches until nicely golden. Set the mushrooms aside. Add the onion to the same pot over medium-high heat and brown slightly, about 6 minutes. Add the garlic and cook until fragrant, about 3 minutes. Remove from the heat. Deglaze the pan with the sherry vinegar. Transfer the mixture to a blender and purée until smooth. Pass through a chinois. Let cool. Measure out 175 g of the purée and combine with the

uni. Season with salt and lemon juice and pass again through a chinois.

Make the silverberry vinaigrette:
In a blender, combine the silverberries, vinegars, honey, and lemon juice and blend for 10 seconds. Pass through a chinois into a bowl. Stir in the celery juice. Season with salt.

Make the scallops and chips:
Using a spice grinder, pulse the maltodextrine, black trumpet and mushroom powders, and vinegar powders until very finely ground. Set the combined powder aside.

Shuck and clean the scallops. Slice each scallop horizontally into 3 discs and arrange 5 slices each around the bottom of 4 bowls. You may eat the remaining slice.

In a medium pot, heat 2 inches/5 cm of oil to 355°F/180°C. Fry the mushroom chips for a few seconds until they bubble slightly and change color. Remove, let drip, then blot.

Dust each chip liberally with reserved powder.

Assemble the dish:
Surround the scallops with 3 pea-size dollops of dulse purée and 5 dime-size dollops of the maitake uni purée. Top with a dusted mushroom chip. Using a spoon or squeeze bottle, fill the bottom of the bowl with about 15 g of silverberry vinaigrette, so it surrounds the rest of the ingredients.

HAKE,
GREEN ALMONDS, DILL

PAIRING:

Berliner Weisse,
Bayerischer Bahnhof
(www.bayerischer-bahnhof.de)

Berliner Weisse is a classically
crisp and clean style of beer,
thanks to its lactic acid tartness
(see TART, page 98). This comes
from Bayerischer Bahnhof in
Leipzig. Built in 1842, the
building was the oldest railroad
terminal but was largely de-
stroyed during World War II.
Since 2000, it's been renovated
and operates as a brewery and
restaurant. Ninety percent of the
beers there are made for
on-premise consumption, but
some—notably this perfect
Berliner Weisse—makes its way
to the States. Its acidity harmo-
nizes with the acidity of the
pickled hake and dill vinaigrette.

SERVES 4

Hake Poaching Liquid:
1500 g Roasted Chicken Stock (Pantry page 247)
750 g Fish Stock (Pantry page 247)
500 g water
275 g fennel, sliced
175 g shallot, sliced
40 g fresh ginger, sliced
40 g garlic, sliced
10 g fresh red chile, sliced
55 g demerara sugar
3 g dried bird's eye chiles
10 g thyme
10 g fresh bay leaves
8 g cubeb peppercorns
8 g white peppercorns
120 g sweet potato vinegar
75 g rice vinegar
90 g verjus
80 g mirin

Watercress Purée:
100 g romaine lettuce
100 g watercress
50 g parsley
Kosher salt
Lemon juice
5 to 6 g instant food thickener

Food & Beer

Dill Vinaigrette:
40 g dill fronds
25 g parsley
10 g chives
10 g chervil
50 g watercress
10 g honey
55 g apple cider vinegar
70 g rice vinegar
160 g celery juice
20 g fresh lemon juice

Hake:
500 g hake steaks, cut into 3-inch/7.5 cm portions
Hake Poaching Liquid (page 158)
20 g almonds, chopped
15 g olive oil
Fresh lemon juice

To Assemble:
30 g Watercress Purée
20 g Pickled Green Almonds (Pantry page 249), sliced
20 g Dill Vinaigrette
4 pieces Sagamité Cracker (page 47)

Make the hake poaching liquid:
In a saucepan, combine the stocks, water, fennel, shallot, ginger, garlic, and fresh chile and bring to a boil. Reduce to a simmer and add the sugar, dried chiles, thyme, bay leaves, and both peppercorns. Steep for 10 minutes then remove from the heat and add both vinegars, the verjus, and mirin. Let steep for an additional 5 minutes. Pass through a chinois then a soup strainer. Let cool.

Make the watercress purée:
In a large pot of salted boiling water, blanch the romaine for 15 seconds and shock in ice water. Blanch the watercress and parsley together for 30 seconds and shock in ice water. Squeeze the blanched greens of excess water and transfer to a blender. Add about 30g of the water from their ice bath, or as much as needed to allow the mixture to spin freely in the blender. Season with salt and a very light amount of lemon juice. Add the food thickener and blend for 30 seconds. Pass through a chinois and store in a squeeze bottle on ice until needed.

Make the dill vinaigrette:
In a blender, combine all the ingredients and blend on high speed for a maximum of 5 seconds; this will ensure there is no oxidation or discoloring of the vinaigrette from the heat of the blender. Pass the vinaigrette through a chinois, then a fishnet strainer. Store in a glass bottle on ice until needed.

Prepare the hake:
In a medium saucepan, poach the hake in the poaching liquid at 150°F/65°C for 10 minutes or until just warmed through. While still warm, pick the hake into large flakes. Discard the bones and skin. Transfer the fish to a small bowl and toss with the chopped almonds, olive oil, and lemon juice.

Assemble the dish:
Make 3 small piles of hake on each of the 4 plates. Dot with watercress purée and finish with 4 to 5 slices of pickled green almonds. Drizzle with the dill vinaigrette and top with a sagamité cracker.

ROASTED SPRING ONION, CORN, CHANTERELLE

PAIRING:

Taras Boulba,
Brasserie de la Senne
(www.brasseriedelasenne.be)

Belgian beers are traditionally known for showcasing the wondrous possibilities of yeast. But in this beer, Yvan De Baets and Bernard Leboucq, the two brewers at this small Belgian brewery, chose, like their brethren at De Ranke, to let the hops shine through. De Baets is often called a German brewer trapped in a Belgian brewer's body. He prizes efficiency, precision, and, above all, balance. Taras Boulba is a light beer—only 4.5% ABV—with an assertive hoppy bitterness, but one that is perfectly balanced with the yeast profile and light body. Because it's so clean and crisp, Taras Boulba threads the needle between the bite of the pickled spring onion, the woodsiness of the mushrooms, and the sweetess of the creamy corn. Oh, as far as the name goes, it refers to a Nikolai Gogol novella, *Taras Bulba*, about a Russian son who falls for a Polish girl, much to the eventually filicidal anger of his father. In this version, however, it's a Flemish boy and a French-speaking Wallonian, a sign of the troubled history of Belgium and the universality of star-crossed love.

SERVES 4

Corn Bisque:
1250 g Vegetable Stock (Pantry page 248)
500 g water
1075 g corn cobs
75 g shallot, sliced
15 g fresh ginger, sliced
15 g garlic, sliced
5 g jalapeño chile, sliced
5 g Fresno chile, sliced
2 g parsley stems
2 g thyme
2 g bay leaf

Nasturtium Vinaigrette:
225 g whey
175 g apple cider vinegar
125 g watercress
50 g flat-leaf parsley leaves
55 g nasturtium leaves
10 g honey
Kosher salt

Pickled Spring Onions:
4 red spring onions
Pickled Hot Peppers liquid (Pantry page 249)

Corn Purée:
650 g corn kernels
150 g whey
150 g quark
Kosher salt
10 g instant food thickener

Israeli Couscous:
15 g olive oil
25 g shallots, minced
5 g garlic, minced
90 g Israeli couscous
150 g Corn Bisque

150 g water
Corn Purée (page 162)
Kosher salt
Fresh lemon juice

Chanterelles:
5 g olive oil
120g chanterelles, cleaned
15g butter
Fresh lemon juice
Kosher salt
Sagamité Crackers (page 47)

Make the corn bisque:
In a saucepan, combine the vegetable stock, water, corn cobs, shallot, ginger, and garlic. Simmer for 25 minutes over low heat. Add chiles, remove from heat, and let steep 10 minutes. The broth should be slightly spicy. If not, let steep another 10 minutes. Strain the liquid into a bowl, add the parsley, thyme, and bay leaf, and let cool. Strain and discard the herbs. (The remaining bisque should be frozen for another time.)

Make the nasturtium vinaigrette:
Blend all ingredients but salt together for 10 seconds. Pass through a chinois and then a soup strainer to ensure that the vinaigrette has no bits in it whatsoever. Season with salt and store in a glass bottle on ice until needed.

Make the pickled spring onions:
If the onions are larger than 1 inch/2.5 cm at their widest point, cut them in half. Char the onions over very hot charcoal. Cool. Combine the onions with the pickling liquid in a vacuum band vacuum seal. Refrigerate for at least 3 hours. An hour before serving, remove the onions from the bag and let the onions come to room temperature.

Make the corn purée:
In a blender, combine the corn kernels, whey, and quark and blend for 30 seconds. Season lightly with salt. Add the instant food thickener and blend for another 15 seconds. Pass through a chinois into a bowl.

Make the Israeli couscous:
In a medium pot, heat the olive oil over low heat. Add the shallots and sweat for 5 minutes, until slightly softened. Add the garlic and sweat 5 minutes more, until aromatic. Add the couscous and toast for 2 minutes. Pour in the bisque and water and simmer over medium heat until the couscous is just tender, about 10 minutes. Remove from the heat and cool the couscous in its broth.

To finish, drain the couscous. Stir in several spoonfuls of corn purée until the couscous is just loose enough to ooze from itself. Season with salt and lemon juice.

Make the chanterelles:
Set a heavy sauté pan over high heat and add the olive oil. Pan-roast the chanterelles for 3 minutes, or until just cooked, tossing periodically. Add the butter and let bubble and brown, while tossing the mushrooms. When you notice a nice nutty smell, arrest the cooking by adding a squeeze of lemon juice and a heavy pinch of salt. Transfer to a towel-lined plate.

Assemble the dish:
Preheat the oven to 355°F/180°C/Gas Mark 4.

On a small ovenproof platter, warm the pickled spring onions for 1 minute. When they come out of the oven, brush each one with some of their pickling liquid. Divide the Israeli couscous across 4 bowls. Top with 1 or 2 spring onions and a spoonful of the chanterelles. Surround the couscous with a ring of nasturtium vinaigrette. Top with large pieces of sagamité cracker.

SQUID,
PURPLE POTATO, DULSE

PAIRING:

Enkir, Del Borgo
(www.birradelborgo.it)

This is another Italian beer, a
Belgian pale ale style from
another brewery pushing the
Italian craft beer scene forward.
Enkir comes from Birra del
Borgo, founded in 2007 in a
small town halfway between
Rome and Lazio. The founder, a
former biochemist named
Lorenzo di Vincenzo, specializes
in brewing beers with unusual
ingredients that still pair well
with food. Enkir, which in
English means einkorn, is one of
the first domesticated grains.
Here di Vincenzo mixes it with
barley to produce an ale that is
uniquely fruity, a product not
just of the Belgian yeast but
unusually of the grain itself.
With little hop bitterness, and
notes of coriander and oranges,
this well-balanced beer is the
turf to accompany the maritime
surf of Daniel's dulse and squid.

SERVES 4

Roasted Potato Chip:
500 g Yukon gold potatoes, diced
Olive oil
45 g onion, sliced
35 g celery, cut into 1-inch/2.5 cm pieces
25 g fennel, sliced
10 g garlic, sliced
925 g Vegetable Stock (Pantry page 248)
45 g usukuchi soy sauce
5 g honey
2 g coriander seeds
1 g bay leaf
1 g thyme
65 g tapioca pearls

Pickled Kohlrabi:
70 g apple cider vinegar
30 g rice vinegar
55 g water
4 g honey
2 g fennel seeds
1 g dried bird's eye chiles
2 g juniper berries
1 green kohlrabi, brunoised

Purple Potato Purée:
200 g purple potatoes, peeled and diced
25 g butter
2 g bay leaf
40 g uni
Kosher salt
Fresh lemon juice

Potato Chip Dusting:
25 g malt vinegar powder
20 g tapioca maltodextrine
15 g dulse powder
5 g malt powder
5 g shichimi togarashi powder

Squid and Vinaigrette:
500 g Fish Stock (Pantry page 247)
25 g rice vinegar
20 g apple cider vinegar
20 g sweet potato vinegar
120 g squid bodies (tentacles, feather, beak, and skin removed)
20 g parsley oil

Assembly:
2 L peanut (groundnut) oil
15 g Dulse Purée (page 155)
Maldon salt

Make the roasted potato chips:
Preheat the oven to 385°F/195°C/Gas Mark 5.

Toss the potatoes in oil, arrange in a baking pan, and roast for 35 minutes or until tender.

Meanwhile, heat some oil in a large, heavy pot over high heat. Add the onion and sauté until browned. Add the celery, fennel, and garlic and continue cooking until highly aromatic and caramelized.

Add the stock, soy sauce, honey, coriander, bay leaf, thyme, and roasted potatoes to the pot. Simmer for 40 minutes.

Meanwhile, bring a pot of water to a boil. Add the tapioca pearls, stirring occasionally to keep from clumping, and cook until only a dot of opacity remains in the center of each pearl. Drain the tapioca (discard the liquid).

Working in batches, purée the potato mixture and its liquid with the tapioca in a blender. Pass through a chinois into a bowl. Cover and refrigerate until cool; peel off any skin that may have formed on the top.

Measure out 95 g of the potato chip base and use an offset spatula to spread it into a thin layer onto a 12 x 12-inch/30 x 30 cm dehydrator sheet. Dehydrate overnight at 135°F/57°C. The next day, carefully peel the chips off of their sheets and break into 6 x 4-inch/15 x 10 cm rectangular pieces. Store in an airtight container to up to 3 days.

Make the pickled kohlrabi:
In a saucepan, combine the vinegars, water, and honey and bring to a boil. Reduce the heat to a simmer, add the fennel seeds, chiles, and juniper berries, and simmer for 10 minutes. Strain the pickling liquid into a bowl and let cool. Add the brunoised kohlrabi to the pickling liquid and marinate for at least 5 hours. Drain.

Make the purple potato purée:
Arrange the potatoes in a perforated pan and steam until tender, about 15 minutes.

In a small pot, cook the butter with the bay leaf over medium heat, stirring frequently, until browned. Remove and discard the bay leaf. Transfer the potatoes to a blender, add the browned butter, and purée. Pass the mixture through a chinois into a bowl and cool. Purée the potatoes with the uni and pass through the chinois a second time. Season with salt and lemon juice.

Make the potato chip dusting:
Blend all of the ingredients in a clean, dry blender until the texture of dust. Store in a cool dry place with an airtight lid.

Prepare the squid and make the vinaigrette:

In a bowl, whisk together the stock and vinegars. Measure out 100 g for the vinaigrette. Reserve the remainder for poaching the squid.

Split the squid in half. Scrape both the inside and out with a sharp knife to remove any membranes. Flatten onto a silicone baking mat and freeze until solid, about 1½ hours.

In a small saucepan, gently warm the 100 g stock-vinegar mixture. Remove from the heat and whisk in the parsley oil. Keep warm.

Slice the frozen squid into 4-inch/10 cm-long batons as wide as the squid flesh is thick. Let sit on the counter until thawed, about 5 minutes.

Assemble the dish:
Right before serving, in a medium pot, heat the oil over medium heat to 355°F/180°C. Fry 4 large pieces of the potato chips. Blot on paper towels and dust with the potato chip dusting, shaking off any excess.

To poach the squid, in a small saucepan, warm the remaining stock-vinegar mixture to 150°F/65°C in a small saucepan.

Meanwhile squeeze five dots of purple potato purée on one side of each of 4 plates. Intersperse 3 pea-size dollops of the dulse purée between the potato purée dots. On the other side, place a small mound of the pickled kohlrabi. Poach the squid in the poaching liquid for 5 to 7 seconds, or until it just turns white but is not fully cooked through. Strain and divide evenly across the kohlrabi mounds. Dress with a generous spoonful of the vinaigrette directly over the squid and salt lightly. Place a dusted chip on top.

BROTHS

The first thing I ever cooked professionally was soup. Broth is soup in its purest form, stripped completely of solids. It is the sublimation of a solid protein. If the thesis of Snacks (page 134) was flavor, and the thesis of the First Servings (page 146) was ingredient, it's fair to say Broths showcase technique. After all, to be able to extract, and abstract, a clear broth from an ingredient is no small feat.

Philosophically, a broth course also embodies the entire project of the Luksus experience. When we serve the broth, pouring it tableside from a glass teapot into a bowl with but a few garnishes, the guests often look up, befuddled. "Surely, there's something more coming," they seem to be thinking. But after that initial spoonful, so intensely flavored with roasted chicken or smoky pork, the realization dawns that there is a there there. And it's quite a there.

Behind each broth are hours and steeping. We've been making what I call "teas" since the very first day, with wildly different ingredients. With time and patience, the flavors of the main protein seep into the broth. Whether it is the deep fungal heartiness of mushrooms or the saline brininess of mussels, each main ingredient has its own combination of techniques to crack open the flavor. Most of the work is done days ahead. At service, we simply try to provide a supporting cast of flavors and textures to better clarify the base broth. With the roast chicken broth, we pair spicy Korean watercress and garlic scapes; with squash, chestnuts. With cold mussel broth, this counterpoint takes the form of crumble made of dulse (an unheralded seaweed) and smoked bone marrow. Incidentally, the crumble looks exactly like sand—the very thing you don't want in mussels. And that really is the point: to pull the diner out of his comfort zone, to make her even more open and sensitive to new flavors. He becomes aware of new ways of tasting; she notices that there can be great depth in a clear bowl of soup.

CHICKEN, WATERCRESS, CURED YOLK

PAIRING:

Why Can't IBU, Stillwater
Artisanal Ales
(www.stillwater-artisanal.com)

Brian Strumke, the gypsy brewer
behind Stillwater Artisanal Ales,
knows about roaming. For years
he was a globe-circling DJ, on
constant tour. These days he's
mostly based in Baltimore,
Maryland, where he develops
recipes for beers like this hoppy
saison. As with many
Belgian-style beers, this one
showcases the spicy, slightly
floral, faintly fruity properties of
yeast but with a broad basin of
hop bitterness below. Interest-
ingly, the broth and the beer are
similarly colored but, as far as
flavors go, the IBU is a tidy knife
that cuts through the soup's
round, rich flavors.

MAKES 4

Pickled Garlic Scapes:
100 g rice vinegar
40 g apple cider vinegar
35 g water
8 g honey
4 g jalapeño pepper, sliced
3 g coriander seeds
5 g bay leaves
250 g garlic scapes, cleaned
    and trimmed

Fennel Broth:
1500 g water
450 g fennel bulb, sliced
240 g Vidalia or other sweet
    onion, sliced
30 g garlic, sliced
30 g fresh ginger, sliced
10 g fennel seeds
10 g coriander seeds
10 g juniper berries
6 g cubeb peppercorns
6 g bay leaves

Chicken Sausage:
1000 g chicken thighs, minced
130 g shallots, minced
125 g usukuchi soy sauce
60 g Japanese black drinking
    vinegar (Rinkosan Kurosu)

30 g oyster mushroom powder
15 g fresh ginger, minced
8 g fresno chile, minced
6 g cracked black peppercorns

Roasted Chicken Broth:
1250 g Fennel Broth
750 g Chicken Sausage

Onion Purée:
Olive oil
300 g Vidalia onion, julienned
8 g sherry vinegar
Kosher salt
1.5 g xanthan gum

To Assemble:
2 Cured Egg Yolks
    (Pantry page 250)
Kosher salt
Japanese black drinking vinegar
    (Rinkosan Kurosu)
12 Pickled Garlic Scapes, cut
    into 1-inch/2.5 cm pieces
100 g Korean watercress
Olive oil
Fresh lemon juice

Make the pickled garlic scapes:
In a saucepan, bring the vinegars, water, and honey to a boil.
Reduce to a simmer and add the jalapeño, coriander seeds, and bay
leaves. Steep for 10 minutes. Strain and cool completely. Fill a
vacuum bag with the garlic scapes and 100 g of the pickling liquid.
Vacuum-seal. Let sit for at least 1 week in the refrigerator.

Make the fennel broth:
In a pot, combine the water, sliced fennel, onion, garlic, and ginger and heat to 175°F/80°C. Reduce to low heat and add the fennel seeds, coriander seeds, juniper berries, peppercorns, and bay leaves. Simmer for 20 minutes. Strain the liquid, cover, and refrigerate.

Make the chicken sausage:
Preheat the oven to 375°F/190°C/Gas Mark 5.

In a bowl, mix all of the ingredients well. Divide between 2 shallow baking dishes. Bake for 15 minutes. Let rest on the counter for 15 minutes. Strain excess liquid and discard. Cover and refrigerate to cool fully.

Make the roasted chicken broth:
Remove the sausage from the refrigerator and break it up. Divide the meat evenly between 2 vacuum bags. Evenly divide the fennel broth between the bags. Vacuum-seal. Check to make sure the liquid does not leak out of bag. Refrigerate the broth for up to 12 hours.

Set the bags of broth in a water bath set to 131°F/55°C. After 90 minutes, open the bags and strain into a bowl (discard the sausage).

Make the onion purée:
While the broth cooks, heat enough olive oil to coat a heavy-bottom, medium sauté pan set over medium-high heat. Add the onions and cook, stirring every few minutes. After 10 minutes, add another splash of olive oil and continue cooking until well-caramelized and very soft, about 30 minutes. Immediately transfer the onions to a blender and purée with the sherry vinegar. Season with salt. Add the xanthan gum and blend for 15 seconds. Pass through chinois into a bowl, and set aside.

Assemble the dish:
Using a sharp knife, slice each egg yolk into 8 very thin strips. Heat the chicken broth over medium-low heat and season with more salt and drinking vinegar.

Place 4 or 5 dots of onion purée around the base of each of 4 warmed bowls. Arrange 1-inch/3 cm pieces of garlic scapes at the bottom of each bowl.

Pan-roast the watercress in a very hot sauté pan, just barely coated with olive oil, for 15 seconds. Salt lightly, add a splash of lemon juice, and blot on paper towels. Divide evenly across the onion purée and garlic scapes. Tuck 4 strips of yolk into the folds of the watercress in each bowl.

Strain the broth through a fine-mesh sieve and pour into the bowls tableside.

PORK,
CHRYSANTHEMUM, RUTABAGA

PAIRING:

Abraxxxas, Freigeist
(www.braustelle.com)

Pork and smoked beer are a
time-tested tradition in Bamberg, Germany, home of Rauchbiers. For this dish, however, we
selected an Imperial Lichten-
hainer Weisse, a beer that takes
the tart lactic acid bitterness of a
Berliner Weisse and weds it to
the smokiness of a now-rare
Polish-style called a Grätzer.
This particular bottle comes
from Freigeist (free spirit), an
offshoot of a small cutting-edge
Cologne brewery called Braustelle. It's a side project by
Braustelle brewers Peter Esser
and Sebastian Sauer to even
further revolutionize the traditionalist notions of German
brewing than they do at Braustelle. It pairs especially well,
therefore, with this pork broth,
which revolutionizes frequently
traditionalist notions about
broth with the addition of
smoky egg whites and lightly
floral chrysanthemum.

SERVES 4

Chrysanthemum Base:
500 g Roasted Chicken Stock
    (Pantry page 247)
500 g water
210 g fennel, sliced
15 g Chinese cinnamon stick
13 g dried chrysanthemum
    flowers
3 g bay leaf

Pork Broth:
500 g Mangalista pork
    shoulder, minced
500 g chicken thigh, minced
62 g shallots, minced
25 g Japanese black drinking
    vinegar (Rinkosan Kurosu)
12 g jalapeño chile, seeded
    and minced
10 g fresh ginger, minced
6 g garlic, minced
4 g shichimi togarashi
1 g freshly ground black pepper
    Chrysanthemum Base

Rutabaga Purée:
500 g rutabaga, peeled
    and diced
Olive oil
70 g shallots, sliced
5 g garlic, minced
15 g demerara sugar
45 g red wine vinegar,
    plus more as needed
150 g Vegetable Stock
    (Pantry page 248), plus more
    as needed
Kosher salt

Smoked Egg Whites:
Cooking spray
150 g egg whites
Applewood smoking chips

To Assemble:
100 g Smoked Egg Whites
Kosher salt
80 g black radish, brunoised
Japanese black drinking vinegar
    (Rinkosan Kurosu)

Make the chrysanthemum base:
In a pot, bring the chicken stock and water to a boil. Add the
fennel and simmer for 15 minutes. Remove from the heat and add
the cinnamon, chrysanthemum flowers, and bay leaf and let steep
for another 15 minutes. Strain and cool.

Make the pork broth:
Preheat the oven to 410°F/210°C/Gas Mark 6.
   In a bowl, combine the pork, chicken, shallots, drinking vinegar, jalapeño, ginger, garlic, shichimi togarashi, and black pepper
thoroughly. Divide the mixture between 2 shallow roasting pans.
Roast for 35 minutes, stirring occasionally. Remove from the oven,
pouring out any liquid, and let cool. Break up the meat and divide

evenly between 2 vacuum bags. Add the chrysanthemum base equal to the weight of the sausage in each bag and vacuum-seal. Refrigerate and marinate overnight. The next day, cook the bags of sausage and broth in a water bath set to 131°F/55°C for 90 minutes. Strain hot through a china cap, then a chinois (discard the sausage). Cool the broth and set aside.

Make the rutabaga purée:
Preheat the oven to 375°F/190°C/Gas Mark 5.

Toss the rutabaga in olive oil and place on a shallow baking sheet and transfer to the oven. Roast until the rutabaga is nicely browned and fully cooked, 30 to 40 minutes.

In a deep, heavy pot, heat some olive oil over high heat. Add the shallots and cook, stirring occasionally, to caramelize, about 5 minutes. Reduce the heat to medium and add the garlic. After 2 minutes, add the demerara sugar. Cook until lightly caramelized, about 1 minute. Add the vinegar and vegetable stock. Cook at a bare simmer until the sugar has dissolved. Add the cooked rutabaga and bring to a boil. While very hot, purée in a blender, adding more hot vegetable stock if needed so that a silky smooth texture is achieved. Season with more vinegar, and salt.

Make the smoked egg whites:
Coat a small disposable loaf mold with cooking spray and add the egg whites. Steam until set, about 7 minutes. Cool and remove from the mold. Line a hotel pan with a triple layer of foil and add a small mound of applewood chips. Use a small butane torch to start the wood chips smoking, then place a perforated hotel pan on top. Place the egg white brick in the perforated hotel pan. Allow the egg whites to smoke for 2 hours, refilling the wood chips as needed.

Assemble the dish:
Preheat the oven to 355°F/180°C/Gas Mark 4.

Bake the smoked egg white for 2 minutes to warm, then press through the fine holes of a medium-fine strainer.

Meanwhile, in a pot of heavily salted, boiling water, blanch the black radishes for 5 seconds, then shock in an ice bath. Drain thoroughly on paper towels.

Mix the egg whites with the black radish. Season the radish and egg white garnish with salt as needed.

Warm the pork broth over gentle heat then strain through, soup strainer to catch any impurities before serving. Warm 4 bowls in the oven and garnish each with a heavy swoosh of rutabaga purée. Add 1 tablespoon of the radish and egg garnish. Season the broth a final time with salt and drinking vinegar and pour into bowls tableside.

SQUASH, CHESTNUT

PAIRING:

Ryan and the Beaster Bunny,
Evil Twin Brewing
(www.eviltwin.dk)

This is a bière-de-miel (miel is French for honey) that I made for the first time with my friend Ryan Witter-Merithew, at that time Brewmaster of Fanø Bryghus in Denmark; these days the actual brewing is happening at Two Roads in Connecticut. The idea was to make a relatively high ABV (alcohol by volume) saison. We added honey late in the process to give the yeast-produced fruity esters a pleasing dry sweetness. Because the squash broth itself is so well balanced internally—with the chestnut purée adding bass notes to the soprano notes of chile pepper and spicy radish—I wanted a beer that filled in the floral and sweet notes. Luckily, I had made one!

SERVES 4

Squash Broth:
1.5 kg Vegetable Stock (Pantry page 248)
250 g Vidalia or other sweet onion, sliced
165 g celery, cut into 1-inch/2.5 cm pieces
75 g shallots, sliced
35 g fresh ginger, sliced
5 g garlic, sliced
25 g kombu
5 g coriander seeds
2 g fennel seeds
2 g bay leaves
5 g Hon Dashi powder
750 g Blue Hubbard squash, sliced on a mandoline, 2 mm thin
5 g serrano chile, sliced 4 mm thin

Chestnut Purée:
100 g frozen peeled chestnuts
15 g olive oil
50 g onions, sliced
150 g Vegetable Stock (Pantry page 248), plus more as needed
Kosher salt
Fresh lemon juice

Radishes and chestnuts:
1 bunch black radishes
Kosher salt
4 fresh chestnuts

To Assemble:
2 tarragon sprigs
2 fresh bay leaves

Make the squash broth:
In a pot, combine the vegetable stock, onion, celery, shallots, ginger, and garlic and bring up to a bare simmer. Simmer for 35 minutes. Remove from the heat and let cool to 150°F/65°C. Stir in the kombu and steep for 15 minutes. Strain, return to the pot, and bring to a simmer again. Remove from the heat and add the cori-

ander seeds, fennel seeds, bay leaves, and Hon Dashi. Steep for 10 minutes, then strain the base liquid and cool.

Weigh the squash and divide into 2 vacuum bags. Measure out the same weight of base liquid and add to each bag; vacuum seal. Refrigerate the bags overnight.

The next day, cook the bags in a water bath set to 130°F/55°C for 90 minutes, then shock in an ice bath. Strain the stock through a chinois into a saucepan (discard the squash). Warm the stock gently, over very low heat, to around 125°F/50°C, then add the chiles and steep for about 10 minutes or until you taste a pleasant mild heat. Pass through a soup strainer. Cool and reserve.

Make the chestnut purée:
Preheat the oven to 355°F/180°C/Gas Mark 4.

Roast the chestnuts until fragrant and browned, about 20 minutes. Let cool to room temperature.

In a medium pot, heat olive oil over medium-high heat. Add the onions and cook, stirring frequently, until caramelized, about 10 minutes. Add the chestnuts and stock and bring to a boil. Transfer to a blender and purée on the lowest setting until very smooth. Adjust with additional vegetable stock as needed to achieve a smooth medium-thick purée. Season with salt and a drop of lemon juice. Let cool at room temperature.

Prepare the radishes and chestnuts:
Wash the radishes well, but leave on the skin. Slice thinly on a mandoline into discs. In a pot of heavily salted boiling water, blanch the discs for 5 seconds. Shock in an ice bath, drain, and dry.

To peel the chestnuts, use a sharp paring knife to trim away one end and pry off the hard shell. Continue by gently scraping the inner skin away from the nutmeat. Slice the peeled chestnuts on a mandolin to 1 mm thin. Select the most beautiful pieces to soak in ice water for 10 minutes, or until curled. Blot dry.

Salt the sliced radishes liberally and let stand at room temperature for 15 minutes. Rinse and strain of excess liquid.

Assemble the dish:
Place the herbs in a teapot. Warm 4 bowls in a hot oven for 1 minute.

Reheat the broth gently over low heat and salt as needed.

Arrange 5 marble-size dots of chestnut purée along one side of each bowl. Cover with discs of salted radish. Top the radishes with 5 to 7 slices of fresh chestnut.

Strain the warm broth through a soup strainer one final time and into the teapot that holds the herbs. Pour the broth into the bowls tableside.

MUSSELS, SMOKED BONE MARROW

PAIRING:

Tripel, Westmalle Abbey
(www.trappistwestmalle.be)

Malle, the small town where the Trappist monastery Westmalle is located, is landlocked. And I doubt the monks there would ever consider serving their Tripel with something like a cold mussel broth with dulse and bone marrow crumble. A tripel is a high-ABV golden Belgian ale. This one, brewed with the same recipe for the last fifty years, has a fruity aroma—thanks to the yeast—a subtle bitterness, and a diffused malt sweetness. The high ABV and hefty body allow it to keep pace with the broth's intensity.

SERVES 4

Smoked Bone Marrow Crumble:
2500 g marrow bones, cut into 2-in/5 cm pieces
100 g wood chips
20 g butter
8 g demerara sugar
10 g malt powder
10 g olive oil
3 g dulse powder
170 g tipo "00" flour
30 g all-purpose (plain) flour
2 g Maldon sea salt

Mussel Broth:
1000 g mussels, scrubbed and debearded
750 g Dashi (Pantry page 247)
75 g fennel, sliced
5 g juniper berries
5 g fennel seeds
4 g white peppercorns
10 g dried mussels
8 g dried scallops
1 g bay leaf
0.5 g cubeb peppercorns

Mussels:
12 mussels, scrubbed and debearded
20 g onion, sliced
10 g fresh ginger, sliced
5 g garlic, pounded
20 g Dashi (Pantry page 247)

Poaching Liquid:
Olive oil
45 g shallots, sliced
12 g fresh ginger, sliced
5 g garlic, sliced
5 g bird's eye chile, sliced
5 g honey
5 g molasses

210 g Dashi (Pantry page 247)
45 g sweet potato vinegar
45 g apple cider vinegar
20 g rice vinegar
20 g maguro shirodashi shoyu
25 g Chinese cinnamon stick
5 g lemongrass
1 g dried bird's eye chiles

Seasoning Vinegar:
30 g Japanese black drinking vinegar (Rinkosan Kurosu)
20 g sweet potato vinegar
5 g maguro shirodashi shoyu

Cold-Smoked Mussel Broth:
12 mussels, cooked
100 g Poaching Liquid (page 181)
Wood chips, for smoking

To Assemble:
220 g Watercress Purée (page 158)
6 Pickled Red Pearl Onions (Pantry page 247), halved

Make the smoked bone marrow crumble:
Soak the bones in ice water, in the refrigerator, overnight. Remove
the marrow meat from the bones in the morning. Place the bone
marrow in a vacuum bag and vacuum seal. Bring a pot of water to
a bare simmer, add the bag, and cook until rendered, about 3
hours. Strain the fat into a wide, shallow pan that will fit into a
larger hotel pan with room on one end. Place the wood chips in a
small metal container lined with aluminum foil and set next to the
pan of fat in the hotel pan. Light the wood chips on fire to start
smoking. Cover the container tightly with foil. Smoke the marrow
fat, stirring occasionally, for 3 hours. Set aside 90 g for the crumble. (The remainder can be frozen.)
    Preheat the oven to 300°F/150°C/Gas Mark 2.
    Bring the butter and smoked marrow fat to room temperature.
In a stand mixer fitted with the paddle attachment, beat the butter
and marrow fat and sugar for 20 seconds. Add the malt powder,
olive oil, and dulse powder. Beat on low speed for 2 minutes. In a
small bowl, whisk together the flours and salt. Add half the flour
mixture to the mixer bowl and beat for 1 minute. Add the second
half and beat for 1 minute, or until a coarse mealy texture is
achieved.
    Gently transfer the dough to a rimmed baking sheet and spread
into a loose, even layer. Bake until the mixture is dry and no longer
tastes of raw flour, about 15 minutes, stirring after 5 minutes to
break up the uncooked dough. Cool uncovered. Use immediately
or freeze in small containers for up to 2 weeks.

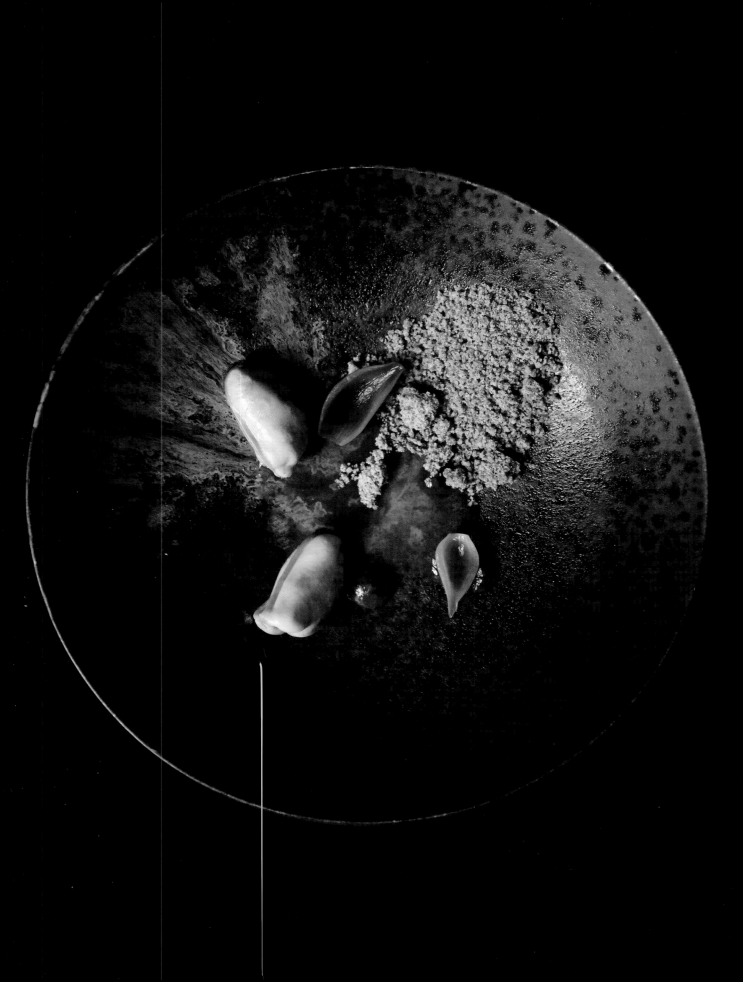

Make the mussel broth:
In a pressure cooker, combine the mussels, dashi, sliced fennel, juniper berries, fennel seeds, and white peppercorns. Close the lid and heat to whistling over medium heat. Reduce the heat to allow a gentle, steady hissing sound. Cook for 10 minutes, then remove from the heat. Let stand, under pressure, for 10 minutes. Then release the steam, strain, and cool in an ice bath.

Measure 800 g of cooled broth and place in a vacuum bag along with the dried mussels, dried scallops, bay leaf, and cubeb peppercorns. Cook in a water bath set to 130°F/55°C for 90 minutes. Strain the broth (discard the solids) and cool.

Cook the mussels:
Heat a large heavy pot so hot, you're sort of scared. Combine the mussels with the onion, ginger, garlic, and dashi and cook until mussels have opened, shaking the pot, about 1 minute. As soon as they do, pour them into a small rimmed baking sheet. Cool, uncovered, in the refrigerator.

Make the poaching liquid:
While the mussels cool, heat some oil in a medium pot over medium-high heat. Add the shallots, ginger, garlic, and chile and sweat until just softened. Add the honey and molasses and cook for another 1 minute, until bubbling. Add the dashi, vinegars, and shirodashi, bring to a boil, then reduce to a simmer. Add the cinnamon stick, lemongrass, and bird's eye chiles and steep for 10 minutes. Strain the poaching liquid (discard the solids) and cool.

Make the seasoning vinegar:
In a small bowl, combine the vinegars and shirodashi.

Make the cold-smoked mussel broth:
Pick the meat from the cooked mussels. (Make sure that the beard is removed!) Place the mussels and 100 g of the poaching liquid in a vacuum bag and vacuum-seal. Cook in a water bath set to 122°F/50°C for 10 minutes, then transfer to an ice bath. Drain the mussels and cold-smoke (See the technique for making smoked egg white on page 175.) This time, set the chips to one side and the mussels on the opposite side. Smoke for between 1 and 2 hours, using a perforated hotel pan until the mussels have a pronounced smoky flavor and have begun to take on a slightly darker hue. Be sure though that the mussels do not cook further.

Assemble the dish:
Season the smoked mussel broth with the seasoning vinegar. Let some smoked bone marrow crumble temper on the counter. Squeeze 4 dime-size dollops of watercress purée into each of 4 bowls. Arrange 2 mussels and 2 pieces of pickled onion around the dollops. Pile a heaping spoon of bone marrow crumble at the top right of each bowl, somewhat flicking it so that it scatters around a bit. Pour the broth tableside using a glass teapot.

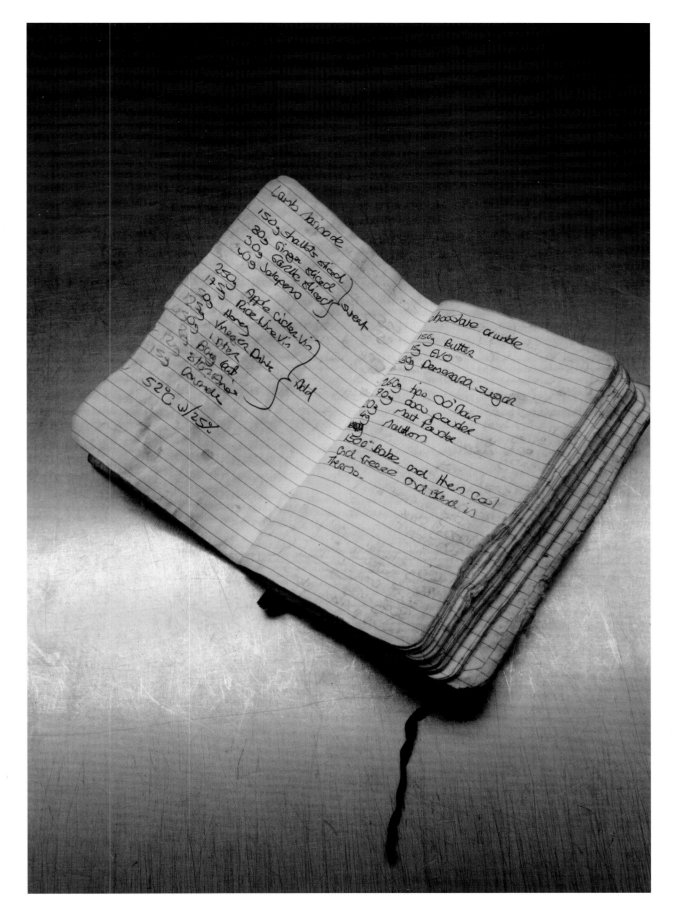

MAIN SERVINGS

Often I find the main serving in a tasting menu to be the least interesting one. A constellation of expectations surrounds it—a holdover, I think, from the 1950s meat-and-potatoes mentality. Main courses tend to lean more conservative than what precedes or follows them. Nonetheless, they still serve a necessary function in the flow of a meal. At Luksus, as we nod to the traditions of a main course, we also try to subvert them.

Let's recap the meal so far. Snacks showcase flavor. First Servings highlight ingredients. Broths emphasize techniques. The Main Course is where everything comes together; it is the synthesis of the preceding arguments. As in many of the offerings at Luksus, what a guest sees on the plate is deceptively simple. The mise en place and preparation, however, are time-consuming and geared toward imbuing the protein with as much flavor as possible. As far as the protein itself—the ingredient that is transformed through technique—the main course is where I really get to play around.

Take, for instance, pork collar. Though it is more common in Denmark where I first came across it, in the United States pork collar is seldom used, since it extends into the more popular Boston butt (shoulder). But the meat, which runs from the neck to the tip of the loin, is densely marbled and immensely flavorful. Because so many guests at Luksus are trying pork collar for the first time, we really want to showcase what makes this cut so special. So instead of just braising the pork, which would still render it delicious, we brine the meat with lots of spices, cook it low and slow, and then roast it to finish. At that point, the question is: What else can we put on the plate to enhance the pork flavor? Scrapple—a loaf made of pork scraps, trimmings, flour, and spices that is little known and even less understood outside the mid-Atlantic states—adds even more heartiness. Millet layers on a rich earthy flavor, while shiso "pesto" and stonecrop contribute bright touches.

In some ways, the main course is the most challenging, because it is so constricted. As the centerpiece of the meal, diners expect a certain format and, I've found, are less tolerant of significant variation. But that's why it's such an enjoyable problem to solve. To present interesting meat in interesting ways makes a chef dig deep into his or her creativity. At Luksus, as with all the courses but especially here, we treat the main course as an opportunity to widen the horizons of the guest. Burned by chewy tacos, he or she might not order beef tongue unprompted or, for that matter, skate, a fish commonly served in brown butter. At Luksus, we do it differently. I like to think we give the skate, or the tongue, or the lamb, the respect and preparation they deserve. This is a function of knowing how to prep the meat, how to cook it, and what other ingredients can make it sing. It's a matter of wise if unexpected combinations, though never sacrificing harmony for novelty. Yes, these cuts might have been considered suboptimal, but I hope after a visit to Luksus, our guests will leave with a newfound respect.

Often we offer a second serving to the main course. Grains or beans served with a different cut of the protein chosen for the main dish. It is a way of exposing the guest to another preparation of the same flavor found in the main course.

PORK NECK, SCRAPPLE, MILLET

PAIRING:

St. Bretta, Crooked Stave
(www.crookedstave.com)

Chad Yakobson, the owner and
brewer of Crooked Stave in
Denver, is a good friend of Evil
Twin. We've collaborated on a
beer together in the past called
Ryan and the Gosling. (Yakobson really looks like Ryan
Gosling!) He also makes beers
worthy of a heartthrob. This one
is a very funky Brett-fermented
witbier (See FUNKY, page 60.)
Yakobson is, in fact, one of the
most esteemed funkmasters,
having written his thesis on
Brettanomyces while at the
International Centre for Brewing
and Distilling at Heriot-Watt
University in Scotland. This beer
is made of a collection of person-
ally cultivated Brett strains and
then aged in oak foeders, which
are larger than the standard
53-gallon barrel. Witbiers,
Flemish for white beers, are an
intriguing style going through a
renaissance in the last decade.
They are made with at least fifty
percent wheat and are often
spiced. At Crooked Stave, Chad
uses seasonal fruit like blood
oranges to add a touch of
fruitiness as well as the nontra-
ditional funky-ass Brett. Daniel's
pork collar is one of the most
complex flavors we have on the
menu. To pair, I chose this
particular beer because it
tastefully cuts the fatty richness
of the collar and the scrapple.
Though aged in barrels, it is still
a clean beer with a relatively dry
finish and a funk that lingers.

SERVES 4

Brined Pork Neck:
2000 g water
90 g coarse salt
75 g demerara sugar
6 g Chinese cinnamon stick
6 g juniper berries
5 g allspice berries
5 g star anise
4 g cubeb peppercorns
3 g bay leaf
3500 g pork neck
125 g butter
3 thyme sprigs

Scrapple:
1 pig head
4 pig trotters
4 yellow onions, quartered
2 garlic heads, crushed
8250 g Roasted Chicken Stock
(Pantry page 247)
Olive oil
80 g shallots, minced
12 g garlic, minced
100 g quinoa
85 g usukuchi soy sauce
40 g apple cider vinegar
Kosher salt

Pickled Salt and
    Pepper Cucumbers:
350 g water
125 g apple cider vinegar
40 g champagne vinegar
85 g granulated sugar
25 g honey
20 g mirin
20 g Fresno chile, sliced
3 g coriander seeds

2 g fennel seeds
500 g salt and pepper
    cucumbers, sliced

Millet:
15g olive oil
50 g shallots, finely diced
15 g garlic, finely minced
Kosher salt
100 g millet
200 g Vegetable Stock
    (Pantry page 248)
6 thyme sprigs
4 pieces fresh bay leaf

Shiso Pesto:
50 g red shiso leaf
50 g olive oil

To Assemble:
75 g Vegetable Stock
    (Pantry page 248)
300 g Millet
Butter
40 g Shiso Pesto
50 g toasted almonds, chopped
Kosher salt
Fresh lemon juice
4 (¼-inch/6 mm-thick) slices
    frozen Scrapple
4 slices Brined Pork Collar
20 g Pickled Salt and Pepper
    Cucumbers
5 g stonecrop

Prepare the pork neck:
In a saucepan, combine the water, salt, and demerara sugar and bring to a boil. Reduce to a simmer, add the cinnamon stick, juniper berries, allspice berries, star anise, cubeb peppercorns, and 1 gram of bay leaf and steep for 15 minutes. Strain (discard the solids) and cool the brine completely.

In a clear plastic container with a lid, fully submerge the pork collar in the brine and refrigerate for 24 hours.

In a sauté pan, brown the butter over medium heat and cool. Remove the pork from the brine. Combine the neck with 50 grams of brown butter and remaining bay leaves in a vacuum bag and vacuum seal. Cook the pork in a water bath set to 125°F/52°C for 12 hours. Let rest for 1 hour on the counter and then move to an ice bath.

When ready to serve, preheat the oven to 355°F/180°C/Gas Mark 4.

In a heavy sauté pan, pan-roast the pork neck on all sides over high heat, about 4 minutes per side. When browned, add the remaining brown butter and the thyme. Baste with the butter as the meat continues to brown. Move the pork to a roasting pan and roast in the oven for 6 minutes. Hold in a warm area to rest (but leave the oven on for reheating the pork before plating).

Make the scrapple:
Arrange the pig head, trotters, onions, and crushed garlic heads in a large pot. Cover with 8000 g chicken stock and an equal amount of water. Bring to a boil, skimming impurities that rise to the surface. Reduce the heat and simmer, skimming frequently, until the meat is very tender, about 4 hours. Replenish the water to keep the meat submerged as needed.

Meanwhile, in a medium saucepan, heat the olive oil over medium-low heat. Add the shallots and minced garlic and sweat until softened, about 10 minutes. Add the quinoa and toast for 1 minute. Add the remaining 250 g chicken stock, bring to a boil, reduce to a simmer, and cover. Cook until all the liquid has been absorbed, about 20 minutes. Spread the quinoa on a rimmed baking sheet to cool.

After 4 hours, remove the pig head to one baking sheet and the trotters to another. Let cool. Strain (discard the solids) and cool, the cooking liquid. Once cool, pick the meat from the head and trotters. Discard the blood pockets in the head, eyes, skin, teeth— all the things you definitely do not want to eat. Mix the cooled, picked meat with 175 g of cooked quinoa, 750 g of the reserved cooking liquid, the soy sauce, and vinegar. Season with salt and mix very well. Line one or two 18 x 13 x 4-inch/46 x 33 x 13 cm rimmed baking sheets with plastic wrap (clingfilm) and pack the mixture tightly on the sheet(s). Cover the top with plastic wrap and weight down with something flat that fits the sheet. Refrigerate overnight. The next morning, cut your scrapple into brick-size blocks. These can be frozen for up to a month.

Make the pickled cucumbers:
In a saucepan, combine the water, vinegars, granulated sugar, honey, and mirin and bring to a boil. Add the chile, coriander seeds, and fennel seeds. Reduce to a simmer and let infuse for 10 minutes. Strain and cool.

In a vacuum bag, combine the sliced cucumbers and cooled liquid and vacuum-seal. Refrigerate and marinate for 12 hours. Open and store the pickles in the liquid.

Make the millet:
In a heavy pot, heat the olive oil over medium heat. Add the shallots and sweat until translucent, about 3 minutes. Add the garlic and a pinch of salt. Sweat for another 2 minutes, or until the garlic is fragrant. Add the millet and cook for 2 minutes. Add the vegetable stock and bring to a boil. Reduce the heat to low, add the thyme and bay leaf, cover, and cook for 15 minutes or until the millet is cooked but toothsome. Transfer the millet to a rimmed sheet pan to cool (discard the thyme and bay leaf).

Make the shiso pesto:
Preheat the oven to 320°F/160°C/Gas Mark 3.

Blend together the shiso leaf and olive oil until fairly smooth, about 2 minutes. Set aside.

Assemble the dish:
In a saucepan, bring the vegetable stock to a boil. Add the millet, return to a boil, and stir frequently until risotto-like in texture; this will take only 30 seconds or so. Remove from the heat, add a strong dollop of butter, and emulsify. Finish by adding the shiso pesto and almonds. Season with salt and lemon juice.

Return the pork to the 355°F/180°C oven for 3 minutes to warm gently through. Place a slice of scrapple on each of 4 oven-proof plates. Place in the oven to warm plate and make the scrapple hot throughout, about 2 minutes.

Spoon the millet mixture on one side of the plate, just overlapping the scrapple. Cut the pork neck into ¾-inch/2 cm-thick slices and place next to the millet. Garnish with the pickled cucumbers and stonecrop.

BEEF TONGUE, ARTICHOKE, FENNEL

PAIRING:

La Roja, Jolly Pumpkin
Artisan Ales
(www.jollypumpkin.com)

Another one of these dishes with a lot going on, the beef tongue has a lot of roasted flavors as well as the earthy intensity of artichokes, garlic, and fennel. It needs a big complex beer to back it up but not one that antagonizes that earthiness. Ron Jeffries, the owner of Michigan's Jolly Pumpkin Artisan Ales, obliges. Jeffries is known for his Brett-forward beers, like this, which have a signature flavor: bready, dry, with a hint of oak and some dark fruit. La Roja is his version of Dark Belgian Ale. With 7.2% ABV, the unfiltered, unpasteurized beer isn't in danger of being overshadowed by the flavors of the dish, but, because it is dry and effervescent, won't compete with them either. La Roja is a blend of newer and older beers. His are aged anywhere from two to ten months. The result is a well-balanced and totally unique brew.

SERVES 4

Beef Tongue:
1000 g water
40 g coarse salt
25 g demerara sugar
3 g black peppercorns
4 g coriander seeds
3 g allspice berries
2 g bay leaves
1 beef tongue

Artichoke Purée:
400 g very young artichokes
15 g olive oil
160 g fennel bulb, sliced thick
85 g Vidalia or other sweet
   onion, sliced thick
10 g garlic, pounded
500 g Vegetable Stock
   (Pantry page 248)
3 g thyme
2 g bay leaf
Juice of ½ lemon,
   plus more as needed
Kosher salt

Roasted Garlic Chip:
30 g garlic, peeled but left
   whole
Olive oil
200 g Roasted Chicken Stock
   (Pantry page 247)
15 g spring garlic
50 g tapioca pearls
60 g Artichoke Purée

Paprika Dusting:
15 g tapioca maltodextrin
5 g shichimi togarashi powder
4 g vinegar powder
2 g cayenne powder
2 g paprika

Fines Herbes Green Sauce:
100 g olive oil
15 g chives, cut into 1-inch/
   2.5 cm pieces
10 g summer savory
8 g tarragon
5 g chervil
10 g capers
15 g garlic, minced

Fennel Salad:
100 g baby fennel
100 g wax beans or young
   green beans
60 g green chickpeas, shelled
Peanut (groundnut) oil
Roasted Garlic Chips
40 g lovage leaves
Kosher salt
40 g Horseradish Vinaigrette
   (page 81)

To Assemble:
Grapeseed oil
3 (½-inch-/1 cm-thick) slices Beef Tongue base
3 (½-inch-/1 cm-thick) slices Beef Tongue tips
35 g butter
160 g Artichoke Purée
Fines Herbes Green Sauce
Paprika Dusting

Cook the beef tongue:
In a pot, combine the water, salt, and demerara sugar and bring
to a boil. Reduce to a simmer, add the peppercorns, coriander
berries, allspice, and bay leaves. Remove from the heat and steep
15 minutes. Cool with the spices in the liquid, then strain (discard
the solids).

In a clear plastic container with a lid, submerge the whole
tongue in the brine. Refrigerated for 24 hours. Drain, place in a
vacuum bag, and vacuum-seal. Cook in a water bath set to
144°F/62°C for 24 hours. Remove the bag and shock in an ice
bath. Remove the tongue from the bag and rinse. Trim the odd
looking parts at the base of the tongue and, using a sharp knife,
remove the outer membrane of the tongue. Halve the tongue
lengthwise. Slice the base of the tongue crosswise into ½-inch/1 cm
slices and the tip into ½-inch/1 cm lengthwise slabs. Set aside.

Make the artichoke purée:
Clean and trim the artichokes, working quickly to avoid oxidation.
In a Dutch oven, heat the olive oil over medium heat. Add the
fennel, onion, and garlic and sweat for 10 minutes. Add the artichokes and sweat for another 10 minutes. Add the stock, thyme,
bay leaf, and lemon juice. Bring to a simmer, cover, and let cook
until the artichokes are tender, about 20 minutes. Remove the
artichokes and set aside. Strain and reserve the cooking liquid
(discard the solids).

Transfer the artichokes to a blender. Add a few spoonfuls of the
cooking liquid and blend to a smooth purée. Season with salt and
lemon juice. Pass through a chinois into a bowl. Reserve in a
squeeze bottle.

Make the roasted garlic chips:
In a medium sauté pan, add enough olive oil to just cover the garlic, and slowly cook over medium-low heat until the garlic is gold-
en. Remove the roasted garlic with a slotted spoon and place on a
tray with paper towels to absorb access oil. Reserve. (We usually
reserve the oil for a staff meal salad dressing.)

In a medium saucepan, bring the chicken stock to a boil, then
reduce to a simmer. Add the spring garlic and cook until tender,
about 10 minutes.

Meanwhile, in a large pot of boiling water, cook the tapioca
pearls, stirring frequently, until there is only a small dot of white
in the center of the pearls. Drain the tapioca (discard the cooking liquid).

In a blender, combine the reserved roasted garlic, the chicken broth (with the spring garlic), and the strained tapioca pearls and blend until very smooth. Pass through a chinois into a metal container and cool in the refrigerator.

Measure out 95 g of the cooled chip base and use a large offset spatula to spread into a 1/16-inch/1.5 mm-thick layer over an acetate or dehydrator sheet. Dehydrate at 135°F/57°C for 12 hours. Use an offset spatula to carefully separate the chip from the sheet. Break into 6 x 4-inch/15 x 10 cm pieces and store in a very dry container in a dry space until needed.

Make the paprika dusting:
Blend all the ingredients together. Transfer to a spice shaker.

Make the fines herbes green sauce:
In a blender, combine 75 g of the olive oil with the chives, savory, tarragon, and chervil until fairly smooth. Add the capers and pulse 5 times to chop roughly. Transfer to a medium bowl.

In a small pot, heat the remaining 25 g olive oil over medium heat. Add the garlic and cook, stirring frequently, until it turns golden brown. Pour the garlic with olive oil into the herb purée. Stir rapidly to incorporate.

Make the salad and fry the chips:
Two hours before dinner, shave the baby fennel on a mandoline into an ice bath. Drain and dry in a salad spinner. Store on paper towels.

In a pot of salted boiling water, blanch first the beans and then the chickpeas for 5 seconds each, then plunge immediately into the ice bath. Drain and dry on paper towels.

In a medium, deep pot, heat 3 inches/7.5 cm of peanut oil to 355°F/180°C. Fry the garlic chips one at a time for only a few seconds. When bubbling at the edges and opaque, remove, let drip a moment, then blot on paper towels.

In a bowl, mix together the baby fennel, beans, chickpeas, and lovage. Season with salt and toss with the horseradish vinaigrette.

Assemble the dish:
When ready to serve, in a heavy pan, heat enough grapeseed oil to coat until almost smoking. Working quickly, fry all the beef tongue slices on each side. Add the butter and pan roast until browned. Remove the tongue.

Warm 4 plates. Line one side of each plate with dots of artichoke purée of varying sizes. Swoosh a hefty dollop of the green sauce across to the center. Next to the sauce, put some salad. Slice the beef tongue into 1-inch/2.5 cm-wide strips and divide across the plates. Dust the chips liberally with the paprika dusting and place a chip atop each salad. Serve warm.

SKATE, STINGING NETTLE, PEPPERMINT

PAIRING:

Oro de Calabaza,
Jolly Pumpkin Artisan Ales
(www.jollypumpkin.com)

This Belgian-style wild ale is the beer that really put Ron Jeffries and Jolly Pumpkin on the map. In 2004 it won gold in the Great American Beer Festival, largely because of its beguiling wild yeast fruitiness augmented by the time it spends in Chardonnay barrels. It's also highly effervescent, which is important in this pairing. Two of the accompaniments to Daniel's skate—itself a very gentle flavor— are stinging nettle and peppermint, both fresh, almost effervescent flavors themselves. A beer like Oro doesn't weigh down the flavors with a crushing body; instead it augment and complements the herbal notes.

SERVES 4

Skate Confit Oil:
1500 g olive oil
85 g scallion, cut into 2-inch/
    5 cm pieces
60 g garlic, sliced
45 g coriander seeds
30 g bay leaves
30 g juniper berries
40 g fresh ginger, sliced
20 g long peppercorns

Spring Garlic Confit Oil:
60 g spring garlic, cut into
    4-in/10 cm pieces
Olive oil

Stinging Nettle Purée:
100 g stinging nettles, cleaned
    and picked (use gloves)
25 g Spring Garlic Confit Oil
12 g flat-leaf parsley
5 g fresh lemon juice
Kosher salt
10 g instant food thickener
0.5 g xanthan gum

Peppermint Vinaigrette:
40 g Fish Stock
    (Pantry page 247)
30 g rice vinegar
12 g flat-leaf parsley

10 g peppermint leaves
5 g tarragon

Poached Watermelon Radish:
200 g watermelon radish
    (about 1 large), thinly sliced
20 g apple cider vinegar
2 g kosher salt

Pickled Spring Onions:
30 g pickling liquid
4 white spring onions, trimmed
    and cut into 4-inch/
    10 cm strips

Poached Skate:
2000 g Skate Confit Oil
4 (100 g) skate wings
Olive oil
Pickled Spring Onions
20 g butter
Fresh lemon juice
Maldon salt
120 g Stinging Nettle Purée
20 discs Poached Watermelon
    Radish
12 oxeye daisies
12 mustard flowers
20 g Peppermint Vinaigrette

Make skate confit oil:
In a heavy pot, combine the confit oil ingredients; steep at 160°F/70°C for 3 hours. Strain, cool, and refrigerate in a nonreactive airtight container for up to 1 week.

Make the spring garlic confit oil:
In a saucepan, submerge the garlic in olive oil and cook over medium-low heat until tender, about 25 minutes. Remove the garlic, cool, and reserve the oil.

Make the stinging nettle purée:
Blanch the nettle leaves for 15 seconds; shock in an ice bath. Squeeze out some water from the nettles; then add back enough ice water to make a combined weight of 325 g. Blend until smooth; pass through a chinois.

Blend the nettle water with the spring garlic confit and its oil, parsley, and lemon juice until smooth. Season with salt. With the blender running at the lowest speed that maintains a vortex, add the food thickener, then the xanthan gum. Blend for 20 seconds. Pass through a chinois; and refrigerate until needed.

Make the peppermint vinaigrette:
Right before serving, blend all the vinaigrette ingredients on high speed for 8 seconds. Pass through a chinois, pressing on solids. Pass again through a soup strainer. Transfer the vinaigrette to a squeeze bottle and keep on ice.

Make the poached watermelon radish:
Cut each radish slice into a disc using a Matfer #30 (1¼-inch/ 30 mm) ring cutter. Bring a pot of water to a simmer. Place all the ingredients in a vacuum bag, vacuum-seal, and cook over medium heat until the radish is tender, about 3 minutes. Shock in an ice bath. Drain and blot the radishes on paper towels. Refrigerate until needed, but keep at room temperature 1 hour before serving.

Make the pickled spring onions:
Combine the spring onions with the compression liquid in a vacuum bag, vacuum-seal, and compress for 3 hours. Remove 1 hour before roasting.

Poach the skate:
In a medium wide pot, heat 2 inches/5 cm of the confit oil over medium-low heat to 185°F/85°C ; maintain a constant temperature. Fold each skate wing in half and lower into the oil. Set a timer for 5 minutes. Meanwhile, warm 4 plates in the oven while heating a sauté pan over high heat.

Coat the bottom of the pan with olive oil and add the spring onions, heavily charring on one side. Add 15 g of the butter, let foam, cook until browned. Remove from the heat and add a splash of lemon juice. Season with salt. Drain on paper towels.

Check the skate with thin metal cake tester; it should slide easily in and out. Remove the fish from the oil and blot on paper towels. Season with salt and place off the center of each plate. Dot the plates with nettle purée on one side. Intersperse 4 radish discs and add 1 spring onion on each plate. Arrange the flowers around the purée and radishes. Garnish with 5 g of peppermint vinaigrette, followed by more olive oil.

RICE BEAN SALAD, SKATE CHEEK

SECOND SERVING

SERVES 4

Rice Beans:
130 g dried rice beans
Olive oil
50 g yellow onion,
    diced very small
15 g garlic, minced
350 g Vegetable Stock
    (Pantry page 248)
2 g thyme sprigs
1 g bay leaf
Kosher salt

Pickled Kohlrabi:
70 g apple cider vinegar
30 g rice vinegar
55 g water
5 g honey
3 g fennel seeds
2 g juniper berries
1 g dried bird's eye chile
80 g kohlrabi, peeled

Parsley & Celery Water:
50 g fresh celery juice
25 g flat-leaf parsley leaves

Rice Bean Salad:
80 g shelled green chickpeas
320 g Rice Beans (recipe above)
80 g Pickled Kohlrabi
50 g Parsley and Celery Water
20 g Castelvetrano olives,
    diced small
Kosher salt
Fresh lemon juice

Pan-Fried Skate Cheek:
90 g quick mixing flour
30 g Crisp Film
4 large skate cheeks, cleaned
    of skin and large bits
    of membrane
Grapeseed oil
100 g butter
Fresh lmon juice
Maldon salt

Make the rice beans:
Soak the beans in cold water to cover overnight.

In a heavy-bottom pot, heat a splash of olive oil over medium-low heat. Add the onion and sweat, about 5 minutes, until translucent. Add the garlic and cook for another 5 minutes.

Drain and add the beans to the pot with onion followed by the vegetable stock. Bring to a boil, skimming surface impurities. Add the thyme and bay leaf, season with salt, cover, and reduce to a simmer. Cook until tender, about 1 hour 30 minutes. Let stand for 5 minutes. Transfer to a wide dish to cool.

Make the pickled kohlrabi:
In a saucepan, combine the vinegars, water, and honey and bring to a boil. Reduce to a simmer, add the fennel seeds, juniper berries, and chiles, and let steep for 10 minutes over low heat. Strain and cool.

Scoop the kohlrabi with a #12 Parisian scoop. Vacuum-seal the kohlrabi with the pickling liquid in a vacuum bag and marinate, refrigerated, for 3 hours. Drain and store, refrigerated, in an airtight container.

Make the parsley & celery water:
In a blender, blend the celery juice and parsley for 20 seconds. Pass through a chinois, then a soup strainer. Refrigerate for up to 24 hours.

Make the salad:
In a pot of salted boiling water, blanch the chickpeas for 5 seconds, then shock in an ice bath. Drain and blot on paper towels.

With a slotted spoon, transfer the beans from their cooking liquid to a medium bowl. Mix in the chickpeas, pickled kohlrabi, parsley and celery water, and the olives. Season with salt and lemon juice. Let stand on the counter.

Cook the skate:
Thoroughly whisk together the flour and Crisp Film. Heat a heavy medium sauté pan over high heat. Roll the skate cheeks in the fry mix until well coated, shaking off the excess. Cover the pan with a thin layer of grapeseed oil and fry the skate on one side until crusty, about 4 minutes. Once the crust has formed, reduce the heat to medium and flip the skate cheeks. Add the butter to the pan. As the butter browns, baste the skate.

Test the doneness of the skate cheeks with a metal cake tester— it should be just warm to the touch. If they are cooked, add a squirt of lemon juice to the pan to arrest browning and remove the cheeks from the pan. If the cheeks are not yet done, keep cooking for a few seconds. Remove the cheeks and blot on paper towels. Season with salt.

To serve, divide the bean salad evenly across 4 bowls and add a skate cheek on the side.

SQUAB, SALTED PLUM

PAIRING:

BeerBrugna, LoverBeer
(www.loverbeer.com)

Just as Daniel built this dish around the salted plum, this beer, from a small brewery outside Turin, Italy, showcases the plum. In this case, Valter Loverier, a homebrewer turned professional, takes inspiration from the wine-rich region, macerating Ramassin plums from Piedmont and adding them to a sour ale, fermented with wild yeasts and bacteria. The result is almost like a kriek, in its mix of sweet and sour. Unlike a kriek however, BeerBrugna—frequently voted one of Italy's best beers—isn't blended. It is allowed to age eight months and the result has a magical balance of sour and fruitiness that complements the sweet earthiness of the plums and beets while adding some tart backbone to the roasted squab.

SERVES 4

Salted Plums:
500 g pitted Italian prune
  plums
40 g coarse salt

Salted Plum Purée:
375 g Salted Plums
5 g red shiso leaves

Beet and Plum Purée:
350 g fresh beet (beetroot) juice
250 g Salted Plum Purée
Instant food thickener
Pinch of xanthan gum

Dried Squab Breast:
2 Pennsylvania Dutch squab

Beet and Carrot Glaze:
1000 g fresh carrot juice
500 g fresh beet (beetroot) juice
10 g English licorice
7 g Chinese cinnamon stick
5 g star anise
1 g xanthan gum

Beet Crudité:
a selection of beets, trimmed

Brown Butter-Poached Carrots:
4 young orange carrots,
  scrubbed and left whole
4 young purple beta carrots,
  scrubbed and left whole
50 g brown butter
2 g bay leaves

Roasted Breast of Squab:
Olive oil
2 dried squab breasts

To Assemble:
Brown Butter Poached Carrots
100 g Beet and Carrot Glaze
15 g butter
160 g Beet and Plum Purée
28 discs Beet Crudité

Make the salted plums:
In a sanitized container with a tight-fitting lid, combine the plums and salt and refrigerate for 2 weeks.

Make the salted plum purée:
Drain the salted plums in a colander for 5 minutes, but do not rinse. Transfer to a blender, add the red shiso, and purée. Pass through a chinois, transfer to a squeeze bottle, and refrigerate.

Make the beet and plum purée:
In a medium pot, cook the beet juice over medium heat, skimming any impurities that rise to the top, until it's reduced to 90 g, about 45 minutes. Pass through a very fine chinois into a bowl and cool.

In a blender, combine the salted plum purée with reduced beet juice and purée. Pass through a chinois and weigh. Add 2% of the passed purée weight in instant food thickener—about 6 grams—and a small pinch of xanthan gum and purée for 25 seconds.

Prepare the squab breast:
Remove the wings and legs from the squabs (reserve to make the Puy Lentils and Braised Squab Legs, page 205). Refrigerate the crowns of squab, uncovered, for 2 days to dry out the skin.

Make the beet and carrot glaze:
In a heavy pot, cook the carrot juice over medium heat, about 30 minutes to reduce by half. Add the beet juice, licorice, cinnamon, and star anise. Continue to reduce until the glaze is a syrupy consistency, about 1 hour. Discard the spices (do not use a strainer or you will lose flavorful bits of carrot). Transfer the glaze to a blender and purée with the xanthan gum until smooth and shiny, about 20 seconds. Cool and reserve.

Make the beet crudité:
Slice the beets paper-thin on a mandoline; store in an ice bath until ready to plate.

Make the brown butter-poached carrots:
Place the orange carrots in one vacuum bag and the whole purple beta carrots in another. Divide the brown butter and bay leaves evenly between them. Vacuum seal and cook in barely simmering water for about 15 minutes. Shock in an ice bath. Drain and blot dry on paper towels.

Make the roasted breast of squab:
Set the squabs out to come to room temperature 1 hour before serving. Preheat the oven to 355°F/180°C/Gas Mark 4.

Heat a heavy pan over high heat and coat the bottom of pan with olive oil. Add the squab crowns, skin-side down. (The goal is to render the skin.) Move the squab, skin-side up, to a baking sheet and finish in the oven for 4 minutes. Remove and keep warm. (Leave on the oven.)

Assemble the dish:
Set 4 plates in the oven. In a sauté pan, heat up the butter-poached carrots in the beet and carrot glaze over high heat, moving the pan constantly. After about 2 minutes, before the pan is dry and the glaze is too sticky, remove from the heat and add the butter. Swirl vigorously to emulsify. Transfer vegetables and glaze to a small tray.

Using a squeeze bottle, make 5 irregular dots of the plum purée over each of the plates and add 1 of each color carrot. Using a small sharp knife, cut each squab breast in half on the bias. Tuck the halves around the carrots. Garnish with the pickled carrots and beet crudité.

BRAISED SQUAB LEG, PUY LENTILS

SECOND SERVING

SERVES 8

Squab Stock:
40 g squab wings and necks
500 g Roasted Chicken Stock
    (Pantry page 247)

Braised Squab Legs:
Olive oil
4 squab legs (thigh and
    drumstick)
100 g yellow onion, sliced thick
50 g fennel, sliced thick
50 g carrot, sliced thick
15 g garlic cloves,
    pounded
Squab Stock
2 g thyme sprigs
2 g bay leaves
1 g black peppercorns

Squab Liver Purée:
200 g squab livers (supplement
    with chicken livers if needed)
Kosher salt
Olive oil
30 g shallots, minced
20 g sherry vinegar,
    plus more as needed
40 g heavy (double) cream
2 g cracked black pepper

Puy Lentils:
Olive oil
50 g yellow onion, diced finely
10 g minced garlic
125 g Puy lentils
500 g squab braising liquid
    from Braised Squab Legs
Kosher salt
1 g thyme sprigs
5 pieces bay leaves
4 pieces lemon zest strips

To Assemble:
Puy Lentils
Reserved squab braising liquid
Braised Squab Legs
50 g Squab Liver Purée
30 g Fines Herbes Green Sauce
    (page 192)
30 g Pickled Carrots (Pantry
    page 248), diced very finely
Fresh lemon juice
Kosher salt

Make the squab stock:
In a small pot, combine the squab wing, necks, and chicken stock and poach over medium heat for 45 minutes. Strain and cool (discard the solids).

Make the braised squab legs:
Coat the bottom of a heavy pot with olive oil. Over high heat, pan-roast both sides of the squab legs until golden. Set aside.

Drain away any excess fat from the pan and add the onion, fennel, carrot, and garlic and pan-roast until slightly colored, about 5 minutes. Return the legs to the pan, cover with squab stock and bring to a boil, skimming the impurities the surface. Add the thyme, bay leaves, and peppercorns. Cover with a tight-fitting lid and simmer until the legs are tender, about 40 minutes. Remove the legs from the liquid and transfer to a baking sheet. Cool to room temperature. When cool enough to handle, pick the meat from the bones. Strain the braising liquid (discard the solids) and save for cooking the lentils.

Make the squab liver purée:
Pat dry the livers with paper towels. Season lightly with salt. In a very hot pan, with a bit of oil, pan-roast the livers on both sides to color and leave medium-rare. Reduce the heat to medium, add the shallots, and caramelize. When the shallots have developed a deep flavor, remove from the heat and deglaze the pan with the sherry vinegar. Add the cream to the pan for 10 seconds, just to warm slightly. While everything is hot, add the black pepper, transfer to a blender, and purée. Taste and adjust the seasoning with salt and more sherry vinegar. Pass through a chinois into a bowl and cool.

Make the Puy lentils:
In a small pot with a tight-fitting lid, heat a bit of oil over medium heat. Add the onion and sweat until translucent, about 8 minutes. Add the garlic and continue sweating for another 5 minutes. Add the lentils and squab braising liquid and bring to a boil. Reduce to a simmer, season with salt, and add the thyme and bay leaves. Cover and cook over medium-low heat until the lentils are just barely tender, about 25 minutes. Pour into a wide container and add in the lemon zest. Let cool in the refrigerator.

Assemble the dish:
In a small pot, warm the lentils over medium heat, moistening with squab braising liquid as needed. When the lentils are hot, remove from the heat and stir in the squab leg meat. Move the lentils to a small bowl and whisk in the liver purée and green sauce. Stir in the pickled carrots and season with lemon juice and salt. Place 2 large spoonfuls in a bowl to serve.

LAMB, PURPLE TOP TURNIPS, SOUBISE

PAIRING

Goudenband, Liefmans
(www.liefmans.be)

The Belgian brewery Liefmans is famous for its fruit beers. In the early twentieth century, the brewery's founder, Jacobus Liefmans, would swap beer with local farmers for their excess cherry crop. Eventually the trade became symbiotic with the result of a delightfully tart kriek beer. Now Liefmans is run by a wonderful woman named Rosa Merckx, a former ballerina turned Belgium's first female brewmaster. One of her favorite—and certainly one of my favorite—beers is the Goudenband, a Belgian red ale. Originally, Goudenband was meant to be kept as provisions and therefore was made especially strong. Today, each bottle, which is carefully wrapped in tissue paper, is still cherished by many. Fermented in open containers—to allow the microflora of the Schelde River to enter—and aged in barrels for between four and twelve months, it is then mixed again with younger fermentation and left to age in the bottle. The notes of apple, cherry, and wood, followed by hints of nuts and raisins, provide the perfect natural habitat for the lamb.

SERVES 4

Marinated Lamb:
2500 g water
95 g coarse salt
87 g muscovado sugar
5 g star anise
5 g juniper berries
5 g Chinese cinnamon stick
5 g coriander seeds
2 g bay leaf
140 g usukuchi soy sauce
70 g mirin
60 g sweet potato vinegar
1 leg of lamb, boned, broken into 3 main muscle sections

Sauce Soubise:
50 g olive oil
400 g yellow onion, thinly sliced
2 g kosher salt, plus more as needed
Pinch of xanthan gum

Turnip Top Purée:
Kosher salt
125 g turnip tops
80 g arugula (rocket)
50 g sorrel leaves
50 g cold water
8 g instant food thickener
Pinch of xanthan gum

Turnips:
Kosher salt
8 Tokyo turnips, small or halved if medium

Lamb:
Olive oil
1 section lamb leg meat

To Assemble:
Olive oil
4 pieces Pickled Spring Onion (page 197)
15 g butter
Kosher salt
140 g Turnip-Top Purée
200 g Sauce Soubise
Maldon salt

Prepare the lamb:
In a saucepan, combine the water, salt, and muscovado sugar and bring to a boil. Add the star anise, juniper berries, cinnamon stick, coriander seeds, and bay leaf and simmer for 10 minutes. Add the soy sauce, mirin, and vinegar and simmer for 1 minute. Strain and cool (discard the solids).

Place the lamb in a clear plastic container with a lid. Add the cooled marinade, cover, and refrigerate the lamb for 24 hours.

Drain and divide the lamb among 3 vacuum bags and vacuum-seal. Cook in a water bath set to 126°F/52°C for 12 hours. Let rest for 1 hour, then cool completely in an ice bath.

Make the sauce soubise:
In a wide heavy pot, heat 25 g of the oil over medium-low heat. Add the onion, stirring frequently. After 15 minutes, add the remaining 25 g olive oil and 2 g of salt. Continue cooking, stirring frequently, until very soft but uncolored, about 50 minutes.

Transfer the hot onions to a blender and purée with the xanthan gum. Season with more salt if needed. Press plastic wrap (clingfilm) directly onto the purée to prevent a skin from forming and let cool.

Make the turniptop purée:
Shortly before serving, in a pot of boiling, lightly salted water, blanch the turnip tops for 10 seconds. Shock in an ice bath. Squeeze excess water from the turnip tops and transfer to a blender.

Add the arugula, sorrel, and water and purée for about 25 seconds. Season with salt. Add the food thickener and xanthan gum and purée into the mix for 15 seconds.

Make the turnips:
In a pot of lightly salted boiling water, blanch the turnips for 1 minute. Shock in an ice bath. Drain and blot dry on paper towels.

Make the lamb:
Preheat the oven to 355°F/180°C/Gas Mark 4.

In a heavy sauté pan coated with oil, pan-roast the lamb, fat-side down, until deep brown. Continue to brown all sides, about 3 minutes per side. Transfer to a baking sheet and cook until the meat is just warmed through, about 6 minutes. Remove and let the lamb rest.

Assemble the dish:
Warm 4 large plates in the oven. In a medium pan, heat a little oil over high heat. Add the pickled spring onions and the turnips and pan-roast, about 3 minutes. Finish with the butter, allowing it to brown, about 1 minute. Season with salt and drain on a baking sheet lined with paper towels.

On one side of each plate, make dots with the turnip-top purée, then intersperse with dots of the sauce soubise. Over the purées, place the onions and turnips, evenly distributing across the plates. Cut 4 slices of lamb, about ½ inch/1 cm thick. Place opposite to the turnip and spring onion garnish. Season with salt. Serve warm.

DESSERTS

One of the most valuable lessons I learned at Noma is that desserts are a continuum of the menu, not a haywire detour into sweetness. It doesn't make sense to spend an entire menu extolling the virtues of balance only to abandon them at the end of dinner. As I discussed in SWEET (page 58), many of my desserts are therefore undersweetened, and purposefully so. They also highlight seasonality far beyond simply using strawberries in the summer. Teasing out the sweetness of root vegetables, like parsnip or sunchoke, means that in winter months, you can still make a seasonal dessert.

The goal of the desserts at Luksus is to present a gradual slide toward sweetness. As a transition, we serve a palate-cleansing course (without a beer pairing) a sorbet, often made with ginger, and a flavored cordial to bridge the gap between the main course and the dessert. Desserts featuring blueberry and corn, or carrot and yogurt, are just on the other side of savory. This idea is the result of how our kitchen is organized. Most fine dining setups, and most professional kitchens, are run in the Escoffier's brigade de cuisine system: Each chef has his own station, whether it's garde manger (cold prep), hot appetizers, meat, or fish. The pastry station is often run as a separate parallel universe. But at Luksus, all chefs do all things, not only out of necessity but out of philosophy, too. This means that one moment David Pegoli, one of our longest-serving chefs, will be breaking down pork collar, and the next, he'll be baking cumin snap cookies for the carrot dessert. When the roles are this fluid, it is only natural that there's a certain osmotic exchange between courses. And while I'm not going to feature mackerel on the dessert menu, we constantly lean ever closer to savory.

If desserts represent the closing statements of dinner, petits fours are its rolling credits. Each night we offer two seatings: For the first seating at 6:30 p.m., as much as we'd like to, we can't let guests linger; it's a tight turnaround. But at 9 p.m., I love when guests relax over coffee at the end of the meal. Our petits fours, meant to be eaten with hands just like the snacks, close the loop and are meant to be playful. Hopefully, by the time the dinner is over, the diner has gone on a journey. At the very least, she's tasted surprising flavors that exceeded her expectations. That experience of a paradigm shift brings one back to childhood, when everything is so new that every experience was a paradigm shift.

The Crunchie Bar is our riff on a frozen Twix, though with a sprinkle of salt to rein in that crush of candy. The Beet Flødeboller (page 240) are a traditional Danish treat that every Nordic child knows, but that Americans can relate to as a refined Mallomar, or what someone in the United Kingdom might know as Tunnock's Teacakes. I have yet to see a guest bite into what looks like a dark chocolate stupa, revealing the bright red meringue filling, and not break into a grin. Seeing that smile is how I know what we've done at Luksus has been a success.

ICES

Ever since my days at The Fat Duck in Bray, England, I have been obsessed with ice cream. Heston opened my eyes to what was possible in terms of making a flavorful frozen dessert with very little fat; I started to refer to them as ices, to differentiate them from traditional ice cream made with egg yolks. Back in the old days, there was a pastry station at the restaurant that was responsible for spinning fourteen kinds of ices for lunch and ten for dinner. I became enthralled with the process of ice production and wanted to learn all that I could. When I went to Noma, I was exposed to a lot of challenging dishes in the form of ice creams and sorbets. There was a walnut dessert in which we served a type of soft-serve ice cream. We also made a carrot sorbet coated in a yogurt gel and a fatty caramel ice cream that needed to be piped onto the plate. Gelato-style ice creams contain less fat than anglaise-style ice cream and are set with a stabilizer (often made from different seaweed) that gets blended into the base. With this method, you don't need to warm up all the milk as you would with the French custard-style ice cream (one that contains egg yolks); thus the end product can be fresher tasting and cleaner than its yolk-based cousin. Most important is that as the lower-fat ice melts in your mouth, and the flavors—without fat globules in the way—are more intense and taste, leaving your palate alert and ready for the next elements of the dish.

Swirling two different ices together is something that harkens to my childhood chocolate-vanilla soft serve. It is also interesting for the guests to observe this manual process in our open kitchen. But the most important thing is to find two ices that will act as complements to one another. The use of a frozen component (sorbet, ice, granite, parfait) in a dessert is something that I've always welcomed and on which I've focused. There is still so much to the science of ice cream making that I want to continue to learn, and perhaps the best way to do so is to make each base its own unique recipe. This way, every ice on the menu can have a slightly different mouthfeel from the others. Each recipe is a new challenge that deserves its own approach and spotlight.

A chef friend, Agata Felluga, introduced me to her friend, the artist Davide Balula. Davide was looking for someone to collaborate with for an art installation where ice cream flavors mimicked his paintings. We made four flavors: River, Dirt, Smoke, and Burnt Wood. For me, it was fascinating to collaborate on a food-based project with someone other than a chef. He brought a completely new perspective to the discussion of the flavor profiles for the four ice creams. I mean, who but an artist would make a dirt-flavored ice? When Davide got invited to Art Basel in Switzerland in 2015, our pop-up gelato shop, featuring our ice flavors, was realized.

Food & Beer

CARA CARA ORANGE, GINGER

SERVES 4

Syrup:
340 g water
145 g sugar
80 g glucose

10 g fresh lemon juice
2½ bronze-strength
    gelatin sheets
2.5 g sorbet stabilizer

Cara Cara Orange Sorbet:
300 g fresh Cara Cara juice
    (about 8 Cara Cara oranges)
155 g Syrup
25 g corn maltodextrin

Ginger Cordial:
10 g honey
25 g fresh ginger, chopped
75 g water
10 g fresh lime juice

Make the syrup:
In a saucepan, combine the water, sugar, and glucose and bring to
a boil. Cook until the sugar is dissolved. Let cool.

Make the sorbet:
Pass the orange juice through a chinois. Transfer the orange juice
to a blender, add two-thirds of the syrup, the maltodextrine, and
lemon juice.

Bloom the gelatin in cold water, drain well, and blot on paper
towels. Whisk the sorbet stabilizer into the syrup remaining in the
saucepan. Bring to a boil, whisking constantly. Remove from the
heat and stir in the gelatin until melted.

Whisk a small amount of the sorbet base back into the stabilized syrup, then whisk the stabilized sorbet back into the base and
combine thoroughly. Transfer to a Pacojet beaker and freeze. Store
in a freezer that holds between -22 to -40°F /-30 to -40°C. Spin the
sorbet for service.

Make the ginger cordial:
In a heavy medium pot, caramelize the honey over medium heat,
about 30 seconds. Add the ginger and cook for 30 seconds, or until
aromatic. Add the water and lime juice. Cook over low heat for 15
minutes. Strain and chill thoroughly.

Assemble the dessert:
Quenelle a small amount of orange sorbet into 4 chilled ice cream
bowls. Pour into each bowl 5 g of well-chilled ginger cordial. Serve
immediately.

BLUEBERRY, CORN

PAIRING

Justin Blåbær,
Evil Twin Brewing
(www.eviltwin.dk) and
Westbrook Brewing Company
(www.westbrookbrewing.com)

I would have to be an idiot to
pair a dessert as wonderfully
blueberrian as this one with
anything but the Justin Blåbær
(see FRUITY, page 116). In
general, these dessert pairings
are more complementary than
contrasting. Where there is fruit,
I'll try to echo that fruit in the
pairing; where there is a tartness, I'll try to echo that tartness. This isn't just because the
pairings work well in each
individual instance, but also
because philosophically, dessert
marks the more comforting stage
of the meal. These are gentle
pairings—not alwaus challenging, but enormously pleasing.

SERVES 4

Blueberry Cookie Dough:
180 g butter
110 g sugar
12 g blueberry powder
270 g all-purpose (plain) flour
1 g Maldon salt
40 g fresh blueberry juice
20 g egg yolks

Corn Cream and Corn Tuile:
150 g corn kernels
400 g heavy (double) cream
Maldon sea salt

Blueberry Ice:
365 g blueberries
125 g blueberry purée (such as Les Vergers Boiron)
475 g milk
80 g trimoline
70 g heavy (double) cream
45 g sugar
38 g corn maltodextrin
10 g fresh lemon juice
2 bronze-strength gelatin sheets
1.5 g sorbet stabilizer

Corn Ice:
310 g fresh corn kernels
485 g milk
80 g heavy (double) cream
70 g trimoline
60 g sugar
55 g yogurt
25 g corn maltodextrin
10 g fresh lemon juice
1 bronze-strength gelatin sheet
3 g sorbet stabilizer

Assembly:
40 g Blueberry Cookie Dough
Blueberry Ice
Corn Ice
120 g fresh blueberries
80 g Corn Cream
Cold-pressed rapeseed oil
4 (4 x 5-inch/10 x 13 cm) pieces Corn Tuile

Make the blueberry cookie dough:
Temper the butter for 20 minutes. In a stand mixer fitted with the paddle attachment, beat the butter, sugar, and blueberry powder together. In a bowl, whisk together the flour and salt. Add the flour mixture to the butter mixture and beat until the mixture has a coarse, mealy texture. In a small bowl, whisk together the blueberry juice and egg yolks until very smooth. With the mixer running, pour the yolk-juice mixture into the dough and beat until just incorporated. Shape into a ¾-inch/2 cm thick block, wrap well in parchment, and freeze for about 4 hours.

Make the corn cream and corn tuile:
Preheat the oven to 320°F/160°C/Gas Mark 3.

In a blender, blend together the corn and cream for 10 seconds, to create a thick paste. Press through a chinois into a bowl, pressing on solids with a ladle to extract as much liquid as possible. Reserving the solids, set the corn cream (the strained liquid) aside and refrigerate.

Roll out the corn solids as thinly as possible between 2 silicone baking mats. Lightly salt. Remove the top sheet and bake the corn until light golden, about 12 minutes. Use a small offset spatula to lift the corn tuile off the sheet into large flakes, at least 4 x 5 inches/10 x 13 cm.

Make the blueberry ice:
In a blender, purée together the blueberries, blueberry purée, half the milk, the trimoline, cream, sugar, maltodextrin, and lemon juice. You may need to do this in 2 batches. Pass the blueberry base through a chinois into a bowl.

Bloom the gelatin in cold water, then drain and blot on paper towels. In a medium saucepan, whisk together the remaining milk with the sorbet stabilizer. Scald the mixture over medium heat, whisking constantly. When the bubbles break the surface, remove from the heat and whisk in the gelatin to dissolve.

Stir about a third of the blueberry ice base into the stabilized milk to temper. Then whisk the milk mixture back into the remaining blueberry ice base. Transfer to 2 Pacojet beakers and freeze. Store in a freezer that holds between 22 to 40°F/-30 to -40°C. Spin the ice for service.

Make the corn ice:
In a blender, purée together the corn, half the milk, the cream, trimoline, sugar, yogurt, maltodextrin, and lemon juice for 25 seconds. Pass the corn base through a chinois into a bowl.

Bloom the gelatin in cold water, then drain and blot dry on paper towels. In a small curved-wall pan, whisk together the remaining milk with the sorbet stabilizer. Scald the mixture over medium heat, whisking constantly. When the bubbles break the surface, remove from the heat and whisk in the gelatin to dissolve.

Stir about a third of the corn ice base into the stabilized milk to temper. Then whisk the milk mixture back into the remaining corn base. Transfer to 2 Pacojet beakers and freeze. Store in a freezer that holds at between 22 to 40°F/-30 to -40°C. Spin the ice for service.

Assemble the dessert:
Divide the 40 g of frozen cookie dough into 8 (5 g) pieces and roll into balls the size of blueberries. Return to the freezer and keep frozen.

Scoop alternating spoonfuls of blueberry ice and corn ice into a frozen 1-liter metal canister. Use a spoon to work the ices around to swirl; do not blend.

Divide the blueberries evenly across 4 chilled bowls. Sneakily nestle the blueberry cookie dough balls among the blueberries, . Pour 20 g of corn cream into the base of each bowl. Drizzle a few drops of rapeseed oil onto the corn cream. Scoop an egg-sized portion of the swirled blueberry and corn ice over the blueberries. Top each bowl with 1 or 2 pieces of corn tuile.

CARROT, YOGURT, CUMIN

'Merica, Prairie Artisan Ales
(www.prairieales.com)

Chase and Colin Healey, the brothers behind Prairie Artisan Ales, frequently just open the doors and windows at their brewery in Tulsa, Oklahoma, and let in America's wild yeasts. I've collaborated with them on a spontaneous fermented beer (see SOUR, page 76), but they also make a range of really complex and wonderful wild farmhouse-style ales. Even the labels are complex, wild, and wonderful. (Colin is a graphic artist.) For this dessert, which as Daniel mentioned just barely qualifies as a dessert, I wanted to pair a beer that corals it closer to sweetness. 'Merica is made of a single hop, the crisp tropical Nelson Sauvin from New Zealand; a single malt, a floor-malted Pilsner; and a combination of yeasts that include those crazy Bretts and a wine yeast strain that yields dryness. The result is a clean, funky aroma and a crisp bitterness in the mouth, both of which echo Daniel's tart yogurt.

SERVES 4

Yogurt Powder Dusting:
25 g yogurt powder
20 g powdered (icing) sugar
10 g vinegar powder
10 g tapioca maltodextrin

Cumin Snap Cookie:
75 g butter
100 g muscovado sugar
140 g all-purpose (plain) flour
4 g baking soda
    (bicarbonate of soda)
1 g kosher salt
4 g cumin seeds, toasted
    and ground
3 g fresh ginger, minced
35 g molasses
15 g egg yolk

Honey Nougatine Powder:
550 g fondant
450 g glucose
5 g butter
50 g honey granules

Seasoned Carrot Purée:
750 g carrots, sliced ⅛-inch/
    3 mm thick
875 g fresh carrot juice, plus
more as needed
20 g apple cider vinegar
4 g fresh lemon juice
5 g honey

Carrot Sorbet:
575 g water
225 g glucose
190 g granulated sugar
875 g carrot juice
160 g Seasoned Carrot Purée
30 g corn maltodextrin
15 g fresh lemon juice
4 gelatin sheets
2 g sorbet stabilizer

Yogurt Ice:
385 g water
160 g glucose
125 g granulated sugar
475 g yogurt
40 g corn maltodextrine
25 g fresh lemon juice
3 gelatin sheets
2 g sorbet stabilizer

Glazed Carrots:
225 g fresh carrot juice
75 g demerara sugar
30 g apple cider vinegar
15 g rice vinegar
10 g honey
4 g cumin seeds
4 purple beta carrots, cut into
    4- to 5-inch/10 to 13 cm-
    long pieces
4 small Thumbelina carrots

Tarragon Purée:
60 g yogurt
16 g tarragon leaves
30 g double Devon cream
0.8 g xanthan gum
35 g buttermilk
3 g fresh lemon juice

To Assemble:
75 g Honey Nougatine Powder
1 Pacojet container Carrot
   Sorbet
1 Pacojet container Yogurt Ice
30 g Yogurt Powder Dusting
120 g frozen Cumin Snap
   Cookie
20g Seasoned Carrot Purée
10g Tarragon Purée
8 pieces Poached Carrots

Make the yogurt powder dusting:
In a blender, blitz all the ingredients together. Store in a shaker.

Make the cumin snap cookie:
Temper the butter for 1 hour at room temperature. In a stand mixer fitted with the paddle attachment, beat together the muscovado sugar and butter on low speed for 3 minutes. In a small bowl, whisk together the flour, baking soda (bicarbonate of soda), and salt. One half at a time, add the flour mixture to the butter mixture. Beat on low speed for another 2 minutes. Combine the molasses and egg yolk. Pour in a slow, steady stream into the running stand mixer until incorporated. Divide the dough in half. Roll each half between 2 sheets of parchment paper and freeze.
   Preheat the oven to 340°F/170°C/Gas Mark 3.
   Bake the cookie dough in a single piece until slightly darkened around the edges, about 12 minutes. Cool fully and break into pieces. Transfer to a vacuum bag and beat with a rolling pin to form a granola-like texture. Store in the freezer.

Make the honey nougatine powder:
Line a large baking sheet lined with silicone baking mats and place near the stove. In a large wide pan, slowly melt the fondant and glucose together over medium heat. Cook, whisking constantly, until the temperature reaches 266°F/130°C on an infrared thermometer, about 25 minutes. Turn off the heat and quickly whisk in the butter until completely melted. Carefully pour the mixture onto the silicone baking sheet. Let stand until completely cool, about 2 hours.
   Using the back of a ladle, break the nougatine into small pieces. Transfer to a blender and blitz to a fine powder. While blitzing, steadily add the honey granules. Sift through a fine-mesh strainer. Store in a dry container.

Make the seasoned carrot purée:
In a saucepan, combine the carrots and carrot juice and cook over medium heat, stirring every few minutes, until almost dry, about 45 minutes. Transfer the hot mixture to a blender and purée, adding a splash of carrot juice if needed to get the mixture to spin freely. Pass through a chinois into a bowl and refrigerate until cool.

Whisk 160 grams of the puree with the vinegar, lemon juice, and honey. Cover and refrigerate for at least 1 hour.

Make the carrot sorbet:
In a saucepan, simmer together the water, glucose, and granulated sugar, stirring constantly, until all the sugar is dissolved. Cool the syrup.

Blend together 300 g of the syrup, the carrot juice, carrot purée, maltodextrin, and lemon juice. Pass through a chinois into a bowl. Set the carrot base aside.

Bloom the gelatin in cold water, then drain and blot dry on paper towels. In a medium saucepan, whisk together the sorbet stabilizer and 225 g of the syrup. Bring to a boil, whisking constantly. Remove from the heat and whisk in the gelatin until dissolved. Whisk in a small amount of the carrot sorbet base, then whisk the syrup mixture back into the base. Stir thoroughly. Transfer to 2 Pacojet beakers and freeze.

Make the yogurt ice:
In a saucepan, simmer together the water, glucose, and granulated sugar, stirring constantly until all the sugar is dissolved. Cool the syrup.

Blend together half of the syrup, the yogurt, maltodextrine, and lemon juice. Bloom the gelatin in cold water, then drain and blot dry on paper towels. In a medium saucepan, whisk together the sorbet stabilizer and the remaining syrup. Bring to a boil, whisking constantly. Remove from the heat and whisk in the gelatin until dissolved. Whisk in a small amount of the yogurt base, then whisk the syrup mixture back into the base. Stir thoroughly. Transfer to 2 Pacojet beakers and freeze.

Make the glazed carrots:
In a saucepan, combine the carrot juice, demerara sugar, vinegars, and honey and bring to a boil. Add the cumin and remove from the heat. Steep for 10 minutes. Strain (discard the spices). Reserving the poaching liquid, drain the carrots and let cool.

Divide the carrots between 2 vacuum bags. Add 100 g of poaching liquid to each, then vacuum-seal. Poach in a pot of simmering water until tender, about 20 minutes. Shock the carrots in their bags in an ice bath. Drain the liquid and dehydrate the carrots in a dehydrator at 136°F/58°C for 1 hour.

Make the tarragon purée:
Blend together the yogurt and tarragon leaves. Add the Devon cream and xanthan gum. Blend until incorporated, about 10 seconds. Strain through a chinois into a bowl. Whisk in the buttermilk and lemon juice until smooth.

Assemble the dessert:
Preheat the oven to 320°F/160°C/Gas Mark 3. Cover a baking sheet with crumpled foil and have at the ready.

Invert two 18 x 13-inch/46 x 33 cm rimmed baking sheets and place a silicone baking mat on top of each. Using a medium-fine strainer, dust a light coating of nougatine powder evenly over the mat. Bake in the oven with a low fan for 1 minute or so, or until the nougatine is glossy and translucent. Remove from the oven and let stand for 30 seconds. Use a small offset spatula to lift up the edges of the nougatine sheet. Lift as large a sheet as possible and drape it over the crumpled foil. Work quickly. If the nougatine becomes too brittle, return it to the oven for a few seconds to make it pliable once again.

Spin the carrot sorbet and then the yogurt ice in a Pacojet, washing the blade between ices. Scoop alternating spoonfuls of carrot sorbet and yogurt ice into a frozen 1-liter metal canister. Swirl gently, but do not blend.

Pick 4 large pieces of nougatine and move to a baking sheet. sprinkle with the yogurt powder dusting, gently tapping off the excess.

Divide the cumin snap cookie crumbs across 4 chilled bowls. Give each bowl 2 large dollops of the seasoned carrot purée and five small dots of the tarragon purée. Place 1 of each type of poached and dehydrated carrot on each dish. Gently place a quenelle of the swirled ices onto the cumin snap cookie. Top with a piece of dusted nougatine.

RHUBARB,
FENNEL, MATCHA

PAIRING

Geisterzug Gose Rhubarb,
Freigeist (www.braustelle.com)

This bottle comes from the same
guys who make the Abraxxxas,
a sought-after sour and complex
beer. Here they resurrect the
Gose style—a style from Leipzig
currently having a bit of a
renaissance—which is known
for its use of both coriander and
salt. For this beer, the brewers
Peter and Sebastian, share my
philosophy that sometimes it's
just better to add the thing to a
beer you want it to taste like
instead of relying on esters. They
filter the wort over spruce and
then condition it with rhubarb,
for a full-throttled flavor after
fermentation. It isn't every day
you get a rhubarb dessert and it
certainly isn't every day you
have a rhubarb beer. So the
pairing is a celebration of the
two minds on two continents
who saw one ingredient and
both decided to innovate.

SERVES 4

Fennel Licorice:
265 g water
70 g granulated sugar
8 g fennel seeds
3 g licorice root powder
7 g pine shoots
60 g honey
40 g glycerin
5 g gum arabic
85 g wheat starch

Rhubarb Purée:
900 g rhubarb, cut into 1-inch/2.5 cm pieces
100 g powdered (icing) sugar
25 g poaching liquid (reserved from cooking the rhubarb)
15 g apple cider vinegar
8 g honey
3 g fresh lemon juice
3 g instant food thickener
Pinch of xanthan gum

Rhubarb Sorbet:
425 g water
225 g granulated sugar
115 g trimoline
425 g Rhubarb Purée
175 g fresh rhubarb juice
35 g corn maltodextrin
20 g fresh beet (beetroot) juice
10 g fresh lemon juice
2½ bronze-strength gelatin sheets
2.5 g sorbet stabilizer

Goat Cheese Ice:
725 g water
265 g granulated sugar
155 g trimoline
340 g goat cheese
165 g yogurt
18 g corn maltodextrin
15 g fresh lemon juice
4 ½ gelatin sheets
6 g sorbet stabilizer

Matcha Crumble:
80 g butter
20 g granulated sugar
4 g matcha powder
180 g all-purpose (plain) flour
1 g Maldon salt
15 g milk

Fennel Licorice Dust:
10 g beet (beetroot) powder
4 g malic acid
2 g honey granules
1 g fennel pollen
80 g granulated sugar

To Assemble:
8 pieces Fennel Licorice
40 g Fennel Licorice Dust
½ beaker (500 ml) Goat Cheese Ice
800g Rhubarb Sorbet
100 g Matcha Crumble)
60 g Tarragon Purée (page 224)
120 g Rhubarb Purée
8 borage flowers or violets

Make the fennel licorice:
In a saucepan, combine 250 g water, 45 g granulated sugar, fennel seeds, and licorice root powder and bring to a boil. Reduce to a simmer and cook for 5 minutes. Remove the syrup from the heat and add the pine shoots. Let stand for 10 minutes. Strain (discard the solids) and cool.

In a medium pot, whisk together 115 g of the syrup, honey, glycerin, and remaining 25 g granulated sugar and 15 g water over medium heat. As soon as the sugar has dissolved, whisk in the gum arabic until incorporated. Whisk in 40 g of the wheat starch until incorporated, then whisk in the remaining 45 g. Whisk until very thick and hard to stir, about 7 minutes. Do not cease stirring.

Remove from the heat and transfer the licorice to a medium sized vacuum bag. Vacuum-seal the bag and cook in a pot of boiling water for 1 hour 30 minutes.

Cut the bag open and roll the licorice between 2 silicone baking mats to a ⅓-inch/8 mm thickness. Transfer the mats to a baking sheet, wrap well in plastic wrap (clingfilm), and freeze.

Once the licorice is frozen (several hours later), you can portion it into batons, about ⅓ x ⅓ x 1½ inches/8 mm x 8 mm x 4 cm. Keep frozen in an airtight container.

Make the rhubarb purée:
Toss rhubarb in powdered (icing) sugar. Pack into a large vacuum bag and vacuum-seal. Cook in a water bath set to 160°F/70°C for 50 minutes. Reserving the cooking liquid, drain the rhubarb and purée in a blender for 15 seconds. Pass through a chinois into a bowl. Measure out 110 g of the pureed rhubarb and freeze the rest.

Blend the reserved pureed rhubarb, the poaching liquid, vinegar, honey, and lemon juice for 10 seconds. Add the instant food thickener and xanthan gum. Blend for 20 seconds more and pass through a chinois into a bowl. Let sit for 2 hours.

Make the rhubarb sorbet:
In a saucepan, combine the water, granulated sugar, and trimoline and bring to a boil, stirring occasionally, until the sugar is completely dissolved. Let the syrup cool.

In 2 batches, combine the rhubarb purée, half of the syrup, the rhubarb juice, corn maltodextrine, beet juice, and lemon juice in a round metal container and blend with an immersion blender. Pass the rhubarb purée through a chinois into a bowl.

Bloom the gelatin in cold water, then drain and blot dry on paper towels. In a medium saucepan, whisk the remaining syrup with the sorbet stabilizer and simmer over medium heat, whisking constantly. Remove from the heat and stir ingelatin, until dissolved. Whisk a small amount of rhubarb purée into the stabilized syrup, then whisk the syrup mixture back into the rhubarb purée. Whisk thoroughly. Transfer to 2 Pacojet beakers and freeze.

Make the goat cheese ice:
In a saucepan, combine the water, granulated sugar, and trimoline and bring to a boil, stirring occasionally until the sugar is completely dissolved. Let the syrup cool.

Blend the 685 g syrup, goat cheese, yogurt, maltodextrin, and lemon juice with an immersion blender in a round metal container. Pass through a chinois into a bowl.

Bloom the gelatin in cold water, then drain and blot dry on paper towels. In a medium saucepan, whisk the remaining syrup with the sorbet stabilizer and simmer over medium heat, whisking constantly. Remove from the heat and stir in gelatin until dissolved. Whisk a small amount of goat cheese base into the stabilized syrup, then whisk the syrup mixture back into the goat cheese mixture. Transfer to 2 Pacojet beakers and freeze. Store in a freezer that holds between 22 and 40°F/-30 and -40°C.

Make the matcha crumble:
Temper butter for 1 hour at room temperature.

Preheat the oven to 320°F/160°C/Gas Mark 3.

In a stand mixer fitted with the paddle attachment, beat the butter with the granulated sugar, about 2 minutes. Add the matcha powder and mix for another 2 minutes. In a small bowl, whisk together the flour and salt, and beat into the butter mixture. When loose and mealy, drizzle in the milk slowly while the mixer runs at low speed. Let run for 1 minute. Place dough evenly into a medium baking dish. Bake until the crumble is light brown, about 20 minutes. Cool on the counter and then freeze. Once frozen (about 2 hours), pulse in a food processor until the crumble has a texture like instant coffee. Return to the freezer.

Make the fennel licorice dust:
In a blender, blitz the beet powder, malic acid, honey granules, and fennel pollen into a thin dust. In a bowl, whisk the dust with the granulated sugar. Store in a dry area.

Assemble the dessert:
In a small container with a lid, shake the fennel licorice with the licorice dust until well coated.

Spin the goat cheese ice and then the rhubarb sorbet in a Pacojet, washing the blade between ices. Scoop alternating spoonfuls of the goat cheese ice and rhubarb sorbet into a frozen 1-liter canister. Swirl gently, but do not blend.

Divide the matcha crumble evenly across the bottoms of 4 chilled wide bowls. Dollop a spoonful of tarragon purée into the center of the bowl. Squeeze 3 quarter-size dots of rhubarb purée around the crumble. Intersperse with the fennel licorice. Place a scoop of the swirled sorbet and ice in each bowl. Using a spoon, form into irregular shapes. Sprinkle lightly with additional matcha crumble and top with flowers.

SUNCHOKE, MALT, THYME

PAIRING

Extra Export Stout, De Dolle
(www.dedollebrouwers.be)

Belgium isn't known for its
stouts but no one told that to the
guys at De Dolle Brouwers
(which translates to The Mad
Brewers), a brewery in the small
town of Esen. Their version
takes that dark-roasted maltiness of a traditional Imperial
stout and pairs it with oerbier
yeast, a blend of Belgian yeasts
and lactobacillus. The result is a
dark, almost black beer with
chocolate, dark fruit, and espres-
so flavors but a mitigating
tartness, developed as it ages in
the bottle from the lactobacillus.

SERVES 4

Malt/Chocolate Ice:
1 bronze-strength gelatin sheet
315 g milk
45 g heavy (double) cream
35 g trimoline
25 g cocoa powder
20 g muscovado sugar
8 g malt powder
3 g sorbet stabilizer
115 g 64% chocolate

Roasted Sunchoke Ice:
500 g sunchokes (Jerusalem artichokes)
Olive oil
430 g milk
70 g heavy (double) cream
50 g trimoline
35 g buttermilk
25 g corn maltodextrin
20 g granulated sugar
5 g milk powder
1½ bronze-strength gelatin sheets
1 g sorbet stabilizer

Sunchoke Dusting:
300 g sunchokes (Jerusalem artichokes), coarsely grated
25 g sunchoke powder
5 g vinegar powder
8 g malt powder
10 g tapioca maltodextrin

Thyme Syrup:
165 g granulated sugar
75 g water
15 g thyme leaves

Thyme Mousse:
1½ bronze-strength gelatin sheets
90 g heavy (double) cream
110 g yogurt
125 g Thyme Syrup
35 g whey
5 g fresh lemon juice
50 g egg whites
10 g granulated sugar

Blackberry Purée:
20 g granulated sugar
90 g water
200 g blackberries
8 g rosehip vinegar
10 g instant food thickener

Arlettes:
Powdered (icing) sugar, for dusting
200 g block Puff Pastry (recipe follows), chilled

To Assemble:
½ recipe Thyme Mousse
1 Pacojet container Sunchoke Ice
1 Pacojet container Malt/Chocolate Ice
100 g Chocolate Crumble (page 66)
80 g Blackberry Purée
4 (6 x 4-inch/15 x 10 cm) pieces Arlettes
30 g Sunchoke Dusting

Make the malt/chocolate ice:
Bloom the gelatin in cold water, then drain and blot dry on paper towels. In a blender, combine half the milk, the cream, trimoline, cocoa powder, muscovado sugar, and malt powder. Blend to incorporate the powders; scrape the sides with a spatula and blend again, for a total of 20 seconds. Pass the malt base through a chinois into a bowl.

In a small saucepan, whisk together the remaining milk with the sorbet stabilizer. Scald the mixture over medium heat, whisking constantly. When the bubbles break the surface, remove from the heat and whisk in the gelatin to dissolve. Whisk a small portion of the malt base, then whisk the milk mixture back into the base.

Set a medium bowl over a saucepan that has ½ inch/1 cm of simmering water in it. Use this double boiler to melt the chocolate. When the chocolate has fully melted, whisk in a small amount of malt base to start tempering the chocolate. With an immersion blender running in the bowl of malt base, stream in the chocolate. Transfer to 2 Pacojet containers and freeze. Store in a freezer that holds between -22 and 40°F/-30 and -40°C.

Make the roasted sunchoke ice:
Preheat the oven to 355°F/180°C/Gas Mark 4.

Toss the sunchokes in the lightest amount of oil and roast until deeply browned but not burned, about 20 minutes. Allow the sunchokes to cool.

In a blender, combine half the milk, the cooled sunchokes, cream, trimoline, buttermilk, maltodextrin, granulated sugar, and milk powder. Pass the sunchoke base through a chinois into a bowl.

Bloom the gelatin in cold water, then drain and blot dry on paper towels. In a small saucepan, whisk together the remaining milk with the sorbet stabilizer. Scald the mixture over medium heat, whisking constantly. When the bubbles break the surface, remove from the heat and whisk in the gelatin to dissolve. Whisk in a small amount of the sunchoke base, then whisk the milk mixture back into the base. Transfer to 2 Pacojet containers and freeze. Store in a freezer that holds between -22 and -30°F (-30°C and -40°C).

Make the sunchoke dusting:
Dehydrate the sunchokes in a dehydrator set to 126°F/52°C for 12 hours or until very dry and can be broken into pieces easily.

Pulverize the dried sunchokes in a blender to a fine dust, about 30 seconds. Whisk together the 3 powders and the tapioca malto-dextrin. Store in a spice shaker in a dry area.

Make the thyme syrup:
In a small saucepan, combine the granulalted sugar and water and bring to a boil until the sugar is completely dissolved. Let cool.

Measure out 130 g of the syrup and freeze until slushy, about 90 minutes. In a blender, blitz the partially frozen syrup with the thyme leaves for 12 seconds on high and pass through a chinois, then a fishnet strainer. Use the thyme liquid that day or freeze to use later.

Make the thyme mousse:
In a large bowl, using a balloon whisk, whip the cream to soft peaks. Reserve in the refrigerator.

Bloom the gelatin in cold water, then drain and blot dry on paper towels. In a bowl, whisk together the yogurt, 75 g of the thyme syrup, the whey, and lemon juice until well incorporated. In a small saucepan, melt the gelatin with the remaining 50 g thyme syrup over low heat. Once the gelatin has fully melted, whisk it into the yogurt mixture. Transfer to the refrigerator to start to set. Stir the yogurt mixture occasionally to help it chill evenly. This process may be expedited by use of an ice bath under the bowl. When the thyme and yogurt has thickened slightly, incorporate the whipped cream.

Meanwhile, in a stand mixer fitted with the whisk attachment, whisk the egg whites and granulated sugar on medium speed to medium-stiff peaks.

Whisk half the whites into the thyme base. Whisk in the re-maining whites, trying to preserve their airiness. Finish the mix-ture by using a rubber spatula to scrape the walls and base of the bowl to insure nothing is left unincorporated. Transfer to a container with a lid.

Make the blackberry purée:
In a small saucepan, combine the granulated sugar and water and bring to a boil until the sugar is completely dissolved. Let cool.

Measure out 45 g of the cooled syrup and transfer to a blender with the blackberries. Blend until smooth, about 15 seconds, then blend in the rosehip vinegar for 5 seconds. Pass through a chinois into a bowl, rinse the blender jar, and return the purée to the blender. Blend with the instant food thickener for 15 seconds and pass through a chinois again. Store refrigerated.

Make the arlettes:
Preheat the oven to 340°F/170°C/Gas Mark 3.

Dust a work surface with powdered (icing) sugar. Lay the block of puff pastry on the sugar and dust the top as well. Use a rolling pin to gently pound the block of dough down to a ½-inch/1 cm thickness. Lift the sheet and dust again underneath and above. Dust the rolling pin and roll away from you three times. Rotate and flip the dough, dusting both sides again, and roll away from you again. Continue rolling, rotating, flipping, and dusting the dough until it is so thin that it is nearly see-through and may start to tear at the edges. This will become a pastry called an arlette. Let the dough sit for 1 minute; then roll again twice in each direction.

Use a bench scraper to carefully lift the dough and move to a flat baking sheet lined with parchment. Top with another sheet of parchment. (If your baking sheet is too small to fit all of the arlette, you can cut it in half and stack the 2 sheets on each other with a sheet of parchment between them.) Top the final piece of parchment with another flat baking sheet and something heavy such as a cast iron pan. Bake until well caramelized throughout, rotating as needed. This can take up to 15 minutes. Remove from the oven and let cool for 1 minute. While the arlette is still warm, use a small offset spatula to break the sheets into irregular pieces about 6 x 4 inches/15 x 10 cm. Store in a very dry area.

Assemble the dessert:
Chill 4 bowls. Gently whisk the thyme mousse to loosen slightly and transfer to a piping bag with an INOX #5 tip. Spin one beaker of chocolate ice in a Pacojet, wash the blade, and spin one beaker of roasted sunchoke ice. Alternate spoonfuls of the malt and sunchoke ices into a frozen 1-liter canister (in a ratio of 1 to 2). Swirl gently, but do not blend. Distribute the chocolate crumble just off center of each plate. Surround with dots of blackberry purée. Pipe 3 to 5 portions of thyme mousse around the blackberry purée. Scoop a portion of the swirled ices onto the chocolate crumble. On a baking sheet, dust the pieces of arlette with the sunchoke dusting, tap off the excess, and partially cover the quenelle of swirled ice with the arlette. Serve immediately.

PUFF PASTRY
Makes 5 blocks
Mix A:
1875 g European-style unsalted butter
750 g all-purpose (plain) flour

Mix B:
550 g European-style unsalted butter
750 g water
5 g white wine vinegar
75 g kosher salt
1875 g all-purpose (plain) flour, plus more as needed

Make mix A:
Temper the butter to room temperature. Incorporate the flour by hand. Portion into five 525 g blocks. Wrap in plastic wrap (clingfilm) and refrigerate for 1 hour.

Make mix B:
Temper the butter to room temperature. In a bowl, mix together the water, vinegar, and salt. In a stand mixer fitted with the paddle attachment, beat together the flour and butter. Slowly stream in the water mixture and beat until incorporated. Portion into five 625 g blocks, wrap in plastic wrap (clingfilm), and refrigerate for at least 2 hours.

Flour your bench and rolling pin lightly. Working with 1 block at a time, roll mix A thinly into an 8 x 8-inch/20 x 20 cm square. Place mix B on top. Roll lengthwise until the dough is about 30 inches/76 cm long and still the same 8-inch/20 cm width. Fold the bottom end up to meet exactly with the top, then fold over itself again. Turn clockwise a quarter turn so that the double fold is on the left handside of your dough. Repeat this process and roll to 30 inches/76 cm long and repeat the double fold. Rest the dough in the refrigerator for 30 minutes. Complete two more of these book folds, making a quarter-turn each time. Now the puff pastry is ready to portion and store. Portion in 200 g blocks.

BEETROOT FLØDEBOLLER

MAKES 12

Licorice Cookies:
250 g butter
160 g sugar
30 g licorice root powder
4 g malt powder
300 g all-purpose (plain) flour
1 g Maldon salt
25 g yolks

Chocolate Coating:
500 g 70% dark chocolate
40 g Mycryo powdered cocoa butter

Beet Meringue:
90 g sugar
70 g glucose
65 g fresh beet (beetroot) juice
115 g fresh beet (beetroot) juice, boiled and then strained, cooled
50 g sugar
20 g powdered egg whites
2 g smoked dulse powder

To Assemble:
12 Licorice Cookies
150 g Beet Meringue
500 g Chocolate Coating

Make the licorice cookies:
Dice the butter and temper for 20 minutes at room temperature.

In a stand mixer fitted with the paddle attachment, beat the butter and sugar together on low speed. In a bowl, whisk together the licorice and malt powders, then beat into the butter mixture. In another bowl, whisk together the flour and salt. Add to butter and work on low speed until mealy, about 20 seconds. With the mixer running, add the yolks.

Divide the dough into 3 even portions. Place each portion between 2 sheets of parchment paper and, using a rolling pin, roll out to a ⅛ inch/3 mm thickness. Freeze for at least 3 hours. Remove

and use a Matfer #40 (1½-inch /40 mm) ring cutter to punch out discs.

When ready to bake, preheat the oven to 320°F/160°C/Gas Mark 3.

Without thawing, bake 12 licorice cookies on a heavy baking sheet until lightly browned, about 13 minutes. Remove from the oven and let cool.

Make the chocolate coating:
Combine the chocolate and powdered cocoa butter in a metal bowl set over a small pot of simmering water. Stirring occasionally, melt the chocolate completely. Remove the bowl to a towel-lined cake pan and store in a cool part of the kitchen. Stir every 10 minutes with a wooden spoon until cooled to 86°F/30°C. Return the bowl to the double boiler set up. Over medium-low heat, stir constantly to bring the temperature up to 91°F/33°C.

Make the beet meringue:
In a small high-walled pot, combine the sugar, glucose, and fresh beet juice over medium-low heat. Stir for the first 2 minutes to prevent any sugar from sticking and burning. Cook to 241°F/116°C, stirring occasionally.

While the syrup is coming to the proper temperature, in a stand mixer fitted with the whisk attachment, gently whisk together the cooled boiled beet juice, sugar, and powdered egg whites. When the egg white powder is wet enough to not puff into the air, increase the speed to 80% of your machine's maximum. When the meringue no longer rises, reduce the speed to low.

When the syrup reaches the desired temperature, cut the heat and swirl to cool for about 30 seconds. With the mixer running, pour a small dollop of syrup into the meringue mixture. Let run for 15 seconds. Repeat twice. Then pour the rest of the syrup in a thin continuous stream. Allow the machine to run until the meringue is only slightly warm. Fold in the smoked dulse powder. Transfer the meringue to a piping bag fitting with an INOX #10 tip.

Assemble the flødeboller:
Transfer the cooled cookies to a wire rack set over a rimmed baking sheet. Pipe the meringue onto the cookies until it comes to the edge. Raise the tip straight up and pipe again. Repeat until there are 4 or 5 layers. Refrigerate for 1 hour.

Remove from the refrigerator and coat with the tempered chocolate. Transfer to a parchment-lined baking sheet and let cool again in the refrigerator. Store in airtight dry containers in the refrigerator until serving.

CRUNCHIE BAR

SERVES 8

Chocolate Chip Cookies:
225 g butter
170 g sugar
345 g all-purpose (plain) flour
1 g Maldon salt
40 g yolks
30 g milk
60 g 70% chocolate, chopped

Crunchie Bar:
Cooking spray
315 g sugar
125 g glucose
60 g water
50 g dark honey
15 g baking soda (bicarbonate of soda)

Ice Cream Sandwiches:
8 (1-inch/2.5 cm) squares Crunchie Bar
300 g Chocolate Coating (page 240)
1 Pacojet container Vanilla Ice (page 66)
8 Chocolate Chip Cookies

Make the chocolate chip cookies:
Dice the butter and let it temper for 20 minutes at room temperature.

In a stand mixer fitted with the paddle attachment, beat the butter and sugar together. In a bowl, whisk together the flour and salt, then add to the butter mixture. Beat until a loose mealy crumb is formed. Add the yolks, one by one, then stream in the milk. When the dough is cohesive, beat in the chocolate pieces until just incorporated.

Divide the dough into 2 balls and flatten into discs. Use a rolling pin to spread the discs between 2 sheets of parchment paper to a ⅓-inch/8 mm thickness. Freeze the sheets. Once frozen, use a Matfer #30 (1¼-inch/30 mm) ring cutter to punch out cookies. Work quickly. Transfer the frozen cookies to an airtight container with parchment between each layer. Keep frozen.

When ready to bake, preheat the oven to 320°F/160°C/Gas Mark 3.

Without thawing, bake the cookies on a baking sheet for 11 to 13 minutes, or until golden. Remove from the oven and transfer to another baking sheet to cool.

Make the crunchie bar:
Coat a very dry and clean 9 x 13 x 2-inch/23 x 33 x 5 cm baking dish with cooking spray.

In a tall pot that you can still pick up and flip one-handed, combine the sugar, glucose, water, and honey. Whisk over medium heat and cook, stirring frequently, until the sugar reaches a temperature of 320°F/160°C. Remove from the heat and vigorously stir in the baking soda (bicarbonate of soda) for 5 seconds. There will be foam.

Pour the mixture into the prepared baking dish, using a whisk to scrape the sugar from the pot. Leave undisturbed for 1 hour. Lift the bar from the dish. Portion into 1-inch/2.5 cm squares. Store in an airtight container in a cool, dry area. Bars will last for up to 3 days.

Make the ice cream sandwiches:
Place the crunchie bar squares on a wire rack set over a rimmed baking sheet and pour the chocolate coating over them to coat all sides (but not the bottom). Spin the vanilla ice in the Pacojet. To serve, scoop a small mound of vanilla ice onto each cookie and top with a piece of chocolate-coated crunchie bar.

PANTRY

In the following pages, you'll find what we typically keep in our larder. As you'll notice, pickles play a prominent role. In fact, a lot of our refrigerator space is occupied by rows of neat plastic containers filled with pickles. For me, pickles are like the punctuation of the recipe. These recipes are good to have on hand. Typically, they make enough to be used in a few applications. But most can be stored.

— DANIEL

BROTHS

ROASTED CHICKEN STOCK | Makes 1.2 L

1000 g chicken wings
140 g cremini (chestnut) mushrooms, thickly sliced
Olive oil
90 g shallots, sliced
15 g garlic, sliced
20 g honey
1000 g chicken stock
75 g usukuchi soy sauce
75 g scallion, cut into 2-inch/5 cm pieces
2 g fennel seeds

Preheat the oven to 395°F/200°C/Gas Mark 6.
Rinse and pat dry the chicken wings. Roast on a rimmed baking sheet until browned, about 35 minutes.
Reserving wings, pour off about 2 tablespoons of chicken fat and transfer to a wide, heavy-bottomed pot. Set the pot over medium-high heat, add the mushrooms, and cook until browned, about 8 minutes. Remove the mushrooms from the pot and set aside.
Using the same pot, coat the bottom with olive oil, increase the heat to high, and pan-roast the shallots until browned, about 6 minutes. Add the garlic and cook another 2 minutes. Reduce the heat to medium. Add the honey and let caramelize lightly, about 30 seconds. Add remaining ingredients and reserved chicken wings, and mushrooms. Simmer, uncovered, for 1 hour, skimming the solids as they rise to the surface. Strain the stock and cool. The stock can be kept covered in the refrigerator for 2 days or frozen for up to 3 months.

DASHI | Makes 1.5 L

1650 g water
50 g fennel, sliced
5 g fresh ginger, sliced
5 g kombu

In a saucepan, combine the water, fennel, ginger, and kombu and simmer over medium-low heat for 20 minutes. Let cool to 150°F/65°C, then submerge the kombu and steep for 15 minutes. Strain and cool. The dashi can be kept covered in the refrigerator for 2 days or frozen for up to 1 month.

FISH STOCK | Makes 750 ml

1000 g fish bones
50 g Vidalia or other sweet onion, sliced
35 g fennel, sliced
35 g celery, cut into 2-inch/5 cm pieces
2 g garlic, sliced
2 g thyme sprigs
1 g bay leaves

In a large heavy stockpot, combine all the ingredients with enough water to just cover and heat to 167°F/75°C. Reduce the heat to low and cook for 10 minutes, skimming the solids as they rise. Remove from the heat and let steep for 10 minutes further. Strain through a china cap and then chinois. The stock can be kept covered in the refrigerator for 2 days on ice or frozen for up to 1 month.

HAM BROTH | Makes 3 L

5500 g water
1250 g ham hock
275 g slab bacon, cut into 2-inch/5 cm strips
150 g onion, cut into sixths
10 g garlic, pounded
2 g bay leaf
20 g coriander seeds
12 g tsaoko fruit
20 g kombu

In a large, heavy stockpot, combine the water, ham hocks, and bacon and bring to a boil, skimming the impurities from the surface. Reduce the heat to medium-low. Simmer for 1 hour, then add onion and garlic. After another hour, add the bay leaf, coriander seeds, and tsaoko fruit. After a further hour, taste—it should be very porky. (If not, simmer slightly longer.) Remove from the heat and let steep for 10 minutes. Submerge the kombu and steep for 10 minutes. Strain the broth (discard the solids). The stock can be kept covered in the refrigerator for 2 days or frozen for up to 2 months.

MUSHROOM STOCK | Makes 400 ml

Grapeseed oil
20 g shallots, sliced
4 g garlic, sliced
100 g cremini (chestnut) mushrooms, sliced
75 g white mushrooms, sliced
500 g Vegetable Stock (page 248)

Set a heavy saucepan over medium high-heat and coat with oil until it shimmers. Add the shallots and pan-roast until they begin to caramelize, about 8 minutes. Add the garlic and cook for an additional 3 minutes. Remove the shallots and garlic and set aside.
Add twice as much oil as before and heat until smoking. Add both mushrooms and cook, stirring occasionally, about 6 minutes. Return the shallots and garlic to the pan. Add the vegetable stock and simmer for 1 hour over medium-low heat, skimming the solids as they rise. Strain stock and cool (discard the solids). The stock can be kept covered in the refrigerator for 2 days or frozen for up to 1 month.

VEGETABLE STOCK | Makes 2.5 L

2000 g water
400 g Vidalia or other sweet onion, sliced thick
225 g fennel bulb, sliced thick
150 g leek, cut into 2-inch/5 cm pieces
150 g celery, cut into 2-inch/5 cm pieces
10 g parsley stems
5 g coriander seeds
3 g fennel seeds
15 g kombu

In medium stockpot, combine the water, onion, fennel bulb, leek, and celery and heat to 175°F/80°C. Reduce the heat to medium-low and simmer for 30 minutes, skimming the solids as they rise. Add the parsley, coriander seeds, and fennel seeds and cook over low heat for 15 minutes more. Remove from the heat and let the stock cool to 150°F/65°C. Submerge the kombu and steep for 15 minutes. Strain stock and cool. The stock can be kept covered in refrigerator for 2 days or frozen for up to 1 month.

PICKLES

PICKLED BEETS | Makes 500 g

160 g apple cider vinegar
50 g rice vinegar
150 g water
15 g honey
5 g black peppercorns
3 g coriander seeds
4 g juniper berries
1 g dried bird's eye chiles
500 g red beets (beetroot), peeled and sliced very thin on a mandoline

In a saucepan, combine the vinegars, water, and honey and bring to a boil. Reduce to a simmer, add the peppercorns, seeds, berries, and chiles, and simmer for 10 minutes. Strain (discard the solids) and cool. Using a Matfer #40 (1½-inch /40 mm) ring cutter, cut the beets into discs. Place the beets and pickling liquid in a vacuum bag and vacuum-seal. Let the beets pickle overnight before use. Store in the refrigerator for up to 1 week.

PICKLED GREEN CABBAGE | Makes about 4500 g

3000 g green cabbage
Kosher salt
850 g apple cider vinegar
475 g rice vinegar
275 g water
80 g honey
75 g sliced shallots
10 g sliced garlic
10 g coriander seeds
5 g black peppercorns
6 g shichimi togarashi powder
2 g dried bird's eye chiles

Core and shred the cabbage. Lightly salt and let sit overnight. Rinse well.

In a saucepan, combine the vinegars, water, and honey and bring to a boil. Reduce to a simmer, and add the shallots, garlic, coriander, peppercorns, powder, and chiles. Let steep for 10 minutes. Strain (discard the solids) and let cool to 176°F/60°C.

Pour over the cabbage in an airtight container and pickle at least 2 days before use. Store in refrigerator for up to 1 month.

PICKLED RED CABBAGE | Makes 1200 g

425 g rice vinegar
275 g white wine vinegar
300 g water
50 g honey
40 g sliced shallots
15 g fennel seeds
10 g sliced seeded jalapeño
12 g white peppercorns
8 g dried chile flakes
5 grams garlic, sliced
4 g fresh bay leaf
1500 kg red cabbage, shredded

In a saucepan, combine the vinegars, water, and honey and bring to a boil. Reduce to a simmer, add the shallots, fennel seeds, jalapenos, peppercorns, chile flakes, garlic, and bay leaf. Let steep for 10 minutes. Strain (discard the solids) and let cool to 176°F/80°C. Pour over the cabbage in an airtight container and store in the refrigerator. Let the cabbage pickle at least overnight, and preferably for 1 week or longer, before use.

PICKLED CAULIFLOWER | Makes 1500 g
450 g rice wine vinegar
400 g white wine vinegar
90 g sugar
900 g water
6 g fennel seeds
6 g juniper berries
6 g black peppercorns
2 kg heads cauliflower, broken into florets

In a saucepan, combine the vinegars, sugar, and water and bring to a boil. Reduce to a simmer, add the spices, and let steep for 5 minutes. Strain (discard the solids) and let cool to 176°F/60°C. Pour over the cauliflower florets in an airtight container and store in the refrigerator. Let the cauliflower pickle overnight before use; store up to 1 week.

PICKLED CARROTS | Makes 3000 g

3000 g carrots
1450 g apple cider vinegar
450 g rice vinegar
400 g mirin
60 g honey
160 g sugar
1300 g water
100 g sliced shallots
14 g white peppercorns

Slice the carrots thinly on a mandoline.

In a saucepan, combine the vinegars, mirin, honey, sugar, and water and bring to a boil. Reduce to a simmer, add the shallots and peppercorns, and let steep for 5 minutes. Strain (discard the solids) and let cool to 176°F/60°C. Pour over the carrots in an airtight container and store in refrigerator. Let the carrots pickle overnight before use; store up to 1 week.

PICKLED CELERY | Makes 200 g

110 g apple cider vinegar
50 g rice vinegar
8 g honey
1 g coriander seeds
40 g water
200 g celery, diced

In a saucepan, combine the vinegars, honey, coriander seeds, and water and bring to a boil. Reduce the heat to low and simmer for 5 minutes. Strain (discard the solids) and cool. Place the celery and cooled liquid in a vacuum bag and vacuum-seal. Store in refrigerator for up to 1 week.

KIRBY CUCUMBER PICKLES | Makes 500 g

175 g sugar
150 g white wine vinegar
120 g apple cider vinegar
240 g water
30 g shallots, sliced
10 g jalapeño pepper, sliced
10 g honey
2 g fennel seeds
1 g dried bird's eye chiles
500 g Kirby cucumbers, sliced ¼-inch/6 mm thick

In a saucepan, combine the sugar, vinegars, water, shallots, jalapeño, honey, fennel seeds, and dried chiles and bring to a boil. Reduce to a simmer and cook for 10 minutes. Cool together and strain. Place the cucumbers and pickling liquid to a vacuum bag and vacuum-seal. Marinate in the refrigerator for 24 hours. Open the bag and refrigerate until needed and for up to 2 weeks in an airtight container.

PICKLED GREEN ALMONDS | Makes 750 g

240 g apple cider vinegar
75 g rice vinegar
450 g water
40 g demerara sugar
20 g honey
8 g juniper berries
4 g black peppercorns
10 g coriander seeds
5 g fennel seeds
5 g bay leaves
5 g lemon zest
500 g fresh celery juice
1000 g green almonds, washed thoroughly, clipped of stems

In a saucepan, combine the vinegars, water, demerara sugar, and honey and bring to a boil. Reduce to a simmer and add the berries, peppercorns, seeds, bay leaves and lemon zest. Simmer for 5 minutes. Remove from the heat and let steep for 10 minutes. Let cool, then stir in the celery juice. Divide the almonds among 4 vacuum bags. Fill evenly with brine. Vacuum-seal and let sit, refrigerated, for at least 1 week.

PICKLED HOT PEPPERS | Makes 200 g

275 g apple cider vinegar
175 g rice vinegar
290 g water
35 g demerara sugar
25 g honey
8 g juniper berries
8 g fennel seeds
3 g cubeb peppercorns
2 g bay leaf
300 g mixed hot peppers, washed and stemmed

In a saucepan, combine the vinegars, water, demerara sugar, and honey and bring to a boil. Reduce to a simmer and add the berries, fennel seeds, peppercorns, and bay leaf. Let simmer for 10 minutes. Strain (discard the solids) and pour the hot liquid over the hot peppers. Let cool. Cover and let sit for at least 1 month. Strain and reserve the liquid.

PICKLED RED PEARL ONIONS | Makes 300 g

300 g peeled red pearl onions
280 g red wine vinegar
145 g sweet potato vinegar
110 g rice vinegar
20 g muscovado sugar
310 g water
10 g coriander seeds
8 g white peppercorns
2 g fresh bay leaf

Peel and halve the onions.
    In a saucepan, combine the vinegars, sugar, and water and bring to a boil. Reduce to a simmer and add the coriander, peppercorns, and bay leaf. Let simmer for 10 minutes. Let the liquid cool completely. Place the onions and cooled liquid in a vacuum-seal bag and vacuum-seal. Store in the refrigerator. Let the onions pickle for at least 2 and up to 6 hours before use.

PICKLED JALAPEÑOS | Makes 700 g

275 g rice vinegar
250 g apple cider vinegar
175 g water
65 g maple syrup
8 g lemongrass
2 g cumin seeds
2 g fennel seeds
1000 g jalapeño peppers, washed thoroughly (but not stemmed)

In a saucepan, combine the vinegars, water, and maple syrup. Reduce to a simmer, add the lemongrass, cumin, and fennel and simmer for 10 minutes. Strain (didscard the solids) and let cool to 158°F/70°C. Remove the stems of the jalapeños and prick the skin multiple times with a sharp knife. Pack the peppers in a snug airtight container. Pour the pickling liquid over the peppers and let cool uncovered. Cover and store for at least 2 weeks in refrigerator before use. Store in refrigerator for up to 2 weeks.

PICKLED RAMPS | Makes 500 g

1000 g ramps
1500 g water
1100 g apple cider vinegar
700 g rice vinegar
80 g demerara sugar
80 g usukuchi soy sauce
70 g fish sauce
40 g honey
16 g dried bird's eye chiles

Clean the ramps by trimming the roots off of their bases and removing any dead, dry, or slimy outer layers. Discard any leaves that are yellowed. Rinse thoroughly in 2 cycles of cold water. Lay out to dry on kitchen towels.

In a saucepan, combine the remaining ingredients and bring to a simmer. Cook for 10 minutes and taste. If the pickling liquid is not spicy, simmer another few minutes.

While the liquid is simmering, transfer the ramps to a deep plastic container that they fit in snugly. Strain the liquid over the ramps while still at a simmer, reserving and adding the chiles to the ramps if you would like a spicier pickle. (This also provides a byproduct of "rampy" pickled chiles, which are nice for marinades and dressings.) Cool, uncovered, and then cover with parchment paper. Weight down with something clean and heavy, like a plastic to-go container full of water wrapped in plastic wrap (clingfilm). Cover everything with a tight-fitting lid and store in the refrigerator. Store in refrigerator for up to 1 month.

CONDIMENTS

CELERY SALT | Makes 400 g

250 g celery root (celeriac), grated
250 g coarse salt

In a small bowl, mix the celeriac with the salt and allow the mixture to sit out overnight. Dehydrate in a dehydrator set to 122°F/50°C for 12 hours. Blitz in a food processor until the consistency of kosher salt. Store at room temperature for up to 2 months.

VANILLA SALT | Makes 275 g

250 g coarse sea salt
75 g granulated sugar
1 vanilla pod, split and seeds scraped out

Pulse the salt, sugar, and vanilla in a blender until fine. Store in refrigerator for up to 6 months.

CURED EGG YOLKS | Makes 12

Syrup:
400 g water
175 g demerara sugar
62 g honey
2 g star anise
2 g fennel seeds
4 g cinnamon stick

Eggs:
100 g Vanilla Salt (page 250)
12 egg yolks, whole (not beaten)
200 g Syrup (recipe above)

Make the syrup:
In a saucepan, combine all the syrup ingredients and bring to a boil. Reduce to a simmer and cook for 10 minutes. Strain and refrigerate.

Make the eggs:
Line a shallow-lidded container with a thin layer of vanilla salt. Clean the yolks as best you can and space evenly over the salt. Top each yolk with 1 tablespoon of vanilla salt. The yolks will not be completely submerged. Refrigerate, uncovered, for 12 hours.

The next morning, rinse the yolks of salt gently in a bowl of cold water. Transfer to a snug container. Pour enough syrup to cover the yolks halfway. Cover with a wet towel and place in a vacuum machine. Run 3 times. Remove the yolks and let drip for a moment. Dehydrate on acetate in a dehydrator set 104°F/40°C for 12 hours. The yolks will keep, covered in the refrigerator, for up to 1 month.

HOT SAUCE | Makes 750 g

500 g Pickled Jalapeños (page 249), plus 250 g of the pickling liquid
90 g mirin
75 g tomato paste (double concentrate purée)
65 g honey
50 g rice vinegar
55 g Worcestershire sauce
15 g fish sauce

Seed the pickled peppers and transfer to a blender. Add the pickling liquid and remaining ingredients and blend for 2 minutes until smooth. Store covered in a nonreactive container in the refrigerator. Store in refrigerator for up to 1 month.

MAYONNAISE | Makes 500 g

65 g egg yolks
30 g eggs
35 g apple cider vinegar
25 g fresh lemon juice
50 g grainy mustard
275 g grapeseed oil
Kosher salt

In a food processor, blend the yolks, whole eggs, vinegar, lemon juice, and mustard for 30 seconds. With the machine running, add the oil in a steady stream to create an emulsion. Season with salt. Store in the refrigerator for up to 4 days.

MIE DE PAIN | Makes 500 g

50 g olive oil, plus more as needed
15 g garlic, smashed
600 g French loaf or Polish rye bread, torn into bits
Kosher salt

Preheat the oven to 320°F/160°C/Gas Mark 3.

In a medium saucepan, heat a splash of oil over medium heat and fry the garlic to a light brown. Place a comfortable amount of the bread in a food processor. Run the food processor while drizzling in the garlic and oil. If you must work in batches, make sure to reserve oil and garlic for the latter ones.

Using a rolling pin, spread this bread mixture thinly between 2 sheets of parchment on a baking sheet. Remove the top layer of the parchment paper, lightly salt, and bake until golden, about 10 minutes. Break into pieces as needed. Store at room temperature, covered, for up to 1 month.

TOMATO RELISH | Makes 400 g

30 g olive oil
50 g shallots, minced
3 g garlic, minced
10 g demerara sugar
25 g apple cider vinegar
20 g usukuchi soy sauce
125 g tomato paste (double concentrate purée)
1 g paprika
1 g shichimi togarashi powder
0.5 g cayenne pepper
100 g Mayonnaise (page 250)
50 g Pickled Kirby Cucumbers (page 249), brunoised

In a heavy saucepan, heat the olive oil over high heat. Add the shallots and pan-roast until caramelized, about 3 minutes. Add the garlic. After 3 minutes, reduce the heat to medium and add the demerara sugar. After 40 seconds, the sugar will begin to bubble. To prevent burning, add the vinegar and soy sauce. Cook over medium heat until the liquid achieves the consistency of syrup, about 3 minutes. Add the tomato paste, cooking to a deep rusty red, about 6 minutes. Stir in the paprika, togarashi, and cayenne and cook for another 2 minutes. Transfer the mixture to a shallow hotel pan and cool, uncovered, in the refrigerator. Once cool, fold in the mayonnaise and pickles.

HOUSE VINAIGRETTE | Makes 250 g

275 g apple cider vinegar
80 g rice vinegar
45 g honey
30 g Dijon mustard
10 g fresh lemon juice
125 g grapeseed oil
150 g whole-grain mustard
Maldon salt

In a blender, combine the vinegars, honey, Dijon mustard, and lemon juice and blitz. With the motor running, slowly drizzle in the oil. Pour the emulsion into a bowl and whisk in the mustard. Season to taste with salt. Use immediately or refrigerate until needed and for up to 3 days.

YOGURT-TOUCHED WHIPPED BUTTER | Makes 500 g

500 g butter
10 g yogurt
1 g Maldon salt

Temper the butter for 3 hours at room temperature or until softened. In a stand mixer fitted with the paddle attachment, beat the butter on high speed until fluffy and lightened in color, about 8 minutes. Add the yogurt and salt and whip for another 30 seconds on medium speed. Taste and adjust salt to your preference. Store at room temperature until serving and for up to 1 week in the refrigerator.

Phaidon Press Limited
Regent's Wharf
All Saints Street
London N1 9PA

Phaidon Press Inc.
65 Bleecker Street
New York, NY 10012

phaidon.com

First published 2016
© 2016 Phaidon Press Limited

ISBN 9 7807 1487 1059

A CIP catalogue record for this book is available from the British Library and the Library of Congress.

Image credit on page 215: Painting the Roof of your Mouth (Ice Cream), 2015; Davide Balula in collaboration with Daniel Burns; Courtesy Frank Elbaz, François Ghebaly / Photo: Raphael Fanelli

Commissioning Editor: Emily Takoudes
Project Editor: Olga Massov
Production Controller: Nerissa Vales
Photography: Gabriele Stabile and Signe Birck
Design: Nazareno Crea
Printed in China

The publishers would like to thank Kate Slate and Evelyn Battaglia for their contributions to the book.

Commonly used ingredients (unless otherwise specified):
Yogurt is whole-milk plain.
Sugar is granulated.
Milk is full fat; cream is heavy (double).
Butter is high-quality and unsalted.
Olive oil is extra-virgin.
Yeast is fresh cake yeast.
Gelatin is bronze-strength leaf.
Eggs are large.
Herbs are fresh.
All fruit powders are freeze-dried and available online or from pastry products purveyors.

Cooking times are for guidance only, as individual ovens vary. If using a fan (convection) oven, follow the manufacturer's instructions concerning oven temperatures.

Exercise a high level of caution when following recipes involving any potentially hazardous activity, including the use of high temperatures, open flames, slaked lime, and when deep-frying. In particular, when deep-frying, add food carefully to avoid splashing, wear long sleeves, and never leave the pan unattended.

Some recipes include raw or very lightly cooked eggs, meat, or fish, and fermented products. These should be avoided by the elderly, infants, pregnant women, convalescents, and anyone with an impaired immune system.

Exercise caution when making fermented products, ensuring all equipment is spotlessly clean, and seek expert advice if in any doubt. When no quantity is specified, for example of oils, salts, and herbs used for finishing dishes or for deep-frying, quantities are discretionary and flexible.

All herbs, shoots, flowers, and leaves should be picked fresh from a clean source. Exercise caution when foraging for ingredients; any foraged ingredients should only be eaten if an expert has deemed them safe to eat.

AUTHOR ACKNOWLEDGMENTS

JEPPE
My wife Maria—for always believing and helping and taking care of Melvin and Elliot when I'm absent. And for her huge help in making this book
My mother, Sonja
Joshua David Stein—curious and sponge-like mind, extreme and intellectual commitment—and let's face it, you are the word wizard that makes it sounds so damn tasty
Daniel Burns—for helping us live out our dreams
Brian Ewing—for making our new life and move to the USA possible; you are my even more Jesus
Ashley Van Valkenburgh—for listening to long and tiring conversations about beer, food, wine etc.
Michael Peyk—for eventyret Ølbutikken
Henrik Boes Brølling—for Drikkeriget and awesome tips on drinks and food
Mike Amedei—for his help with this book
Joey Pepper—for his help with this book
The Westbrooks and the team at Two Roads Brewing—for brewing space and taking Evil Twin to where we are today
Ryan Witter-Merithew—for being an awesome partner and collaborator when we first started
Aaron Porter—for being an amazing friend
Scott Shor and Rich Carley—for inviting me into their lives
Emily, Emilia, and Olga at Phaidon—thank you for inviting us into the Phaidon family

DANIEL
In loving memory of my mother Arlene—my inspiration, and by far the best home cook I have ever seen
My brothers Sean and Bryan for the love and constant support
To the entire team at Tørst and Luksus, past and present, for your hard work and dedication—in particular to Lincoln Clevensen, David Pegoli, Joshua Plunkett, Veronica Treviso, Houston Stock, Jesus Cervantes; Mike Amedei, Joey Pepper, Ramon Hung, Fernelly Sarria, Ryan Mauban, Anthony Sorice, Graham Saylor, James Mhaoir, Margaret Cam, Arielle Gardner, Laura Carlson, Lilly Gibson, Christina Scott, T Jay Richards, Alexis Cloud
Joshua David Stein for his professionalism, intellect, wit, and penmanship; and for captaining the ship on this amazing voyage
Matt and Julie Orlando for being the most amazing people always
James "Jocky" Petrie for giving me the opportunity of a lifetime. I will never forget
JJ Basil and Ken Van Dyk for their help in the photo shoot kitchen
Lauren Utvich for the fantastic job with the recipe testing
Jeppe and Maria for the continued support

JOSHUA
Ana Heeren, for her patience when I disappeared into myself for weeks on end; my kids, Achilles and Augustus, for understanding that Daddy needed to work
Obviously Daniel and Jeppe and Maria (and Melvin, and Elliot, and that goddamn dog)
The whole crew at Tørst / Luksus, but most of all to Joey Pepper and Lincoln Clevensen without whom the book would not have gotten done. Even a little bit
Nathaniel Jacks, flame-headed agent extraordinaire
Emilia Terragni, may what started over gin and tonics in San Sebastian live on forever
Emily, Olga, and the whole team at Phaidon
Gabriele and Signe, of course, the Twinned Weegees of Tørst

This book was brought to you by the letter Ø.